NEGRO TALES FROM PINE BLUFF, ARKANSAS,
AND CALVIN, MICHIGAN

NEGRO TALES FROM

PINE BLUFF, ARKANSAS,

AND CALVIN, MICHIGAN

by Richard M. Dorson

Bloomington 1 9 5 8

Indiana University Press

Reprinted with the permission of the original publisher
KRAUS REPRINT CORPORATION
New York
1968

INDIANA UNIVERSITY PUBLICATIONS

FOLKLORE SERIES NO. 12

Indiana University, Bloomington, Indiana

Library of Congress catalog card number: 58-63484

Publication Committee

Richard M. Dorson, Editor
John W. Ashton, Consulting Editor
W. Edson Richmond, Assistant Editor
Thomas A. Sebeok, Assistant Editor

The Folklore Series of the Indiana University Publications was founded in 1939 for the publication of monographs
and occasional papers in the field of folklore. This volume
was composed at the Indiana University Research Center
in Anthropology, Folklore, and Linguistics.

Printed in U.S.A.

ACKNOWLEDGMENTS

President Lawrence A. Davis of Arkansas Agricultural, Mechanical and Normal College and his Director of Public Relations, John Howard, offered me hospitality and assistance which immeasurably facilitated my fieldwork in Pine Bluff. My introduction to the section on Suggs originally appeared in Michigan History, titled "The Astonishing Repertoire of James Douglas Suggs, A Michigan Negro Storyteller," XL (June 1956), pp. 152-166, and I wish to thank its editor, Dr. Lewis Beeson, for permission to reprint it here in revised form. The Graduate School of Indiana University has made possible the publication of this work by generously providing funds for a Folklore Monograph Series.

INTRODUCTION

NEGRO TALES FROM PINE BLUFF, ARKANSAS, AND CALVIN, MICHIGAN

The present work explores from two directions the incomparably rich narrative lore of the Southern Negro. One method employs the technique of the concentrated field trip to an alien region. A foray deep into the Mississippi Delta, to a teeming Negro community in southeastern Arkansas, garnered sheaves of tales from a score of informants. Ninety-three of these texts, over half the hoard, are here presented, including examples of the little known genre of the protest tale, whose mocking humor cloaks the deepfelt reactions to Jim Crow. The other approach consists in recurrent visits during a period of two years to a single outstanding storyteller, J. D. Suggs, who lived three hours by car from my home in Michigan. More than one hundred of his tales, some two-thirds of his total, appear here. Suggs himself belonged by birth and culture to the Mississippi Delta, and his comprehensive repertoire ranges over the same themes displayed in the Arkansas collection.

Our knowledge of American Negro tales remains surprisingly incomplete. The old storylore has gathered momentum since plantation days, when Joel Chandler Harris identified the slave tale exclusively with Brer Rabbit and the rest of the "creeturs." While the work of Elsie Clews Parsons, published in earlier Memoirs of the American Folklore Society, still stands as a storehouse of Negro texts and comparative references, she undertook her major field work in the Carolina coastal islands, the Bahamas, and the West Indies, at the geographical and cultural periphery of United States Negro tradition. Further, we know nothing of her informants, and little of the circumstances of her collecting. She made perfunctory contact with her storytellers, and worked too often through the medium of schoolchildren and teachers. Almost all tale-collectors similarly slight their human sources.

In the course of thirty years since Parsons collected, the Negro repertoire has notably changed and expanded. Increased education, mobility and social contacts have broadened the themes and heightened the fluency of Southern Negro storytelling. At the same time the plantation culture has retained a tenacious hold on the minds and imagination of the children and grandchildren of slaves. Today the narratives of Southern colored people embrace historical memories, floating jests, occult experiences, spectral encounters, realistic horrors, and antique fictions. The two collections presented here sample this diversified yet homogeneous body of folktales.

CONTENTS

LIST OF TALES

PART I

II

ANIMAL AND BIRD STORIES

III

OLD MARSTER AND JOHN

IV

SPIRITS

V

JOCULAR TALES

III

WHITE MAN AND COLORED MAN

IV

SUPERNATURAL EXPERIENCES

V

HOODOOS AND TWO-HEADS

VI

CURES AND SIGNS

VII

TRUE WONDERS

VIII

PROTEST TALES

IX

SCRIPTURAL TALES

X

TALL TALES

XI

IRISHMEN

XII

PREACHERS

XIII

NOODLES

XIV

JOCULAR TALES

XV

RIDDLES

PART I.

NEGRO TALES FROM

PINE BLUFF, ARKANSAS

IN THE FIELD

Although folklorists in the United States enjoy no such facilities as speed up collecting say in Ireland, they can employ means to create a favorable field situation. Sympathetic institutions, agencies, and key individuals may open up routes to the prized informants one usually seeks by haphazard meanderings. Such was my experience on a field trip in southern Arkansas, when in eight days (June 23-30, 1953) I netted one hundred and sixty Negro folktales, in an area new to me and where I lacked any acquaintances. The lucky breaks that made this possible could be systematically cultivated on other field projects.

A speaking engagement to the Arkansas Folklore Society had taken me down to the University of Arkansas, deep in the Ozark hills. Before returning north I wished to supplement my Michigan Negro work with some Southern Negro comparisons. But the enthusiastic group I met at Fayetteville, and their leading collectors, Vance Randolph and Otto Ernest Rayburn, specialized in folklore of the rolling Ozark country, where few Negroes lived. A Negro graduate student I fell in with at the student union suggested my seeing the president of the Arkansas Agricultural, Mechanical and Normal College, Lawrence A. Davis, who was taking a summer course at the University. President Davis spoke with me most cordially, saying he had himself written a master's thesis on Negro folk sermons, and came to hear

my talk on "A Fresh Look at Negro Storytelling." The
young and energetic president proved a benefactor indeed; he invited me to headquarter at his all-Negro college in Pine Bluff, explained its situation in the heart of
the cotton-growing flatlands, where colored folk lived
densely, and telephoned ahead to make arrangements
for me. Accordingly I drove two hundred and fifty
miles southeast, and took up residence in the new modern student union building, where I lived among Negroes, being the only white person on campus.

Except for the hundred degrees heat, this base of
operations served my purpose admirably. President
Davis had requested his director of public relations,
the painter John Howard, to assist me; Mr. Howard, ur-
bane and impressive, introduced me to other faculty
members, who pooled their wits in my behalf. The A.
M. and N. College was established in 1875 as a Negro
agricultural college, but since the presidency of
Lawrence Davis it has expanded, physically moving to
its present attractive semi-circular campus, and intel-
lectually moving toward a broader humanities curricu-
lum. As is usually the case with a faculty group, close
bonds with the "folk" did not exist, but the college community provided me with some initial contacts in town,
chiefly professional men, and still more important, ap-
proved my credentials and made possible my smooth
entry into a tension-ridden society. (An anthropologist
friend of mine teaching in the South once complained
that he and his students were unable to pursue field
work among Negroes because of White suspicion and
pressure.) Furthermore, by being around and visible
for a period of time, I constantly reminded my hosts of
my quest, who came up with suggestions which had not
occurred to them on our first meeting.

A friend and former teacher of Mr. Howard's

living close by the college turned out to be a fine informant. Reverend Silas Altheimer, a wrinkled, sharp-
featured, soft-spoken, lightskinned old man, still remembered clearly the slavery-time tales he had heard
from his mother. His father had come from Germany
to farm in Arkansas, and developed the plantation which
grew into the village of Altheimer, twelve miles outside
Pine Bluff. There he met the ex-slave woman who bore
him a family. "They didn't stop their old habits after
slavery time, you know," the elderly man said in his
gentle way. Despite his long educational background,
Reverend Altheimer had absorbed completely the traditions of Southern Negro culture, and related comic fictions, grim accounts of slavery life, and supernatural
legends. Surprisingly he believed in hants and hoodoos,
and argued spiritedly with his son about a ghost-ridden
orchard behind the ancestral home; the boy contended
the strange screams and shakings were psychic phenomena, while his father stoutly maintained they were hants.
At the end of each visit Altheimer said he knew no more
stories, but after we talked a little on my return he remarked, "That brings one to mind," and was off again.

Between interviews and scoutings I cooled off at
the Lion's Inn, a cafe on the edge of campus where most
of the college community drifted in at one time or another to snack, drink ice tea or cokes, and listen to a
thunderous jukebox. The owners, Mr. and Mrs. A. A.
Mazique, soon understood my mission, and introduced
me to likely prospects. Shrill and voluble Mrs. Mazique
loudly trumpeted my demands for old tales, and Mr.
Mazique, a large, curly-haired Louisianan with French
blood, told me a couple himself, and suggested a splen-
did informant, E. M. Moore, who lived right by the college in a small cottage. All the faculty knew Moore, an
engineer with a fluent tongue, and seemed puzzled at

their oversight in not giving me his name. Moore had
owned one of the most beautiful homes in town, but sold
it to finance a new type of excavator he had invented.
His Indian blood showed clearly in oval features and
short black hair, and he spoke with the lucidity of an
elocution teacher. Why Moore had not immediately occurred to the faculty circle soon became apparent, for
his stream of anecdotes sidestepped the conventional
plots about Brother Rabbit and Old Marster, to center
on the racial situation, in realistic and wryly humorous
fashion. Actually Moore was relating a seldom collected narrative form, the Negro tale of social protest.

Sitting around one evening in the Lion's Inn when
my leads had run out, I met A. J. King, Jr., a youthful
graduate of the college, wiry and energetic, who inter-
ested himself in my project at once. He had noticed
and remembered the announcement of my lecture at the
University in the Little Rock paper, because it dealt
with a Negro subject. He said that he was a West Indies
Negro, and so smarter than the Southern born Negro,
and he talked in lively fashion, keeping the group around
him convulsed with laughter. That night he drove
me out to Barnes Settlement, where he taught school,
and introduced me to an eighty-nine-year old grandmother, Maria Summers, as a likely prospect. But
young King himself gave me more tales than the matri-
arch.

One day Mr. Howard assigned the college photog-
rapher, Geleva Grice, a tall, bushy-haired young man,
as my guide to inspect the outlying villages. He took
me to nearby Altheimer (named for the Reverend Silas's
father), to see the Negro farmers and their families
come to town on Saturday afternoon, a cherished custom
of the Southern Negro reflected in folktales. A wide,
dusty highway separated the depot from a string of low,

flat-roofed stores joined to an arcade screening the
pavement from the burning sun. A dense crowd shuffled slowly up and down under the arcade. Among the
stream of brightly clothed Negroes stood out an island
or two of sunburned white farmers, and a gang of Mexi-
cans, imported under contract to help with the rice and
cotton planting. Grice knew no one in the throng, so we
went up cold to two colored men talking quietly by themselves and asked if they knew stories. Naturally they
looked at us with surprise, but one of the pair (who I
later learned was a master mason just returned from a
score of years in Chicago), directed us to Ben Jones in
Gethsemane, who could keep us listening from morning
to night. This seemed like a dodge to get rid of us, but
the man insisted, and gave us directions, and off we
went, nine miles of mostly gravel road through flatlands
all planted to cotton, until we reached the gas station
that passed for Gethsemane, and found Ben Jones at
home on his farm (he didn't own an automobile), a fair-
skinned, jaunty Irishman to all appearances, with a
twinkling tongue sure enough, popping out jokes and
tales in a steady flow, many of them "rough."

One morning a professor of Foreign Languages I
had met casually asked how things were going, and
would I like to talk to his class. I wanted this particular opportunity, and Professor Oliver Jackson kindly
introduced me to his freshman composition class of
some twenty students, half of whom were older women,
presumably in-service school teachers, and urged them
to assist me in gathering Negro tales. I told some sam-
ples, and after the class six students came up to contrib-
ute stories of their own.

Right from the first Mr. Howard and other faculty
members suggested I visit the colored Old Folks Home.
Previous collecting experience had taught me that this

idea, seemingly so plausible, contains little merit.
Your informant must first of all possess a keen and active mind and tongue, and institutionalized old people
are often senile and witless. But since Mr. Howard had
made the appointment for me, I drove out east of town
through an increasingly ramshackle colored neighborhood, until I reached the home, a clean, fresh-painted
little building set back from the road. Reverend Mrs.
Toler greeted me, the founder of the home and minister
of its adjoining chapel, an active, durably built lady
with a remarkable career of teaching, preaching, and
social work in the Deep South. She writes in her magazine, "I started on my mission one cold day in March,
1942. I was told of one Mrs. Ollie Hill who lived alone.
She was like Job, full of sores, bedridden; a very un-
pleasant odor met me at the door. I was glad to bring
her with me, bathe, feed and care for her."* So started
the project that Mrs. Roler had now built up into a well
equipped nursing home able to care for one hundred persons. Her inmates covered most species of human pa-
thos, the paralyzed, the blind, the feeble-minded, a man
who could only crawl, another who couldn't sit, the forgotten, the forlorn, the destitute. Mrs. Toler had culled
the few not bedridden for the storytelling party, and
these gathered in the chapel expectantly. In the ensuing
exchange, as I anticipated, I did most of the talking and
they gave little response, a handful of short texts, each
followed by an outbreak of childish laughter. But the
day was surprisingly saved by Mrs. Toler herself, who
tried to stimulate the group with some excellent tales
from her own background in the Mississippi hills, including my only version of the well-known West Indian

------

*The Echo, A Magazine For The Aged And De-
pendent, ed. Rev. Mrs. L. R. Toler (Pine Bluff, Ark.,
vol. VII, May 1953).

type, "In the Cow's Belly." This experience strengthened my conviction that the best informants possess superior mental gifts.

For all the assistance the college circle gave me, my richest strike in Pine Bluff came from a chance contact before I even reached the campus. The Courtneys, a father and son and their wives, belonged socially and economically to the small wage-earner class, below even the tenant farmer, who chopped and picked cotton by the day, and did what odd jobs one could in a city. Tobe Courtney had just gotten to his feet after eleven months on his back from a stroke, and sat all day on his little porch in a rocking chair; his wife Sally worked in the fields; their son John, who lived next door, although a big, sturdy-looking fellow, held an incurable cancer in his stomach, according to a doctor's letter he showed me, and could do only light jobs like paper-hanging or a little barbering on the sly; his wife Julia was nursing a fourth baby and confined to the house all day. Each of the four told me stories, making up a large and absorbing family collection, and yet at first meeting the auspices appeared wholly unfavorable.

Arriving late my first evening in town, I checked in at a motel, and wandered around the nearby streets after supper. I had chosen a Negro section to stop in, and through the evening haze could discern figures seated or standing on the porches that fronted each squat dwelling. My first attempt to start a conversation failed, but my second scored a ten strike. I asked the white-haired, roundfaced old man rocking in a porch chair, did he know any tales? "No," he answered, "I stopped telling them since I became a Christian convert in 1915." In a few minutes however I had invited myself onto the porch, and chatted amiably with Tobe Courtney the rest

of the evening. Tobe spoke with laborious slowness,
but he had a good deal stored in his head that gradually
transferred to my notebooks during the week. Tobe
could do nothing except sit on his porch and greet pass-
ersby, clasping and unclasping his hands spasmodically,
and his wife or son had to dress and undress him, so
feeble were his arms.

Tobe soon forgot his earlier objection to storytelling, and brought me deep within his own folklore-laden
surroundings. Sitting with him one afternoon on the
porch, I saw a briskly walking stranger stop short, inquire as to Tobe's health, and then suggest he treat his
twitching hands by splitting a frog down the middle and
tying one half to each wrist; as the frog died, the mis-
ery would leave. After the man had gone, I asked Tobe
why he didn't try the remedy; because his wife and son
were both terrified of frogs, he said, and he couldn't
tie them on himself, with his stroke. Another time talking of witches and spirits, he mentioned a case of witchcraft that had befallen his wife, and summoned forth the
timid woman, wornout from the cotton fields, who described the episode in full detail without a moment's
hesitation. At one point big, ambling John Courtney,
Tobe's son who lived next door, and spoke as slowly and
softly as his father, drifted over, and related to his dad
at length a vision of buried treasure that was obsessing
him. John could not place the spot, but Tobe recognized
it instantly, and John planned to go digging the next rodeo day when everybody would have gone to town. A
chance reference Tobe made to a Baptist revival being
held a couple of blocks away resulted in my accompany-
ing him that night. The only white person present, I
marveled at the fervent spontaneous singing of the congregation, the hortatory talents of the ministers, the
tears of the mourners, and the shouts of the happy.

Whoever has attended a Southern Negro revival will understand the wealth of Biblical allusion in the daily
speech and the Scriptural folktales of Negroes, and the
chanted interpolations these so frequently contain.

After hearing John's hidden-treasure dream, I
turned his way and found that he quite exceeded his father as a narrator. In spite of his labored, rambling
way of talking, John knew his texts thoroughly and in extensive detail, and his deadpan delivery sent his audience into spasms of laughter. One night I recorded half
an hour of John's narration, and surprisingly his wife
Julia also contributed a couple of tales into the micro-
phone, although John had stated that she knew no stories,
being a good Christian woman. Julia at first seemed on
the severe side, a sturdily built, efficient, positive woman, quick of gesture and speech, the complete opposite
of John. Her two stories, crisp and idiomatic, stuck in
my mind, and now I found myself dropping back to see
Julia. She talked six times faster than the average person, so she said, an inheritance from both sides of her
family, and while nursing her baby burst into a streak
of storytelling that had me writing till my fingers
cramped. My last evening in Pine Bluff I stopped in to
record Julia, and the excitement that recording always
generates stimulated John to produce fresh tales, and
even old Tobe thought up another, and I recorded and
wrote until after midnight. As I shook hands to say
goodbye, Tobe said, "I was proud to have you visit me,"
with a moving sincerity that quite embarassed me; all
four Courtneys came to the gate and waved as I drove
away.

Another relationship I formed off the street de-
teriorated instead of improving. Wandering around the
heavily Negro section of town by the railroad depot, I
spotted two lean men of middle age on a bench in front

of a rooming hotel, and attempted to strike up a conversation. I had however failed to notice their white canes,
and one had to explain to me they were blind. He could
tell by my voice that I was Northern, and white. "We
don't associate the same way down here." Still after
this awkward start both told a John tale, and the smaller
man launched off into further yarns. He was Harrison
Stanfill, a war veteran with apparently an adequate pension; he knew a "gang of stories," and agreed to tell me
more, but on return visits I found him steadily less cooperative. Once his blind friend deterred me from going upstairs to Stanfill's room, saying he was drunk,
and when I returned next morning Stanfill protested that
he had a clean record and asked me to leave him alone;
nor could I allay his suspicions. The fact that no one
around the hotel knew me, that I asked Stanfill for the
details of his birth and occupations, and perhaps that il-
licit transactions were conducted in the hotel, which
bore a curious air of mystery within its winding corri-
dors, blunted this contact.

Had I been planning a book of Southern instead of
Northern Negro tales, the Pine Bluff situation could
have been more intensively manipulated. The network
of leads and associations built up in the eight days would
have paid increasing dividends; I could have spoken to
more classes, located people out of town or away from
home when I called, taken trips to surrounding plantations and villages or even distant places where the Pine
Bluff faculty had friends and relatives. Each field project presents a different set of circumstances, but the
inevitable barriers in the field can be reduced through
a strategic entree into the community.

ANIMAL AND BIRD STORIES

1. Stealing the Butter (Maria Summers)

This Negro favorite, which I found far
more popular than "Tar Baby," occurs in
Antti Aarne and Stith Thompson, The Types
of the Folk-Tale (Helsinski, 1928), as Type
15, "The Theft of Butter (Honey) by Playing Godfather"; see also Stith Thompson,
Motif-Index of Folk-Literature (Bloomington, Ind., 1932-6), Motif K372, "Playing Godfather," and K401.1, "Dupe's
food eaten and then blame fastened on
him"; and Thompson, The Folktale (New
York, 1946), p. 221, which describes the
tale's wide distribution. Elsie Clews
Parsons gives texts and references in
her Folk-Lore of the Sea Islands, South
Carolina, MAFLS XVI (1923), no. 3, pp.
8-10, "Playing Godfather: Tell-tale
Grease"; and Folk-Lore of the Antilles,
French and English, Part 3, MAFLS XXVI
(1943), no. 73, pp. 94-97, "Playing Godfather." For long texts in which the rabbit also puts the blame on the bear, see
my "Negro Tales," Western Folklore,
XIII (April 1954), pp. 79-81, from John
Blackamore, and the opening tale in my
Negro Folktales in Michigan (Cambridge,
Mass., 1946; hereafter NFIM), pp. 33-35,
from J. D. Suggs, and see note 1 in NFIM
204. The final incident in the present
text resembles many in which the trickster

kills the stupid ogre; see Motif K7142, "Victim tricked into entering box," which gives
three American Negro references.

One time a man had his butter down in the spring
where it could keep cool—people didn't have wells in
them times—and the Rabbit he saw it. And the Bear
and the Rabbit was hunting partners for things to eat,
and the Bear found it first, and was calling it his'n.
And the Rabbit was always the sharpest y'know, and he
told the Bear he had some babies to christen (we call it
baptize now). And the Bear asked him how many. And
he said, "Four." So he would get up early that morning,
would get down to the spring, ate one part of the butter.
When he went back the Bear said, "Where you been,
Brother Rabbit?"
"Been christening the baby."
"What did you name him?"
"One Part Gone."
So next morning he went again.
"Where you been, Brother Rabbit?"
"I been christen another baby."
"What the baby name?"
"Two Part Gone."
He goes off again, and the same thing happen. He
calls the next baby "Three Part Gone." The last one is
"All Gone and Lick the Bottom."
And so the Bear went down there to the spring to
get the butter. And when he come back he asked the
Rabbit, had he been down to the spring to et the butter.
The Rabbit said, "No, no, I tell you what to do. First
one get up in the morning with the belly grease et the
butter."
So they both went to bed, and both went to sleep.
And the Rabbit got up that night and he greased Old

Bear's belly right good. And he said to the Bear, "I told you I said the first one get up in the morning with the belly grease et the butter. So you et the butter." So the Bear commenced getting mad, and the Rabbit was scared. He knowed the Bear could whip him, so he said, "There's going to be a party here tonight." He went to jumping around and dancing. And so he had a large box, said, "Brother Bear, you better get in the box and stay here tonight, while I run over and get the girls and bring them back." So Brother Bear jumped in the box, and the Rabbit locked him up.

He could see out, he said, "Brother Rabbit, what you doing with all the vessels on the fire?"

He said, "I'm going to scald you, that's what." He commenced hollering and going on, and at last the Rabbit scalded him and that was the end of that.

2. Stealing the Butter, Hiding in the Log (John Courtney)

This is a truncated version of Type 15 above, plus two additional episodes. The first is the "Fire Test," for which see Parsons, Sea Islands, no. 7, p. 14, and NFIM 33-35, "Who Ate Up the Butter?" by J. D. Suggs, in which the Terrapin, not the Rabbit, fakes the jump. Richard Smith's variant, "Mr. Rabbit in Partners," similarly uses a jump test to determine the thief, but not over a fire ("Richard's Tales," recorded by John L. Sinclair, transcribed by Stella A. Sinclair, in Folk Travelers, ed. Mody C. Boatright el al., Publications of the Texas Folklore Society XXV, 1953, pp. 220-224). The second episode follows an independent tale, explaining how the Buzzard became bald, where the Buzzard traps the Rabbit or the Fox in a hollow tree;

cf. NFIM 41-42, "The Reason the Buzzard
Got a Bald Head," by Sarah Hall, and note
9, p. 206. The three narrators in Michigan
whom I heard tell the buzzard tale, Sarah
Hall, St. Elmo Bland, and J. D. Suggs, all
recited the conversation between the captive and captor animals in sing-song.
Courtney's thinner text follows this de-
vice to the extent that the Rabbit answers
in progressively weaker tones. Under Motif K714.3, "Dupe tricked into entering hollow tree," Thompson gives one reference,
to Joel Chandler Harris, Nights with Uncle
Remus, no. 14 ("Brother Terrapin deceives
Brother Buzzard"). Actually the tale—analogue is in Harris, Told by Uncle Remus,
no. 9, "Why the Turkey Buzzard is Bald-
Headed."

Brother Fox, Brother Bear and all of 'em was picking cotton. And they were all staying in the same house,
and they'd buy their groceries together. So every evening they'd come in they'd go to the store. Brother Rabbit's money was kinda short, he wasn't making much
that day 'cause he felt a little ill. So they was all going
to book their money in and buy some butter. Brother
Rabbit he didn't eat butter, and he was short. So they
went on and bought them two pounds of butter. They all
went to the field next morning. There they worked all
the next day. They come in, Brother Rabbit was the
first to go to bed. He'd catch them all sleeping; he'd
get up and eat some butter. And next morning Brother
Rabbit'd be up early smoking his cigar with his legs
crossed.
    And they were going on to the field and work that
day. So when they come in they missed that butter.
Say, "Who was eating that butter? We didn't eat all that
butter!"

Brother Fox said, "We won't work tomorrow, we'll
have a test on the butter. One eat that butter we'll find
him out."

So they built a great big fire next morning. And
then Brother Buzzard he was going be the captain, the
boss of it. Because practically everywhere he go he
flew. So they got the fire built, a great big log heap fire.
So Brother Buzzard says, "Okay, Brother Fox, you may
be first." Brother Fox he backed up and he lit out—
Woody, woody, woody. And he jumps, he jumps it clear.
And he comes on back. Brother Buzzard says, "Okay,
Brother Rabbit you're next." Brother Rabbit he backed
up, pulled his derby off, and he hits it just as hard as he
could go right toward the fire. And Brother Rabbit got
close to the fire—Boody, boody, boody, boody—then
whipped his belly agin the ground and run around the
fire. And they thought they heard him hit the other side.
Brother Buzzard say, "Okay, Brother Bear, you're next."
So Brother Bear he backed up and he lit out. And he
leaps right in the fire.

Brother Rabbit say, "Yeah, I told you Brother Bear
eat that butter."

So Brother Bear walks on back close to Brother
Rabbit, and he made a break at him, and it was a hollow
log right down close to him. So Brother Rabbit run in
that hollow log, wasn't but one way in. So Brother Bear
fastened up the other end of that log with Brother Rabbit in. "I'll show you about tricking me." And they all
went on and left Brother Rabbit in the log.

Next morning they went down to see about it.

"Brother Rabbit." [High]

"Hunh." [Loud]

"Oh let's go on back and forget about you." So they
went on back and Brother Rabbit stayed in there. They

went back to see him again. So they called him again,
"Brother Rabbit."

"Hunh." [Weak]

He answered like he was nearly about gone. "O yes,
nearly about got him." They went away and left him.
So next morning would be the end of the week he'd been
in there. "I know he'll be dead this morning." They
went down to see about it.

"Brother Rabbit." [High]

Brother Rabbit wouldn't answer. He'd done study a
trick on them.

"Brother Rabbit." Call him twice.

"Oh yeah, we got him." Brother Fox, Brother Bear
they pulled that chunk out of the log. Brother Fox
reached up in there to get Brother Rabbit. Out come
Brother Rabbit, out by Brother Fox's hands.

"Oh yes, you son of bitches think you're smart, I
can be your schoolteacher yet."

3. Tar Baby (Julia Courtney)

See Parsons, Antilles, no. 24, pp. 48-51,
"Tar Baby," for texts and extensive references. In my "A Negro Storytelling Session
on Tape," Midwest Folklore, III (Winter,
1953), pp. 202-204, E. L. Smith of Calvin, Mich-
gan, joins the Playing Godfather and Tar
Baby episodes in a text that also sets the
tar baby before a spring. The present abbreviated variant lacks the usual sequel of
the "Mock Plea," in which the Rabbit obtains his freedom by begging the animals
not to throw him into the briar patch. The
tale-type is no. 175 in Aarne-Thompson,
"The Tarbaby and the Rabbit," and Motif

K741 in the Motif-Index, "Capture by tarbaby," which gives references to the mono-
graphic literature.

Was a long summer drouth among the animals.
And Brother Rabbit played like he'd get up every morning and lick the dew off the grass. That's why he stayed
so slick and fat. So Rabbit had found a spring, and he
wouldn't tell none of the rest of the animals. Every
morning he would get up real early and go down to the
spring and get a drink of water. Next morning he got up
just a little bit earlier and went down to the spring, and
got him a drink of water. But Brother Fox beat him up
and followed him down there. Brother Fox come back
and told the rest of the animals how dirty Brother Rabbit was. All the animals got together and made them a
tar baby, and put it in front of the spring.
    And the spring was very small spring. Brother Rab-
bit couldn't go round the tar baby to get no water. So
when he got there he stooped down, and he could see the
tar baby standing there. He thought it was someone.
Brother Rabbit walked up to it and told him to move out
of the way. And he repeated again, "Move out the way.
If you don't I'll slap you." So he hauled off and slapped
him with one front paw. That one stuck. Brother Rabbit said, "Turn me loose. I have three more paws."
So he slapped him with the other one. Brother Rabbit
said, "All right, you better turn me loose. I have two
more." Slapped him with one more. He said, "I have
one more." And he slapped with the other one. Then
he said, "If you don't turn me loose I'll butt you with
my head." So all the animals caught Brother Rabbit
stuck to the tar baby.
    (By him pulling the tar would give, and he thought
it was someone there.)

4. Rabbit and Bear Inside the Elephant (Mrs. L. J.
   Toler)

    Helen L. Flowers, A Classification of
the Folktale of the West Indies by Types
and Motifs (Indiana University doctoral
dissertation, 1952), describes an independent subtype of Type 676, "Open Sesame,"
for which she finds 22 variants in the West
Indies (nos. 14-35). She comments, "Here
the distinguishing feature is the use of the
password to gain entrance into a living animal for the purpose of cutting meat from
it." Flowers draws her material from
Parsons, Antilles; see no. 26, "In Cow's
Belly," pp. 52-56, for the 22 texts, and
comparative references, to Louisiana,
Canada, France, Portugal, and Africa.
Flowers nos. 17, 22, 27, and 29, Parsons
E, D, R, U (Guadaloupe, Dominica, St.
Martin, Haiti) are closest to the present
text, which has lost the magic password
motif but otherwise follows the basic plot
fully. In the four texts above, Rabbit and
Zamba, Rabbit and Tiger, Jack and his
greedy brother, and Bouqui and Malice
all enter a cow. The substitution of the
elephant for the cow in the Toler text is
curious. Ludwig Bemelmans in Hotel
Splendide (New York, 1941), pp. 65-66,
relates a Senegalese story of a Hare
that jumps inside the Elephant's mouth,
eats his bowels and heart, and escapes
from his intestines. The Joel Chandler
Harris version, in Uncle Remus, His
Songs and his Sayings, no. 34, "The Sad
Fate of Mr. Fox," follows the West Indies
form in having the fox and the rabbit jump
inside a cow, and in retaining the magic
password, which is "Bookay," the name

of the cow, and obviously a carryover from
"Bouqui," the trickster in the Haiti texts
(Parsons, p. 56). Harris has "maul" where
Mrs. Toler has "melt" for the hiding place
of the trickster's dupe, properly milt, or
spleen. A text from Creoletown, La., has
"Bookee" and "La Pain" (A. H. Fauset,
"Negro Folk Tales from the South," JAF,
XL, 1927, no. 235, p. 242, "In the Cow's
Belly").

This story clearly has closer affini-
ties with the Thumbling-Petit Poucet complex, where the tiny hero is swallowed by
a cow (see Grimm no. 45, "Thumbling as
Journeyman) or even with Jonah and the
whale, than with Open Sesame, to which
it is linked only by one stray motif.

Mr. Bear and Mr. Rabbit were good friends. Mr.
Rabbit came up one day with a bucket of lard. Mr. Bear
wanted to know where he got it, he wanted some.

Mr. Rabbit said, "Oh, Mr. Lion and Mr. Elephant
and all of 'em down there telling big tales. Mr. Elephant laughed so long and loud, opens his mouth so wide,
I jump in, go and get me a bucket of fat, jump out before
he can shut it."

Mr. Bear decided he could do the same things. So
both of 'em went down with their buckets, sitting by the
side of Mr. Elephant, waiting for him to laugh. Soon Mr.
Elephant laughed, in jumped Mr. Rabbit, in jumped Mr.
Bear, began tearing out the fat. Mr. Elephant closed in
on 'em before they could get out.

Mr. Rabbit said, "He never done this before."

Mr. Bear said, "What we gonna do?"

"You go in the melt, I'll go in the bladder."

Pretty soon Mr. Elephant took sick and died. Then
his friends begin to wonder what killed him so quickly,
better have an examination. Had a meeting, decided to

cut him open and see what his trouble was. They cut
him open, first thing they come across was the bladder,
and they threw it down the hill. When they threw it
down it crushed.

Out jumped Mr. Rabbit, and hollered up to them,
"Look out, don't throw your nasty mess down on me.
What's the trouble up there?"

"Mr. Elephant's dead."

"What's the trouble?"

"Mr. Rabbit, we don't know."

Said, "Where's the malt?"

"We threw it down the hill."

Then Mr. Rabbit said, "Show it to me. All right,
get you some switches every one of you. Beat on it till
I tell you to stop."

Beat him into a jelly. Lifted the veil off it, found
Mr. Bear in there dead.

Mr. Rabbit said, "That's what killed Mr. Elephant."

5. Take My Place (John Courtney)

The popularity of this tale can be
seen from the extensive references and
many texts provided by Parsons, Antilles,
no. 23, pp. 41-47, for "Substitute Victim
(Take My Place!)." The key motif here,
K842, "Dupe persuaded to take prisoner's
place in a sack: killed," appears in several international folktales with human
characters, but has become entrenched
in the American Negro animal cycle; Joel
Chandler Harris uses the plot four times
(Uncle Remus, His Songs and His Sayings,
no. 23, "Mr. Rabbit and Mr. Bear," and
no. 29, "Mr. Fox Gets into Serious Business"; Nights with Uncle Remus, no. 31,

"In some Lady's Garden," and no. 32,
"Brother Possum gets into Trouble").
These last two examples interestingly
juxtapose two variants, one from Uncle
Remus and one from African-born Daddy
Jack, who claims he heard the tale dif-
ferently. Uncle Remus philosophically
comments, "One man, one tale; 'n'er man,
'n'er tale. Folks tell um diffunt" (Nights
with Uncle Remus, Boston and New York,
1883, p. 189).

Courtney has combined the substitute-
victim story with a separate incident, the
first Negro folktale I ever heard, from St.
Elmo Bland (born in Mississippi) in Calvin, Michigan, in March, 1952. His text
follows.

The Fox called the Buzzard, "Mr.
Buzzard." [Very loud]

The Buzzard wouldn't answer.

Mr. Fox said, "I was just going to
tell you where you could find some dead
carr'on."

So the Buzzard slowly turned around
and said, "Whu-u-u-t?"

The Fox told him where there was a
young mule dead in the field (he was only
asleep), and how to get him away. "Tie
a rope around your head and around the
colt's legs." The Fox tied the rope so,
and tested the colt. Colt woke up, and
started running. Fox began to laugh and
call out, "Hold him, Mr. Buzzard, hold
him."

Buzzard said, "How the devil can
I hold him if my feet ain't touching the
ground?" (Cf. "Richard's Tales," in
Folk Travelers, pp. 241-242, "Dead
Colt Comes to Life"; Motif K1047,
"The bear bites the seemingly dead
horse's tail"; Harris, Nights with

Uncle Remus, no. 2, "Brother Fox Catches
Mr. Horse.")

Once there was a Brother Rabbit and he'd found
out where there was a big garden of greens. So he
would go up every morning and he'd tell the little girl
her father had said turn him in the garden, and at
twelve o'clock turn him out. So he would make it his
business to go there every morning and call the little
girl. "Little girl, father said turn me in the garden,
twelve o'clock come turn me out."

So the little girl said, "Okay." So they begin to
miss those greens.

The girl's father say, "Somebody's eating these
greens up around here. I can't tell where my greens
is going to." So he asked the little girl.

She told him she said, "Father said Brother Rabbit come here every morning and turn me in the garden,
and twelve o'clock turn me loose."

He say, "When he come today just turn him in, when
twelve o'clock come just let him stay till I come."

So when twelve o'clock come Brother Rabbit called
the little girl, "Little girl, oh little girl." Say, "Little
girl, twelve o'clock, turn me out. Dang-dong, dang-
dong."

So up come the girl's father. "Brother Rabbit,
what you doing in there?" Say, "Okay, I'll just fix you."
Say, "I'll send you Brother Fox and Brother Bear."
When Brother Fox and Brother Bear got there, girl's
father say, "Brother Fox, who's been getting my greens?"

Brother Fox say, "I haven't had a mess of greens
this year."

And Brother Bear say, "You know I've been away
up north."

So he say, "Well that leaves it up to Brother Rabbit."

Brother Rabbit sitting there saying nothing, studying his way out. So he takes Brother Rabbit out there and tied him up to a great big old limb. And when he climbed down he left Brother Rabbit swinging. That's the way he was going to punish him. Brother Rabbit he swung and he swung and he swung, by the limb.

"I'm going to heaven in a swing-swing-swing.
I'm going to heaven in a swing-swing-swing."

Brother Fox and Brother Bear heard him singing. So Brother Fox told him, "Let's go up there, Brother Bear, and see about Brother Rabbit."

When Brother Fox and Brother Bear got there Brother Rabbit called, say, "Brother Bear, I haven't had a drink of water since that man tied me up here." Say, "You come up here and let me tie you up here until I can get a drink of water. I'll be right back." So Brother Bear let him tied him up there. But Brother Rabbit stayed so long till Brother Bear went to singing. Brother Bear couldn't think of the song Brother Rabbit was singing.

"I'm going to heaven in a dang-alang-alang.
I'm going to heaven in a dang-alang-alang."

And the girl's father heard Brother Bear singing. He knew that was a different voice. He was going back and see about that. So when he got there Brother Bear in the tree. And he said, "Brother Bear, what you doing up there?"

Brother Bear said, "Brother Rabbit got me to stay till he come back."

He said, "I'll just fix you, taking Brother Rabbit's

place." He took Brother Bear down and give him a good
beating. Brother Rabbit done gone on home.

So Brother Bear he was crying and he gone down to
the house and Brother Rabbit was sitting up on the
porch, smoking a cigar with his legs crossed, his derby
on. (He was a hard sport.) And Brother Bear he
jumped at Brother Rabbit and missed him. Brother Rabbit told him, "I tell you what, I know just where we can
get some meat at." So they went on down there.
Brother Rabbit told Brother Bear, "There's a dead
mule." Say, "Brother Bear, your tail's longer than
ours, and heavier too, I'll just tie your tail to the mule's
tail." When he got his tail tied, Brother Rabbit reached
down and got a flail, and lammed the old mule in the
side. So the mule jumped up and started running. And
Brother Rabbit commenced to hollering, "Hold him
Brother Bear, hold him." [High]

He said, "How in hell can I hold him with ne'er foot
touching the ground?"

(That mule had his tail up and was knocking him
with his hocks.)

   6. Rabbit and Hedgehog (Julia Courtney)

        For the distribution of this tale see
     Type 1074, "Race"; Motif K11.1, "Race
     won by deception: relative helpers"; The
     Folktale, p. 196; Parsons, Antilles, no. 50,
     pp. 78-80, "Relay Race." A close text from
     Mary Richardson, who was raised in Ten-
     nessee and Mississippi, "Rabbit and Hogs-
     head [sic] have a Race," is in NFIM 37-38.
     Cf. my "Negro Tales from Bolivar County,
     Mississippi," no. 2, "Tapin and the Deer"
     (Southern Folklore Quarterly, XIX, June
     1955, p. 106). May A. Klipple, African

Folktales with Foreign Analogues (Indiana
University doctoral dissertation, 1938, abstracted by Stith Thompson) gives 38 references, seventeen coming from the East
African cattle areas. Flowers, A Classification of the Folktale of the West Indies,
adds two African examples to Klipple, and
cites 10 West Indies texts.

Rabbit and Hedgehog lived 'jining farms. And
every day the Rabbit would go down and make fun of the
Hedgehog's babies. And he would tell them:

> "Short leg long wit,
> Long leg not a bit."

Every day he would come down and tell them that
same thing:

> "Short leg long wit,
> Long leg not a bit."

So he made Old Lady Hedge mad. And so the Rabbit told the Hedge they'd have a race. (That's the way
they had of evening up things.)
And that night Old Lady Hedge talked it over with
her husband and daughter. And the next day Brother
Rabbit came over to their home. Old Lady Hedge was
ready the next morning, she and her daughter. They
had a mile run. Old Lady Hedge got on one end, and
she on the other.
So the Rabbit told the Hedge, "Are you ready?"
She said, "Yes."
So they begin running. And the Hedge went toddle
toddle, and Brother Rabbit was so busy running, he
didn't miss her when she stopped.

When he got near the other end, Old Lady Hedge's
daughter raised up and said, "I'm here."

So the Rabbit said it wasn't dead fair. "We'll try
it over."

So they started running again. And the little Hedge
went toddle toddle. This time the Rabbit still didn't notice the Hedge toddle. When he got to the other end, Old
Lady Hedge raised up, and said, "I'm here."

(He had to quit making fun then you know. Them
legs is so slow the Rabbit couldn't see her when she
stopped, she's so low down. A hedgehog is a short
thing.)

7. Mr. Rabbit and Mr. Frog Make Mr. Fox and
    Mr. Bear Their Riding-Horses (John Courtney)

Other variants were told me by Tobe
Courtney and Mrs. L. J. Toler. The present text is unusual in having two riders
and riding horses. This is Type 72, "Rabbit Rides Fox A-courting," and Motif K1241,
"Trickster rides dupe horseback." See
Parsons, Antilles, no. 47, pp. 73-76, "Riding-Horse." Klipple under Type 72 suggests Motif K1241.1, "Trickster rides dupe
a-courting," and provides five African references. Martha W. Beckwith describes the
story as "very common in Jamaica and presents no local variations from the form familiar in America" (Jamaica Anansi Stories,
MAFLS XVII, 1924, p. 235, note to no. 3,
"Tiger as Riding-horse," pp. 5-6). The Joel
Chandler Harris version appears in Uncle
Remus, His Songs and His Sayings, no. 6,
"Mr. Rabbit Grossly Deceives Mr. Fox."
This latter tale presents Brer Rabbit smoking like a "town man," in the same conception John Courtney gives in no. 5, above,

"Take my Place," where he describes the
Rabbit as a "hard sport."

Mr. Rabbit and Mr. Frog were courting two girls,
and Mr. Bear and Mr. Fox were liking them too. Mr.
Fox and Mr. Bear they had the best going, the girls
cared most for them. So Brother Rabbit went down to
Brother Frog's house, and built up a scheme to play on
Brother Bear and Brother Fox. So they set a night that
they were going to the girls' house, an off night from
what Brother Bear and Brother Fox were courting.
And so they went on a Friday night, and they told the
girls, "Brother Fox and Brother Bear's our riding-
horses. You're crazy about them boys but there ain't
nothing to them."

So the girls says, "Oh no, I can't believe that."

So Brother Rabbit told them, says, "I'll prove it if
you'll be my girl friend." And Brother Frog said he
would too. So they set a night that they was going to
prove it, in the next following week. So that evening
Brother Fox and Brother Bear come over to Brother
Rabbit's house.

Brother Rabbit say, "You just the man I want to
see." So Brother Rabbit say, "We ought to go to some
extra girls' house tonight, we need some more girls."
So they finally made it up and begin to get ready. They
carried them a saddle apiece, Brother Rabbit and
Brother Frog, and hid them by Brother Bear's girl
friend's house. So they went on that night down to this
extra girl's house. So they stayed there till nine o'clock.
Brother Bear and Brother Fox they had to stay by their
girl friend's house. So they all got ready and started
out. Brother Rabbit took sick. Brother Rabbit was so
sick, Brother Bear 'cided to try to tote him. So Brother
Frog he had a bellyache. So that made him sick too.

So Brother Fox said, "Well we'll just tote them two
guys up here and we'll stop over."

Brother Bear told them, says, "Crawl up on my
back, Brother Rabbit, I'll tote ya." And Brother Fox
told Brother Frog to crawl up. Both of them was so
sick, he could get up there but he couldn't stay up there.

Brother Rabbit told him, says, "I just can't stay on
your back. I gotta get something to hold to." Brother
Rabbit told him, "I know what, I see the very thing I
can hold to." [Excited] Brother Frog say the same
thing. So Brother Rabbit say, "Here's some saddles
here, here's the very things we can hold on to." So
they put the saddles on, and Brother Rabbit and him
climbed up in the saddle. Both of 'em was so sick they
couldn't hardly stay in the saddle.

And when they got to the girls' house, Brother Bear
say, "Now you've got to get down, Brother Rabbit, at
the steps. That is far as I can carry you."

So Brother Rabbit told him, says, "You take me to
the top steps, we can make it." He had done put him a
pair of spurs on he and Brother Frog. So when they
got up to the top step, Brother Rabbit popped them
spurs to Brother Bear. Brother Bear ran right on
in his girl friend's door. Brother Rabbit said, "I told
you Brother Bear was my riding horse, I told you
Brother Bear was my riding horse."

Brother Frog said, "I told you Brother Fox was
my riding horse."

8. Rabbit and Fox Go Fishing (Maria Summers)

Two popular tales are joined here. For
"Playing Dead Twice in the Road," see
Parsons, Antilles, no. 9, pp. 29-31, for ten
West Indies text summaries, and her

discussion in Folk-Lore, XXVIII (1917),
pp. 408-414, "The Provenience of certain
Negro Folk-Tales," where she attributes
the migration of the tale to a comparable
incident in "The Master Thief" (Type
1525), transmitted by Portuguese traders
to Gold Coast Negroes and thence to
Southern slaves. I printed a variant from
John Blackamore in "Negro Tales,"
Western Folklore, XIII (April 1954),
pp. 83-84, "The Rabbit, The Fox and the
Bear: Playing Dead in the Road."
    The second episode is Type no. 2,
Motif K1021, "The Tail-Fisher." A variant in which the rabbit tells the fox to
fish with his feet in a bucket of water is
in my "Negro Tales from Bolivar County,
Mississippi" (Southern Folklore Quarterly,
XIX, 1955), pp. 105-106, no. 1, "Brer Rabbit an' Brer Fox." The rabbit is deceived
by the fox in NFIM 38-39, "Why the Rabbit has a Short Tail," from Sarah Hall. In
The Folktale, pp. 119-120, Stith Thompson
cites the study by Kaarle Krohn on the
thousand-year history of the tale.

    The Fox and the Rabbit was staying together, and
so they went out fishing. The Rabbit was too lazy to
fish so he run on ahead and lay down like he was dead.
The Fox come along, say, "Here's one of Brother Rabbit's people. If I seen another one I'm going to lay my
fish down and go back and tell Brother Rabbit." Rabbit
jumps up and runs around and gets ahead of him again,
lays down like he was dead. And the Fox laid his fish
down and went back to tell Brother Rabbit. After he got
out of sight Brother Rabbit jumped up and carried his
fish home and was cooking 'em when Brother Fox come
in. Brother Fox say, "Hey Brother Rabbit, where you
get all these fish?"

"I caught 'em."

And the Fox say, "I had a string of fish and I saw some of your people dead, and I went back and I couldn't find either your people or the fish."

The Rabbit said, "I ain't got 'em. I went down to the creek and th'owed my tail in the creek, and every hair had a fish hanging to it. You better go try."

He went to the creek and the water friz around his tail, and he thought he had a lot of fish. Brother Rabbit come by and say, "Hey Brother Fox, how many fish you got?" He said he had so many that he couldn't pull 'em out. The Rabbit he listened.

"What's it?"

"It's that man yonder with his fox dogs."

·"Pull, Brother Rabbit, pull."

The Rabbit he was grunting like he was pulling but he wasn't doing nothing. "Unh, unh." So he said he'd go get the ax and cut his [the Fox's] tail so he could get loose before the dogs get there. And so he cut the tail off, and the Rabbit said to the Fox, "Oh yes, you got a short tail like me."

(Looks like he oughta know the Rabbit couldn't th'ow his tail in the water and get those fish—he didn't have no tail. Looks like everything ignorant but the Rabbit.)

9. Rabbit and the Ashes (Sally Courtney)

This bare plot is characteristically elaborated by Joel Chandler Harris in Uncle Remus, His Songs and His Sayings, no. 30, "How Mr. Rabbit Succeeded in Raising a Dust."

They had a contest, the one dance the dust outa the

rock got the girl. And so everybody had done danced
but Mr. Rabbit. Mr. Rabbit was getting hisself into action, he was dipping hisself into ashes — they wasn't paying him no attention. (The ashes was in the chimney.)

Say, "Well Mr. Rabbit, it your turn now to dance
the dust out the fire."

He come up dragging hisself like he didn't care.
"Well, I don't know whether I can dance or not." Heading on up there, and shuck hisself a little bit, and the
ashes just flew. And he jumped right on up in the girl's
lap. "That's my girl."

10. Quail and Rabbit (Silas Altheimer)

The Quail and the Rabbit were out hunting fruit.
The Rabbit would run from place to place, but the Quail
would fly. So finally the Quail found a patch where
there were ripe peaches and ripe canteloupe and ripe
watermelons and ripe plums and a field of ripe peas
nearby, all of which the Quail liked, especially the peas.
But he didn't want the Rabbit to share in it. So the Quail
rose and flew in the direction the Rabbit went until she
saw the Rabbit, then she fell to the earth, and ran all
around, shuffling her wings, and fall down and roll.
The Rabbit said, "Mr. Quail, what's the matter?"

And the Quail shuffled her wings and rolled around
and said, "Mr. Rabbit, we'd better leave here, and run
as hard as we can. I went down that way and a great
big man met me. He beat me half to death. I wouldn't
have gotten away had I not flown."

And so the Quail began to run a little bit and fly,
run a little bit and fly, and the Rabbit ran too, and he
carried the Rabbit in the opposite direction. After getting the Rabbit considerably away the Quail got some of

his friend quails and flew back to the orchard and pea-
field, where they feasted on peas and ripe plums.
    So that's one time Mr. Rabbit was beaten.

11. Bear and Buzzard (Tobe Courtney)

        Ordinarily this yarn falls within the Old
    Marster and John cycle. See J. Mason
    Brewer, "John Tales," in Mexican Border
    Ballads and Other Lore, Publications of the
    Texas Folklore Society XXI (1946), pp. 92-93,
    "John, McGruder, and the Bear in the Corn-
    field"; Zora N. Hurston, Mules and Men
    (Philadelphia and London, 1935), pp. 100-101,
    "Massa and the Bear"; and NFIM 71-72,
    "John, the Bear, and the Patteroll."
        A popular Negro folktale incident, telling
    how the buzzard became bald, has been neatly
    added. For a full text see NFIM 41-42, "The
    Reason the Buzzard is Got a Bald Head," by
    Sarah Hall, but a variant told me by J. D.
    Suggs comes closer to the present form, in
    that the buzzard scrapes his head by flying
    into a tree in panic. See post, no. 1, pp. 158-160.

I don't know just who it was tied the Bear, but I
think it started like this. There was two mens in the
woods hunting. Well they was a good little piece apart.
So the Bear was coming out of the cornfield. So the
man was sitting down on a log, and the bear slipped up
on him, he was 'bout half asleep you know, had been
hunting all night. And he commenced hollering for the
other fellow was out there with him. And he run round
a tree (now look at me). The bear tried to catch him,
and this was a pretty good man, he jumped behind the
tree. And the bear was reaching at him, and he caught
the bear's foot, both of 'em. And he holding the bear

and hollering for his friend in the woods, the other man.
And when the other man come he say, "Now you hold
him, and I'm going to tie him."

Well when that other fellow got hold of him, he so
weak and tired he sat down and said, "Now when you've
hold him as long as I have, then I'll tie him." Finally
he decided he'd get up and tie him you know, and they
left him out there. They wouldn't kill him, they left
him tied.

So Mr. Buzzard he flew around, till the Bear got
weak you know. He found out where his meal was at.
So finally one day he flew down at him. And when he
flew down on him, the bear hit him with his foot, and
knocked that patch of hair outa his head. He knocked
him kind of crazy and he flew backwards into a tree,
and knocked off the rest of that patch. And he been bald-
headed ever since.

12. Bullfrog and Terrapin (Sally Courtney)

    This suggests the Aesopic fable of Motif
J955.1, "Frog tries in vain to be as big as ox."
Cf. Ray B. Browne, "Negro Folktales from
Alabama," Southern Folklore Quarterly, XVIII
(June 1954), no. 12, p. 134, "The Frog that
Wanted to be Big." Klipple gives five African examples of this motif. A text given me
in Calvin, Michigan, "The Frogs and the Elephant", combines the fable and the present
incident. The mother frog bursts in trying
to emulate the elephant. Next day the elephant
steps on the baby frog at the creek. "Am I
very heavy?" "No, not so heavy, but you're
so hard on my eyes." ("Negro Tales of
Mary Richardson," Midwest Folklore, VI,
1956, no. 5, p. 9.)

Mr. Bullfrog and Mr. Terrapin was having a race.
One went one road, the other went this one, and at the
forks of the road they was going to meet up. The bullfrog jumped in a rut, and a truck come along over him,
and busted both eyes. Along come Mr. Terrapin, crawling.

"Well Mr. Bullfrog, you made it?"
He said, "Yes I made it, mighty hardest."
Says, "What's the matter with your eyes?"
Says, "Oh, just a little straining on them."
(The terrapin didn't have sense enough to know the
bullfrog hop faster than he could crawl.)

13. Meeting Man

This is Type 157, "Learning to Fear
Men," and Motif J17, "Animal learns through
experience to fear men." For sixteen vari-
ants that I collected from Negroes in Michi-
gan, including one by Suggs, see my "King
Beast of the Forest Meets Man," Southern
Folklore Quarterly, XVII (June 1954), pp.
118-128. A tape-recorded text from Mary
Richardson is in my "A Negro Storytelling
Session on Tape," Midwest Folklore, III
(Winter 1953), p. 202. Walter Winfrey of
Inkster, Michigan, told me three distinct
versions, one of which is given in NFIM
40, "The Lion and the Cowboy." For other
American Negro references see note 7 in
NFIM 205-206. Martha W. Beckwith gives
a version from Jamaica where the Tiger is
led by the Lion to attack Man; at first the
Tiger thinks Mr. Ram-Goat is Man:
Jamaica Anansi Stories, MAFLS XVIII,
1924, pp. 67-68, "Man is stronger," and
note, p. 262.

13a. Meeting Man (Bertha White)

The Bear asked the Rabbit about a man. He hadn't
ever seed a man. The Rabbit told him to meet him at
a certain point in the road near the forest, at sunrise.
They arrived the next morning and the little boy come
down the road whistling.
The Bear said, "Is that a man?"
The Rabbit said "No, that's a gonner-be." So next
an old man with a stick.
The Bear said, "Mr. Rabbit, I see a man now."
And the Rabbit said, "Oh no, that's a has-been."
The soldier was coming with a rifle.
The Bear said, "Mr. Rabbit, a man's coming."
The Rabbit looked, and he said, "Yes Mr. Bear,
that is a man, and I'm going."
The Bear stepped out in the opening. The soldier
stopped and said, "Why that's a bear." He pointed his
rifle and shot the Bear in the face. The Bear turned to
run, and he shot him in the rear.
The Bear ran to the Rabbit and said, "Mr. Rabbit,
a man is mighty. He can thunder at one end and light-
nin' at the other, and shoot a bear all in his face and
rear."

13b. Meeting Man (James Heard)

Panther wanted to see a man, and he said to the
Bear, "Now I want you to show me a man." Bear took
the Panther to the road. Along came a little boy, and
Panther said, "Is that a man?"
"No, that's a will-be."
"Well I want to see a man." Along came next an

old man. Panther said to Bear, "What is that, is that
a man?"

"No, that's a have-been."

"Well, I want to see a man."

Come along a man thirty-five years old, right in
his prime, had a double-barreled shotgun, so he [the
Bear] says, "There's a man."

He says, "I'll just see." So the man got there he
went out to see him, man th'owed up and cut down on
him. He lit out then and he th'owed the next load into
him, and he lit out on into the woods, where the Bear
was.

So the Bear asked the Panther, "Did you see a
man?"

"Yes, I did see him, he filled me full of splinters."
He didn't want to see another man.

14. Elephant and Jackal (Harold Lee)

> For a close variant on "Jackal and the
> Camel" see my "Negro Tales of Mary
> Richardson," no. 6, p. 9. Klipple, African
> Folktales with Foreign Analogues, gives
> one example from Madagascar of Motif
> J2137.6, "Camel and ass together captured
> because of ass's singing." In the African
> story the dog barks to retaliate on the croco-
> dile.

It was actually India, but I put it in Louisiana.
That's the center point for ribbon cane. So they'd ate
all the vegetation on one side of the river, and the
Jackal wanted to go on the other side, but he couldn't
swim. So the Elephant could swim, and the Jackal begged him to carry him over to the other side. Elephant

said, "If I carry you over there will you promise to be
quiet, so the farmers don't hear me?" The Jackal
promised, so he kneeled down for the Jackal to jump on
his back. Away they swim. Got over, start eating.
Jackal got full, Elephant was still eating, he started to
holler. Farmers came and beat the Elephant real good.
The Elephant said, "Mr. Jackal, you promised not to
holler."

Said, "After I eat with a full stomach I just got to
holler, Mr. Elephant."

Several trips the Jackal did the same thing, made
the Elephant get a good whipping. So the Elephant
waited till he got in the deepest part of the stream. So
he started turning over in the water. The Jackal said,
"Mr. Elephant, why are you turning over? I can't swim."

"After I have a full stomach I've got to take a bath."

15. Calf Follows Bull (James Heard)

Man had a cow and a calf. And he's carrying his
cow and calf home. And an old bull come along, belling,
and went up to him, and the man thought he'd hurt his
calf, and he drewed back his big switch and struck him
'cross the back, and he lit out. And that calf right behind (a young calf will foller anything). So he went
down the hill and up the hill, and that calf right behind.

The man commenced hollering, "So-o-o-o calf,
here's you mammy." Up the hill and down the hill the
calf went behind the bull. So the calf wouldn't come
back to him and his mother.

So the man said, "Go on calf, you'll find out who
you with when sucking time come."

16. Preacher and Fowls (Tobe Courtney)

Similar texts I collected are in NFIM
47-48, "The Preacher and the Guinea," from
Suggs; "Negro Tales from Bolivar County,
Mississippi," no. 6, pp. 107-108, from Rev.
J. H. Lee, "Preacher and Fowls"; "Negro
Tales of Mary Richardson," no. 8, pp. 10-11.
In addition I have seven unpublished variants
from Michigan, and two variations that also
employ the motif of the speaking fowls. (One
by Suggs is given post, no. 10, pp. 170-171, "Fowls
at the Crap Game.") Ernest W. Baughman
assigns the motif X459.2*(b), "Fowls hide
when preacher comes to visit," in A Comparative Study of the Folktales of England
and North America (3 vols., Indiana University doctoral dissertation, 1953). For
references see note 17 in NFIM 208.
Printed texts cannot convey the marvelous mimicry that flavors this anecdote.

You see the preacher has been coming to the house
every Saturday evening for the service Sunday. Old
rooster say, "Preacher'll be here tomorrow." [High]
Old hen say, walking around, "I think he's coming
now."
Guinea say, "Not yet."
And the old gobbler, he's standing around out, you
know how a gobbler struts, he's looking from the
bushes, says, "Yon come a couple of them son-of-a-
bitches." [Deep]

17. Poll Parrot

Other parrot jests I collected are in
NFIM 48 and "Negro Tales of Mary

Richardson", no. 9, p. 11, "Parrot and
Sow." These Arkansas and Michigan texts
are interconnected through the theme of
the parrot spying on slaves or on the colored
maid in more recent forms, with the punishment motif, J551.5, "Magpie tells a man that
his wife has eaten an eel." (He has his
feathers plucked out for tattling, and thinks
a bald man has also tattled.) Motif J2211.2,
"Why the sow was muddy," also involves
the magpie in the same sort of misconcep-
tion. European and American references
are given in note 18 of NFIM 208, and note
19 pp. 208-209 discusses my eleven texts.
Scatological parrot jokes are still popular
today in urban White circles.

17a. Poll Parrot (Silas Altheimer)

The slaves had no overseer, and yet the Master always knew who did or didn't do, who lagged behind or
didn't keep up, who talked against the Master. Without
seeing them in the fields he could always tell what went
on. So one day a hawk came along, and lifted the old
parrot out of the tree. The parrot used to sit in top of
the tree, at the turn row, and he could listen and see
what they were doing and saying. Hawk caught and carried him off, and as they flew across the field they
came to a bunch of ploughing men, and he was familiar
with one, who was the hostler boy, fed the horses and
waited around the house. He says, "Jim, I'm riding."
Jim says, "Ride home then."
The hawk flew off with him into the woods and con-
sumed him. From then on the Master had to come out
into the field himself to see what the men were doing.
(He was one of those kind [of] men that didn't use over-
seers.)

17b. Poll Parrot (Grace Bedford)

Back in slavery days Old Marster and his wife
would go to town to shop. And the slaves'd take the
time to have a big party—there was so much food it
wouldn't be missed. They would cook cakes and pies
and potatoes and kill chickens and bring out their fiddle and dance. But no matter how they pledged themselves to secrecy, Old Marster would know all about it
when he came back. And then one day one of the maids
who worked in the house heard the poll parrot review-
ing all the things they had done at the last party.
     "Pass the 'tater pie."
     "Gimme another piece a chicken."
     "This is good cake."
     "Are you going to dance now, are you going to
dance now?" [Croaky]
     "Swing your partner."
     (They go off—they lose interest in the conversa-
tion.)
     So they knew how the Marster knowed about them—
Polly had told them. They had gradually stopped the
parties, and Marster thought soon it would stop alto-
gether. Next time Marster went to town they draped a
black cloth over his head and put him under the wash-
pot. When Marster came back he asked Polly what
she'd seen.
     "Polly don't know. Poor Polly been in hell all day."
(Darkness is her idea of hell.)

17c. Poll Parrot (Edna Nelson)

The cook was cooking in the kitchen, some rolls
for herself. And she heard the mistress coming in, so

she put them under the chair, the stove-chair they had
back in slavery times. And mistress came and sat in
the chair talking. So the parrot said, "Miss, bis' burn
you. Miss, bis' burn you." And continued to say that
till she began looking around to see, and found the hot
rolls.

17d. Poll Parrot (Maria Summers)

Ol' Missus had cooked her some tea cakes, and
she didn't give the poor colored lady none. And she
stepped out, so she goes and cooks her some. And she
hadn't seen the poll parrot. And Missus come back in,
and she just had cooked her one panful. And she emptied them in a cloth in a chair. And Missus come in
and sit down and poll parrot said, "Missus, burn your
ass." And the poor colored woman run outdoors, she
said she was going to kill the poll parrot.

17e. Poll Parrot (A. J. King)

Marster had quite a few poll parrots in among his
slaves, to watch them if they were doing anything wrong.
So the parrots began treading the hens, and the slaves
told on them. And the wife was crazy about working jig-
saw puzzles, and she would even crack the eggs and put
the shells back together on the shelf. And she had to
go away to visit her daughter, who was the belle of the
community. And while she was away the husband decided he would cook breakfast. He began to crack the
eggs, and didn't anything come out the shells. So he
just rushed to the parrots and said, "I told you to stop

treading those hens, and the least you can do is use a
prophylactic."

17f. Poll Parrot (Grace Bedford)

This actually happened in Pine Bluff. The woodman
would come around with his load of wood, and the parrot
would call, "Wood, wood. Drive around to the back and
throw it off."
This one lady had installed gas, and while she was
out the parrot called the woodman. He drove around to
the back and threw his wood off and went back to the
front to collect. He knocked and knocked, then went
next door to find out where the people were. The parrot
said it again, and he saw it again. He was going to
wring its neck, when the lady came home and paid him.

III

OLD MARSTER AND JOHN

Most persons associate American Negro Tales with
animal characters, but Old Marster and John figure in
at least as many stories as Mr. Rabbit and Mr. Fox.
The plantation owner, Old Marster, and his roguish
slave John, engage in a perpetual battle of wits, with
now one and now the other emerging victorious. John
resembles two other traditional American scape-
graces, the Indian trickster and the New England Yan-
kee, in his combination of low cunning and obtuse stu-
pidity. The Old Marster cycle reflects the circumstances and relationships of plantation life with often
surprising detail. In the variants that deal with a fight
between two strong slaves on neighboring plantations,
for example, the plots hinge about an instututional feature of slavery, the selection by the planter of a husky
hand for breeding purposes and general strong-arm
duty. Curiously, for all their localized references and
apparent origin in actual historical situations, many
Old Marster narratives issue from Europe, Africa, and
the British Isles, and adapt themselves skilfully to the
features of antebellum life. Emancipation and the crea-
tion of freedmen failed to alter the basic relationship
between Old Marster, who now becomes Old Boss or
the Boss-man, and his hired hand, who still attempts to
shirk his work and fool the Boss.

18. Master's Gone to Philly-Me-York (Silas Altheimer)

The Old Marster cycle of American
Negro tales is imperfectly represented in
field collections, which have tended to em-
phasize animal stories. See however, J.
Mason Brewer, "John Tales," in Mexican
Border Ballads and Other Lore, ed. Mody
C. Boatright, Publications of the Texas
Folklore Society, XXI (1946), pp. 81-104;
Brewer, "Juneteenth," in Tone the Bell
Easy, ed. J. Frank Dobie, Publications of
the Texas Folklore Society, X (1932),
pp. 9-54; Arthur H. Fauset, "Negro
Folk Tales from the South. (Alabama,
Mississippi, Louisiana)," JAF XL (1927),
section IV, "Ole Marster Stories," pp.
262-267; Lay My Burden Down, ed. B. A.
Botkin (Chicago, 1945), "Fooling Master
and Catching John," pp. 3-9; and ch. 4
in NFIM, "Old Marster and John."
For variants of the present tale, see
Fauset, above, pp. 266-267, "Master Gone
to Philanewyork"; Zora N. Hurston, Mules
and Men (Philadelphia and London, 1935),
pp. 112-113; Portia Smiley, "Folk-Lore
from Virginia, South Carolina, Georgia,
Alabama, and Florida," JAF XXXII (1919),
no. 8, p. 362, "Master Disguised"; and
NFIM 59, "Old Marster Takes a Trip,"
from Walter Winfrey. I have another
variant from Katy Pointer of Mecosta,
Michigan in which the partying slaves
sing, "Massie's gone to Philly-me-jinks,
going to be gone three long weeks." They
throw chicken bones to a ragged white man,
their disguised master, who is amused and
does not reveal himself.

Slave named John was in the confidence of his Master, a trusty. John did everything, melted out the

rations to his slaves—Master didn't use a slave-driver
—John kept his accounts, in his head. He couldn't
read or write, but he had a wonderful memory. So his
Master would often go away on a big trip, would stay
sometimes as much as a month. And so his Master was
finally warned by some of his neighbors that John didn't
always behave as he ought, that he often had frolics with
the neighboring Negroes when his Master was away. So
his Master resolved to find out if John was betraying
his trust. He and his wife and daughter feigned to go
to New York on a visit. And so John as usual barbecued
his pork, barbecued a lamb, or calf, or kid, whatever
he could get his hands on, and sent a runner to tell his
friends on neighboring plantations to come to a big
dance, a big barbecue.

The slaves all dressed in their best, came in early
that night to the frolic. So the dance began in the dance-
room in the big house. John always stayed in the big
house to take care of things. And of course the dance
would be carried on by his comrades while he would be
out superintending the tables, having the food placed on.
And so after John get things arranged so and eating
could begin, he'd go in and observe the dance hisself.

In the meantime his Master had slipped in in dis-
guise, his hands blackened, his face blackened, and a
cap on his head. And so while his Master was observ-
ing all this he went in and began to shout:

> "Joy yourself, joy yourself,
> Master's gone to Philly-Me-York."

Then Master disappeared and took the soot off his
hands and his face. When he returned John was patting
and stamping and hollering:

"Joy yourself, joy yourself,
Master's gone to Philly-Me-York."

And when he came out again he saw his Master,
and recognized him fully. And as a matter of course
his feathers fell, and the slaves fell out of the windows,
and that broke up the party, and John was left on his
knees begging his Master's forgiveness.

19. John and the Horse (John Courtney)

In Lay My Burden Down, pp. 5-6, "The
Boots That Wouldn't Come Off," a slave houseboy borrows not only Old Marster's horse but
his boots. When the horse dies, he has to
walk home, his sore feet swell up in the
tight boots, and he has to cut them off.
Luckily Old Marster was amused. The
University of Arkansas Folklore Archives
has a variant (item 7 reel 167, told by
Mrs. Lula Campbell in Brinkley, Arkansas,
14 Nov. 1953, collected by Mary Celestia
Parler) close to that of John Courtney, except that John is not asked to move the dead
horse. Mrs. Campbell says the slave involved was one of her ancestors who worked
for the Rook family.

John went out for a dance one night. They'd let
him out for enjoyment, and he was getting a little better treatment than some of 'em, he was out from under
the belt, he was the handy boy. But he was always trying to he'p some of them and he'd get caught. Boss
let him go to the dance and John stole the Captain's
horse, to make a showdown. And riding to the dance,
John had big time. He came out from the dance to go
home, and found the horse, Mollie, stiff dead.

So John called two or three of the boys there, says, "Listen," says, "What am I going to do?"

And boys say, "I don't know what you going to do."

And John say, it come to him right away, "Just help to get the horse on my shoulder, down to the big gate anyhow." And after he got him to the big gate, that's as far as the other boys could go. They all got to beat it home so they could give an account of theirself, it getting close to daylight. Old John said, "Listen here, you can't leave him here, you-all got to help get him on my shoulder, so I can take him to the stable."

So they all got around him and helped get Mollie on his shoulder, so John could carry him to the stable. And John get him into the stable, he thought about all the tracks he'd made from the gate to the stable, so he got a broom and dusted out all the tracks. Then he lie down.

Just about that time the Boss called him to get up. John generally feed in the morning. So John got up, went in the stable, come tearing back to tell the boss about it.

"You know Boss, old Mollie's deader'n hell out there."

So Boss says, "What seemed to be the matter with her?"

"I don't know Boss, just stiff dead."

So Boss he got up and put his clothes on and went out there. He kind of searched over, and felt to see whether she was warm or sweating you know.

So Boss let it slide for two or three days. Then he called John in question about it. "John, wasn't Sam riding over to the dance the other night?"

And he said, "Nossir, Boss."

And Boss said, "Well I was told there was two seen riding together, Sam and another one."

"Nossir, Boss."

So he say, "Now John, don't tell me no damn lie."

And John owned up, "Yessir Boss, I did ride him over."

"John, how did you get the horse back in the stable?"

John said, "Boss, I just picked him up on my shoulder and carried him over there."

"Well John, if you picked him up you'll have to pick him up again this morning."

John said, "Boss, I'm a little sick this morning, I can't pick him up this morning."

"Okay, John."

He went into the house and got that gin belt. (That's a big old thick belt they whip 'em with.) And he called John. John ran out and answered the Boss. The Boss was going towards the lot. John knowed it was going to be hell then.

Boss says, "John, I want you to pick up that horse this morning."

Then John say, "Boss, I-I can't pick that horse up."

"Didn't you tell me you brought that horse from that big gate?"

He says, "Yessir, Boss, but I had a hell of a lot help with it."

20. Dividing Souls (A. J. King)

Two well-known tales are cleverly intertwined here. The story of the passerby who thinks he hears the Lord and the Devil counting souls in the graveyard enjoys extraordinary vogue: Vance Randolph says he knows fifty persons in the Ozarks who

can tell it (Who Blowed Up the Church House?
New York, 1952, p. 204.) Stith Thompson comments on its European and American popularity, in The Folktale, p. 214, and provides
references under Type 1791 and Motif X424,
"The Sexton Carries the Parson." See also
note 38 in NFIM 213-214. In United
States Negro texts the slave houseboy sometimes carries his crippled Old Marster down
to the graveyard, who in fright runs home under his own power; thus see the variants by
E. L. Smith in my "A Negro Storytelling
Session on Tape," Midwest Folklore, III
(Winter 1953), pp. 205-206, and by John
Blackamore in my "Negro Tales," Western Folklore, XIII (April 1954), pp. 91-93,
"Old Boss and Mac," reprinted in NFIM
68-71. (Grimm no. 59, "Frederick and
Catherine," concludes with a similar incident). A text without the lame listener
motif appears in my "Negro Tales from
Bolivar County, Mississippi," from Billy
Jack Tyler, Southern Folklore Quarterly,
XIX, 1955, p. 111, "Counting Souls." Many
other variants have been told me by Michigan and Arkansas Negroes. The second incident present here is discussed in the following note.)

During the period of slavery time Old Marster always kept one slave that would keep him posted on the
others, so that he would know how to deal with them
when they got unruly. So this slave was walking around
in the moonlight one night. And he heard a noise coming from the cemetery. And it was two slaves counting
apples, which they had stole from Old Marster's orchard. They couldn't count, so they were exchanging
'em. "You take dis un and I'll take dat un. Dis un's
yours and dat un's mine."

So this slave hear them, and he listened, and he
ran back to Old Marster. And running he fell over a
skeleton head, and he spoke to the skeleton head. "What
you doing here?"

And the skeleton head said, "Something got me here
will get you here."

So he told Old Marster when he got to the house that
the Devil and the Good Lord was in the cemetery counting out souls. "Dis un's yours and dat un's mine, dis
un's yours and dat un's mine."

Old Marster didn't believe him, but he went with
him to the cemetery. And Old Marster told him, said,
"Now if the Devil and the Good Lord ain't counting out
souls, I'm going to cut your head off."

Sure enough the slaves had gone and Old Marster
didn't hear anything, and he cut John's head off. Then
John's head fell beside the skeleton head. Then the head
turned over and said, "I told you something that got me
here would get you here. You talk too much."

(That's one my daddy would tell us when we were
talking too much.)

21. Talking Turtle (Julia Courtney)

        Ernest W. Baughman assigns Motif
    B210.2, "Talking animal or object refuses
    to talk on demand. Discoverer is unable
    to prove his claims; is beaten," in A Com-
    parative Study of The Folktales of England
    and North America, and lists five Negro
    variants. A detailed text appears in my
    "More Negro Tales of John Blackamore,"
    Western Folklore, XIII (Oct. 1954), pp.
    256-258, "The Talking Mule," reprinted
    in NFIM 63-65, and see note 33 on pp.
    212-213. Vance Randolph gives an Ozark

variant of the talking turtle in the Tennessee
Folklore Society Bulletin, XIX (Dec. 1953),
pp. 102-103, "A Folktale from Arkansas,"
which he used for the title story in The
Talking Turtle And Other Ozark Folk Tales
(New York, 1957), and see the references
by Herbert Halpert, pp. 179-180.

Every day John had to tote water from the bayou,
and every time he'd go to the bayou he would start fus-
sin'. "I'm tired of toting water every day." The next
day he went to the bayou and he repeated the same thing
(you know just like you repeat the same thing). So last
one day John went to the bayou, the turtle was sitting
on a log.

Turtle raised up and looked at him, and told John,
"Black man, you talk too much."

So John didn't want to think the turtle was talking.
He went back to the bayou, got another bucketful of
water. The turtle told him the same thing. John
throwed the buckets down, took and run to the house,
and called Old Marster, and told him the turtle was
down there talking. And so Old Marster didn't want to
go because he didn't believe it. But John kept telling
him the turtle was talking. So finally Old Boss 'cided
he could go. But he told John if the turtle didn't talk
he was going to give him a good beating. So they all
went on down to the bayou, and when they got down to
the bayou the turtle was sitting on a log with his head
back halfway in his shell.

And so John told the turtle, "Tell Old Marster
what you told me." So John begged the turtle to talk.
So the turtle still didn't say anything. So Old Marster
taken him on back to the house, and give him a good
beating, and made him git his buckets, and keep totin'
water.

When John got back down to the bayou, the turtle
had his head sticking up. John dipped up his water, and
the turtle raised up and told him, says, "Black man,
didn't I tell you you talked too much?"

22. John Praying (Harrison Stanfill)

Baughman assigns this incident Motif
J217.0.1.1, "Trickster overhears man praying for death to take him," and gives seven
Negro and two White references. A variant
that merges the several forms the tale takes
is in NFIM 61-62, "Efan Prays," from J. D.
Suggs, and see note 31 on p. 212. Sometimes Old Marster comes to John's quarters dressed as the Lord to take him away,
or John prays for death for the white folks,
and when the trickster drops an object upon
him, asks the Lord if he can't distinguish
between white and colored people.

This old Boss-man said he was going to whip John
within an inch of his life on Wednesday night. John
started praying every day from Sunday to Wednesday.
On Wednesday evening that was his last prayer. He told
him, "Lord, I been praying every day since Sunday and
you've never failed me. I want you to take me away this
evening." The boys heard the prayer and they went
down and climbed the tree with a ladder rope. So when
John made his final prayer that night he said, "Lord I
got to go, because I've only got fifteen minutes before
my execution."
So they said, "Okay John, you'll have to come by
way of the rope because my chariot is broke."
He said, "All right Lord, let it down, I'm willing to
go any way you carry me."

Old Marster and John

Little boys up in the tree put down the rope,
"John, put your head in this loop." So they comm_.._.._u
tightening on the rope, and he commenced praying fast.
"O Lord, didn't you say you know everything? Well,
don't you know damn well you choking me?"

23. A Dime for the Sack (Harrison Stanfill)

> Sometimes in the praying-tree stories
> John comes out on top of Old Marster. Cf.
> Hurston, Mules and Men, pp. 112-114, "How
> the Negroes Got Their Freedom," where the
> Philly-Me-York tale is joined with that of
> John and his accomplice in the praying tree,
> who plays the Lord and frightens Old Massa;
> the same idea occurs in NFIM 65-67, "Old
> Boss and John at the Praying Tree," from
> Tommy Carter, and see note 35 on p. 213.
> Motif J1473.1, "Man prays for 1000 gold
> pieces. Will trust god for one," furnishes
> the trick here.

Old Boss had all kinds of confidence in John, and
said that anything he asked Jesus for he'd sent it to him.
John had been a favorite around for a while and Boss
was going to give him $100 for his holiday. And he
called John in and asked him, "John, you go on down
and pray the Lord to send you $100 for your holiday,
and if he send that, I'll have all kinds of confidence in
you." So Boss-man sacked up $99.90 and give it to
two of his little boys. So they saw John going down to
the tree that evening and they went along ahead of him
and climbed the tree.
John got on his knees and said, "O Lord, I'm praying to you to have a brilliant Christmas, I wants $100."
No quicker said than done, the little boys dropped a sack

of dough alongside of John. John grabbed the sack and
got off his knees and went hopping off to the house and
said, "Master I got it, I got it."

So Master said, "You sure, John, you got it? "

"Yes Master, I got it."

"Well now, pour it out on the counter and see how
much you got." So John couldn't count but $99.90. "So
you can see John, you only got $99.90."

"That okay Boss, he did what he said he did, but
he charged me a dime for the sack."

24. Mike and Peter (Silas Altheimer)

The same situation appears in NFIM
55-56, "The Fight," from Charles Brown,
and note 23 on p. 210 describes a variant
from Joe D. Heardley still closer to the
present text. Heardley's tale has the
small slave bluff the big one by yelling
to St. Peter and the Virgin Mary to move
over before he throws the thousand pound
maul skyward; five Negro examples are
cited by Herbert Halpert in his note to
"Jack in the Giants' Newground" in Richard
Chase, The Jack Tales (Boston, 1943), p.
189. For the strong man throwing a horse
and his rider over the wall, see my Johnathan
Draws the Long Bow (Cambridge, 1946), p.
126 and n. 14 (told on George Washington
Briggs), and Thomas F. Waters, Ipswich
in the Massachusetts Bay Colony (2 vols.,
Ipswich, Mass., 1905-7), vol. I, p. 242
(told on Jonathan Wise).

Two men had slaves, one named Mike and the other
Peter. And they often met and discussed the strength
of their slaves, how they were giants and so forth.

Finally they made a bet on them, and all their friends
made bets. So they appointed a day to fight in the town
square. But they built an enclosure in the town square,
so all the people could see them fight to a finish. On
the day set a great crowd gathered. One man had come
in and seeing the enclosure, but not knowing it was the
place for the fight, he carried his horse on in the enclosure and hitched him. So when Mike and Peter went
inside, the first thing Mike did was go to the horse that
was saddled and pick him up and lifted him over the
fence.

When Peter saw that he said, "No fight."

25. Big Feet Contest (A. J. King)

During slavery time the Old Marsters would get
together and brag which of their slaves had the largest
feet. And one of the slave Marsters said, "My slave's
feet are larger than yours."

And the other said, "No, my slave's feet are longer
than yours."

So the other slaveowner says, "Give me proof that
your slave's feet are larger than mine."

So this was his proof. He says, "Whenever I buy
shoes for my slave, they come in separate boxes, and
they send a pair of oars with them."

So the other slaveowner gave his proof. Said, "You
know the five hundred acres I own? You know those
field mice was on those five hundred acres?" Says,
"John was plowing at one end of the five hundred acres,
and I hollered, 'Field mouse.' And John raised his
foot. And I said, 'Did you get him, John?'

"And he said, 'Yes, if he's anywhere in the field.'"

26. Watching the Pot

Herbert Halpert notes to a text in Folk-
tales and Legends from the New Jersey
Pines: A Collection and a Study (2 vols.:
Indiana University doctoral dissertation,
1947), "Something in the Pot" (vol. II, no.
162, p. 653) eleven references, one each
from Texas, Illinois and Newfoundland,
two from the West Indies, and six from
England. Baughman assigns Motif J1813.8*
to the incident. The variant by Maria
Summers is close to that in "Richard's
Tales," Folk Travelers, ed. Mody C.
Boatright et al., Publications of the Texas
Folklore Society XXV (1953), recorded by
John L. Sinclair, transcribed by Stella A.
Sinclair, pp. 243-245, "Sheep-Head Dumplings." Halpert remarks, "It is interesting
to note that several collectors have thought
this a purely local story."

26a. Hoghead and Peas (A. J. King)

During the period of slavery Old Marster always
kept a little boy to watch the pot on the stove while the
family attended church. So when they went away to
church this Sunday they had a new boy, so they told him,
"When all the peas go to the bottom, the dinner is done.
So you watch the peas, John."

So the little boy start playing and forgot about the
peas. So when he did take a look the peas had all gone
to the bottom, and the hoghead mouth had opened. And
two or three peas passing across the mouth. All he
knew he was going to get a good beating if all them peas
were gone. So he lit out for church. When he got to
church he ran in with both hands up and mouth open,
calling, "Oh Marster, oh Marster. That hoghead done

ate all those peas and got his mouth open trying to catch
them two or three bubbling round on top."

26b. Sheephead and Dumplings (Maria Summers)

The little boy's mother was at the church, and she
told them to notice the meat in the pot. And the little
boy saw it boiling over so, he thought it was the sheep-
head. Along them times people made dumplings to
meat. And the little boy went to the church to tell his
mother; she becked her hand for him to go back.

He told her, "You needn't to wink, you needn't to
blink, 'cause the sheephead at home knocking all the
dumplings out the pot."

(She might had some meat there and he thought she
had dumplings in the pot, and the water boiling over was
the dumplings jumping out the pot.)

27. John and the Tigercat (Harrison Stanfill)

In olden times Old Boss liked to hunt. He had one
of his Negroes his name was John, so he was a great
fur-hunter, hunt for coons and such. At last one night
they went out and John put the wrong thing up a tree—
happened to be a wildcat. So John went up the tree to
bring him down, like all the other little animals he went
up after, like coons and possums. John went up, and the
wildcat went up too, till he seen he couldn't go no further. So he decided he'd come on back down. When he
got down the tigercat would slide around. So he slid
around enough to tear John's butt with his paws. So
John let the tigercat alone and slid down the tree to
meet his boss. Boss asked him what the trouble was.

He said, "I got one up the tree."

"Why didn't you bring him down?"

So John told him, "No, you'll have to shoot that son-of-a-bitch, he carries a razor."

28. Lazy John (Clara Parker)

> Cf. Hurston, Mules and Men, pp. 125-126,
> "You Think I'm Gointer Pay You But I Ain't,"
> and NFIM 60-61, "Marster Paying Off John,"
> which employ Motif J1172.2, "Payment with
> the clink of the money."

Uncle Tom had some men working for him. John was the shirker in the crowd. Every time the Boss would go away John would not work. Old Boss was watching but John did not know. When Old Boss would leave John would say, "Old Boss think I'm working but I ain't." He'd sit down and not do anything. He'd do this every day till payday come. And when payday come all the men marched around to get their pay checks.

So Old Boss says, when the men was marching around, and John got in sight, "Old John think I'm going to pay him but I ain't."

29. John Outspells Master (Bertha White)

> The same idea is presented in Hurston,
> Mules and Men, pp. 62-63, "How to Write
> a Letter."

It's about John and his Boss in slavery. John was very smart. Boss liked to show him off because he was a good speller. His master had company one day. He

said, "John, come and spell some for us." John took
his seat. He called John several little simple
words. John spelled all he called. John finally got
tired of his Master's entertaining.

And he said, "Master, you spell some now. Let me
try you."

Master says, "All right John, I can spell anything
you call."

Then John says, "All right, stand up, Master." He
says, "Spell tstststschtsch."

"John, what you take me for, a fool?"

John say, "Yessir Master, take your seat."

30. John's Courtship (Julia Courtney)

John's Boss-man had a boy, and he and John was
long together. His Boss-man's boy would go see his
girl reg'larly. Last one night John went to see his girl,
and the next day he was out in the field plowing. So the
boy went down in the field where John was. So John got
to the end of the road he [the boy] said, "Hi John. What
do you say when you see your girl?" (That's what he
asked John.)

And John said, "We just play." See John was
shamed to tell him what they were talking about. So
John axed the boy, "You said you went to see your girl
friend last night." Said, "What did you tell your girl
friend last night?"

The boy said, "I talked co'tship."

John axed him, "What is co'tship?"

He says, "Man, when I went to my girl's house last
night, you know what I told her?"

John said, "No."

He said, "Well I told my girl, 'Good mo'ning.'

(Said) 'Now, sit down.' And I told her, 'Your eyes look like dove eyes. Your cheeks look like a blood red rose. Your teeth look like pearl. Your breath smell like the best thing in the world. And I'm good mind to kiss you.'" So he kissed her.

So that evening commenced to getting late. John had learnt something to tell his girl friend. John couldn't wait till the sun go down hardly. He went to the lot, put his mules in the lot, and went running home. Took him a good hot bath, put his clean clothes on, and lit out to his girl's house in the biggest kind of hurry. John had waited so long till he done forgot what the boy told him. But he didn't think he had. John went on in his girl's house. Before she could get a chance to rest his hat he said, "Hi."

She said, "Hi." [Sweetly]

John couldn't sit down before he started to talking. He say "Yo' eyes look like dove eyes. Your cheeks look like a blood red rose." He say, "Your teeth look like garden rakes. Your breath smell like burnt garlic." Then John drawed his hand back and said, "I'm good mind to slap the hell out of you."

That's what he told her. And he hit her. And she quit him.

(That was told in cou'tship. That's a cou'tship story. People couldn't party out in the country like they could in town.)

31. Saturday Night

This story derives its point from reality. Geleva Grice in driving me around Pine Bluff and Altheimer Saturday afternoon particularly wanted me to see the great clusters of

country Negroes come to town, to congregate
and relax. The idea that the Negro wage-
earner lives from Saturday to Saturday,
when he gets his pay check, appears in a
separate cycle of jests; see my "Negro
Tales," Western Folklore, XIII (April
1954), pp. 96-97, "Colored Man, Jew,
and White Man," from John Blackamore,
reprinted in NFIM 77.

31a. Saturday Night (A. A. Mazique)

Fellow was working on Saturday in a furniture
store, and the boss had some deliveries he just had to
get out that night. And he offered to pay him time and
a half to do the work. John said, "Any other day but I
just can't do it tonight." Then he offered him double
time. John said he still couldn't do it tonight—any
other night but tonight.

"Well John, what's wrong with tonight, that it's different from any other night?"

"Well Boss, if you could be a nigger one Saturday
night you'd never want to be a white man any more."

31b. Saturday Night (E. M. Moore)

The O. H. Harden Furniture Company of McGeehee,
Arkansas, were working practically all Negroes, and
they had very competent help. They got in a carload of
furniture. The car came in on a Saturday morning.
(This happened in 1937.) They wanted to get the car unloaded that Saturday to save the demurrage on it. Mr.
Harden asked his workers if they would work that Saturday and Saturday night. If so they could unload that car

and save this demurrage. So one man that had worked
for that company twenty years told him he'd work that
Saturday, but he wouldn't work that Saturday night. Mr.
Harden wanted to know why he couldn't work Saturday
night.

Said, "I just have to go out on Saturday night."

He said, "Well tell me, what is it you people do
on Saturday night?"

"Well I don't know, but if you would get out and be
a nigger one Saturday night, you never would want to be
a white man again."

IV

SPIRITS

The group of stories in the present section involve supernatural beliefs, and are all told for true. Southern Negroes encounter well-intentioned spirits who visit them in dreams to inform of buried treasure, malevolent witches who disturb their sleep, and fearful hants which infest the shadows. The vast body of lore which Puckett has described in Folk Beliefs of the Southern Negro provides the basis for many personal narratives about spooks and specters.

32. Spirit of the Orchard (Silas Altheimer)

For Southern Negro accounts of spirits and hants, see Drums and Shadows, by the Savannah Unit of the Georgia Writers' Project (Athens, Ga., 1940), passim; Newbell N. Puckett, Folk Beliefs of the Southern Negro (Chapel Hill, N. C., 1926), ch. 2, "Burial Customs, Ghosts, and Witches"; and NFIM ch. 8, "Spirits and Hants."
A haunted orchard that frightens off a thief is in A. M. Bacon and E. C. Parsons, "Folk-Lore from Elizabeth City County, Virginia," JAF XXXV (1922), no. 49, p. 289, "Haunted House."

Mrs. Lou Cooper, my uncle's wife, a large stout woman, told this as a true ghost story, in Cleveland

county, Arkansas, 1877. A slaveowner named Box had
died in the big farmhouse—Box's place—and my stepfather rented the place and stayed there one year, made
a crop. Good land, but he didn't stay there but one year.
I used to hear something walking—tap, tap, tap on the
floor, like a chicken, come right up to the bed.

The thing that brought the matter to a head was my
aunt coming to the field one day to get fruit. We had a
large orchard, ten acres or more (forty acres fenced
in, and half of it was in fruit). And he'd let people come
and get the fruit without charge, apples, peaches, plums.
But four white Indian peach trees, big ones, he had
marked with a string for family use, and told them not
to take those. She said as soon as she pulled the fruit
she heard this loud groaning at the house. She pulled
half a dozen or more of those large peaches and put
them in the bottom of her basket. She took the basket
and went on to the plum orchard. He had it fenced off
so the hogs wouldn't get in. The groaning stopped at
the house. But as soon as she put the basket down the
plums began to rain down. I never have seen such an
orchard; the trees were so thick they just overlapped.
(Box made his slaves put them out; sometimes you got
two different kinds of apples off one tree.) She didn't
know how she got out of there; she heard the groaning
up above in the tree, and the basket was filled (so that
looks like the spirits had action). She didn't come to
herself till she was a quarter of a mile from the house
(the orchard was back and east of the house) going home,
and she never did come back. She was almost frightened
to death when she got home. She told that because she
was almost out of her wits.

We moved away the next year.

33. Tobe Courtney Has a Bad Evening (Tobe Courtney)

Similar scares are presented in my "A
Negro Storytelling Session on Tape," Mid-
west Folklore, III (Winter 1953), pp. 209-211,
by Mary Richardson and Mrs. E. L. Smith,
reprinted in NFIM 122-124, "Hants at
Dusk." Selections of Negro hant tales can
be found in Follow de Drinkin' Gou'd, ed.
J. Frank Dobie, Publications of the Texas
Folk-Lore Society VII (1928), pp. 121-128,
"Confidences from Old Nacogdoches," by
Martha Emmons, part 2, "Hants"; The
Frank C. Brown Collection of North Caro-
lina Folklore, Vol. I (Durham, N. C., 1952),
pp. 669-689, "Ghosts and Hants" (mixed
White and Negro); Botkin, Lay My Burden
Down, pp. 39-48, "Hants"; Puckett, Folk
Beliefs of the Southern Negro, pp. 116-118,
"Negro 'Ha'nts'."

When I was a young man, about sixteen, seventeen
years old, living in Collins, I went to a dance. And long
about nine, ten o'clock I reckon, fellow came in with a
Winchester and broke it up, shot 'em up, and folks flew.
I was the only one stayed in there, after everyone got
out, bartender and everyone, and I filled up my pockets
with cakes and candies and apples. And I coming up the
railroad by myself, and I just eating to beat ya. And I
got way up in a barpit (high banks along a railroad), and
I heard a racket. I thought it was some of the boys trying to scare me, and I commenced cussing. And closer
I got, I saw kind of a whirlwind, leaves and dust around,
and something inside like a bell going "Loopty-loop,
loopty-loop." And my hair got so tight, it stood up
straight on my head, and I done some running—if ever
you saw a little old dark man running, that was me. I

run till I get to the station, and I had to stay there and
rest.

Then along come another man, riding a mule, a
friend of mine. And we went on down through the tan-
yard together, about a mile from town. And that's
where I saw the natchal spirit, that white girl. And I
knowed she was dead. And she was just as natchal as
I looking at you. She was just as if walking back to her
home place. That was a solid spirit.

She was Seefie Courtney. They was white
Courtneys, they raised my father. And long in slavery
times people went in under Marster's name. We grew
up together. She'd been dead about two year—was
about twenty-one, I reckon. The other fellow run off,
he knowed it was a hant. But I stood there and looked
at her till I saw who it was—I'd done run enough that
night. She just kept on going back to her home house.
If Dave Sanders was living today he could tell you the
same thing.

She came on from behind that tree and kept on walking to her father's house. That's why I tell folks there's
hants, there's spirits. Dressed in a long white robe,
and holding that up in one hand. Maybe come back to
visit her father or mother, either one.

34. Haunted House in New Orleans (Silas Altheimer)

Jeanne deLavigne in Ghost Stories of
Old New Orleans (New York and Toronto,
1946) elaborates two score spectral legends
based presumably on reports such as the
present text. In "The Haunted House of the
Rue Royale" (pp. 248-258) a wealthy French
lady sadistically tortures her slaves, whose

shrieks thereafter echo through the man-
sion for more than a century.

Professor Perkins told me this in 1929. He was
principal of sixty teachers.
The story was that a lady of French origin, of
French descent, visited often in Paris and Mobile and
in New Orleans. So on one occasion she came and found
her mother dead. She decided however that some of her
slaves had killed her mother. In spite of their protest
of innocence, she believed they had perpetrated the act.
So she called her trusted slaves, especially her coachman, to put to death her slaves, to make them divulge
the death of her mother. To the last they denied it. She
killed thirteen. People would hear their screams and
groaning, and never saw her slaves again. When some
of the slaves informed the citizens what was taking
place, and the citizens were preparing to punish her,
she took all her money, and had her trusted coachman fly
to Mobile with her. From Mobile she fled to Paris, and
never returned.
The house stands today, and is known as the haunted
house. It is said that people still hear cries and groans
in the house, so no one dares to live there or to take
possession of the property.
My friend, a graduate of Alcorn, carried me there,
in the daytime. I wouldn't go in the nighttime, not under those circumstances.

35. Testing to be a Two-Head (Silas Altheimer)

Tobe Courtney also told me about the
two-head test. "I heard a fellow say once
he paid twenty-five dollars to take that test.

He had to go through a house with a big
hallway, and rooms on each side. And
every room had different things in it,
different performances, fearful looking
animals. He said if you weren't a mighty
brave man you wouldn't go through. . . .
After that, tricks he wanted to work, he
could work them." In NFIM 116, Mary
Richardson gives an esoteric formula
for "Becoming a Two-Head."

My stepfather told me this. He could tell them all
night. His name was Frank Tallbert. That was in Cal-
houn County. He knew this two-headed man. A man
wanted to be two-headed hisself. And so he went to his
house and offered him money, to give him knowledge so
he would be two-headed. (Two-headed really means
two minds.) So he told him he couldn't stand it. "You
couldn't stand to be made a two-headed man." He told
him he could, he could stand it.

So the first thing the two-headed man did was to
make this dinner table walk all around the room and
leap from one end of the room to the other. And then
he made the chairs chase each other around the table,
the whole set of half a dozen.

So he sent him down by a worm fence, and when he
leaned against it the fence fell down. And when he
scraped himself up the fence would build itself up again.
He endured that all right. And all the horses in the pasture came up and neighed, and they would kick and run.
And he still stood his ground. And then the wild foxes
came—many of them in that section—and barked and
barked. And he stood still, determined to be two-headed.

Next a large rattlesnake came and crawled through
the fence where he was, and shook his rattles, striking
at him as he passed. He got out of the way. (That was
the old man sending all those things to test him out.)

Next all the worm fences were surrounding him, and
building themselves up, and falling, and building themselves up. And he got scared, and ran and went back to
the house. The two-head told him he couldn't be a two-
headed man, because he couldn't stand all the tests and
trials that was put on him.

(That's purely imaginative, you can see how their
imagination works. My stepfather said he knew the man
who could do that. I think that's the way the man
learned, by standing the test under some other man.
My stepfather'd tell me that when I was a little boy, and
I'd listen big-eyed till I was afraid to go to bed.)

36. Plagued by Witch (Sally Courtney)

> Accounts of being ridden by witches are
> given by Mr. and Mrs. E. L. Smith and Mrs.
> Mary Richardson in my "Negro Witch Stories
> on Tape," Midwest Folklore, II (Winter 1952),
> pp. 229-241, reprinted with slight editorial
> changes in NFIM 139-144. Note 94 in NFIM
> 221-222 refers to similar American Negro
> experiences.

Seems like it was a little bitty woman in a black
skirt and a white waist and a white rag on her head, and
she'd git up on me and just walk on me from my feets
up, up to my head. She'd just smother me kind of, and
I was trying to talk, till I got hold of her, and throw her
over behind the chifrobe. Then I wakened up, and got up
and sit up on side of the bed.

I sent for old Mrs. Long, midwife, lived about as far
from here as Gray's Motel. She'd been doing that way
for several nights. I said, "Why don't you quit 'noying

me?" I said, "Every night you come down here and
get on me."

She said, "Daughter, I ain't been on you."

I said, "Well yes you sure do, every night I throw
you over behind that chifrobe."

She told me, "Take that baby out from the bed and
it won't bother you."

After that I took the baby outa the bed and it didn't
bother me no more, till I put it back in. Then it came
in the form of a little bitty boy. He got up on top of
me and held his arms out, and wanted me to tote him.
So I picked him up and toted him and then I put him
down. And then the hounds got after him and run him
on off. And that's the last I ever saw him.

They just 'peared up all at once and got behind him.
He was running from them. I carried him off to keep
him from bothering me.

She told me, "He just come in the form of me," told
me not to be scared. She was a friend of ours, a neigh-
bor, died in '30.

(Tobe Courtney: They just shorten your breath—
hah, hah, hah —until it looks like you can't wake up,
until you do wake up. Sometimes I just tetch her [Sally]
and she wake right up. Some people say you can put a
horseshoe over the door can stop them.)

37. Treasure Dream (John Courtney)

For spirits that lead Negroes to treasure and hants that frighten them off see
three texts in NFIM 133-136; and "The
Haint's Treasure," in Tennessee Folklore
Society Bulletin, XIX (Sept. 1953), p. 66,
in an article on "Negro Folklore from
Fayette County." A ghost in a haunted

house discloses the whereabouts of treasure, but the digger quits because of the
cold, in Harry M. Hyatt, Folk-Lore from
Adams County, Illinois (New York, 1935),
no. 10470, p. 610. Other references appear in note 92 in NFIM 221. Familiar
Motifs here are N531, "Treasure discovered through dream," and N538,
"Treasure pointed out by supernatural
creature."

I lived in a place there was a horseshoe over every
door, right off Altheimer, to stop the spirit. I seed it
every night. He was a heavyset man, about my size
now, a white fellow, an I'shman. My wife and I used to
see him, we was just young married then. He'd be at
the north side of the cedar tree, outside my yard by
my woodpile. And he'd just stand there and vanish
away, on down to the ground.

Then one night he came to me in a vision, and he
gave it to me then. He had a colored man with him, a
spare-made fellow. He knocked and he come in and I
asked him what he want. And he told me, some money,
at the spot where I'd seen him. I never did see him but
once again. I used to hear that when they was two
travel like that, they'd kill one — the colored fellow —
and he'd be the one to watch. The white man owned the
money.

My wife's uncle and I 'tempted to get it one night,
but as soon as we put shovel in the earth, that's when
they would 'pear up. They looked just like buffalo cows,
big cows like in Texas, fearful looking; they come up in
the shape of those, big horns, eyes big as a teacup.

So I told a white feller about it. I told him I
wouldn't go near the place, but I'd show him where it
was: three feet north of the root of the tree. After I
showed him the spot I backed off, and I heard a noise,

and I seed it just as he did, just as soon as he put the
shovel in the earth. And I beat him back to the car. I
figured that was what was going to happen. He offered
me five dollars to go back and pick up his instrument;
it cost him $ 1,000—it was a locator. He said I could
make five dollars and I said I wasn't going to make anything except tracks.

(One night after I came from church, I was getting
ready to move, and he 'peared up at that place.)

38. Another Treasure Dream (John Courtney)

About three months ago I had a vision. There was
a man, unknown colored man (kind of favored Ben King
a little bit), and a boy who'd been killed twenty-one,
twenty-two years ago—he got stabbed with a knife, they
got into him on the corner here. They came up to the
gate here, and called me—"John."

Seemed like I knowed them. I said, "Come on in."

He said, "I'm so tired and worried, I been getting
around."

I said, "I been tired too, I been working a little bit
today."

He came in and sat down on the side of the bed.
His name was Luke. I kinda turned my head one side
when I seed him, 'cause I knew where he was supposed
to be. This other fellow said, "I got something for you."

I said, "Something for me?"

I just got up and slipped my pants on, zipped them
up. They went on out the door, and we got on over the
fence, and come on down to the road, and saw an orchard over on the left, a puccawn [pecan] grove, and a
pump sitting right on the edge of the puccawn grove.
The road was coming from the highway to the house; in

the vision I was living in the house. He went to this place, right by the pump, and looked like he just raked it over, and I saw four bushels of money, in a great big oldtime pot, a round pot, deep. And he give me all that.

That whole family's died out. He said he didn't have anybody to leave it to. (They's passed you see.) I wish I knew where that was. I been all over the county looking for it.

[Tobe Courtney says the place is on highway 65 leading up to Mr. Phillips' house.]

When there's a big holiday or rodeo and the people's on the west side of town, I'm going out there.

39. The Mermaid (Silas Altheimer)

See NFIM 147-148 (Suggs) and "Negro Tales of Mary Richardson" no. 19, pp. 17-18, for two printed variants. I have five more unpublished texts, four from Michigan and one from Tobe Courtney in Arkansas, for this hitherto unreported legend. All my eight variants follow the same basic story outline. They are discussed in note 98 in NFIM 223, "The Mermaid." In the present text Altheimer uses a motif not present in the other examples, classified by Baughman as Motif B81.13.4*, "Mermaid gives mortals gold from sea bottom," with one reference from Shropshire.

When my grandmother told me about the mermaid, I said I never wanted to go on the sea. She was reared in New Orleans, and had come to Maryland by steamer. She was on my mother's side.

The mermaid would swim alongside the water at some distance, where she could see the men walking on

deck, and pick out the one she wanted. She'd always
pick a goodlooking young man. And so she would demand him, and if he wasn't thrown overboard she would
threaten to turn the ship over. She'd hear his name,
in time of storm, when they were putting up the rigging,
or taking it down. To prevent her from turning the ship
over, and losing all the passengers and cargo, the
sailors would cast him to her. So as soon as he hit
the surface she would take her long hair and wrap it
around [gesture], yet arrange it so that he could
breathe. And she would soon dive to the bottom of the
ocean, to the confines of her home. Then she reared
children by him. She would give him anything he
wanted except fish—if he asked for fish he would die.
(She would kill him I guess; that's the way I got the
story.) She and the young mermaids would go out together, and leave him at home, but he could have everything his heart could wish. She would make the sailors
throw them to her—fruit, groceries of all kind, barrels of flour, sack of sugar. She'd dart away, and
bring them back, and return, until she was satisfied.
She didn't take all from one ship however.

　　And finally when he grew old, and wanted to return to his old home, she would take him with a bag of
gold, and put him on the shore of the sea nearest his
old home. The fish part kept her human part alive and
active; she just got bigger, the fish part. So he lived
a free man, freer than a sailor, and got all that gold.

V

JOCULAR   TALES

Visibly the Southern Negro possesses a hair—trigger sense of humor. He relishes a joke hugely, meets
it more than halfway, and laughs with body and soul at
even a simple wheeze.[1] Such at any rate has been my
experience on numerous field trips. While the dirty
joke travels among Negroes as readily as among
Whites, unsoiled jests enjoy great favor with colored
people. One special theme for Negro comedy origi-
nates in the fear that colored folk feel about spirits
of the dead. But if they will run from a ghost or a hant,
in the warmth of their homes amid a friendly circle
they can roar about the experience, and enjoy fictional
incidents involving eerie frights. Favorite scare-tales
deal with the dead man who apparently revives, and
the series of horrors that confront the hardy soul who
stays overnight in a haunted house.

Other miscellaneous jests enter into the Negro
repertoire. Southern Negroes retell quantities of
jokes about stupid Irishmen, as do the residents of
certain isolated white communities. Another jocular
pattern involves the gullible and credulous country Negro who comes to town and sees his first train or
streetcar, and reacts in ludicrous fashion. One joke-
cycle deals with the different races, usually the Negro,

---

[1] Newbell N. Puckett comments in similar vein on
Negro humor, in Folk Beliefs of the Southern Negro
(Chapel Hill, 1926), p. 49, "Negro Jokes."

75

the Jew, and the white man, and accounts with wry humor for the lowly estate of the colored man.

In his selection of European folktales, the Negro
again shows a penchant for ridiculous scenes. He de-
lights in those Old World fictions that tell of simple-
minded girls and old maids who commit follies in
quest of husbands, in preference to well-known Märchen, which rarely appear in the thousand texts I have
collected. Fools, simpletons, and numskulls parade
through the various categories of Negro humorous
tales.

(Comic scare tales follow in nos. 40-43; jests
principally of fools and Irishmen in nos. 44-53; and
complex tales of noodles in nos. 54-57.)

40. I'm Going to Fall (John Courtney)

> See the references under Motif
> H1411.1, "Fear Test: saying in haunted
> house where corpse drops piecemeal down
> chimney. Dead man's members call out to
> hero, 'Shall we fall, or shall we not?'"
> This trait also occurs as an episode in
> Type 326, "The Youth Who Wanted to
> Learn What Fear Is," and appears as
> tale no. 4 in the classic collection of
> Household Tales by the Brothers Grimm.
> Mention of variants of Type 326 where
> the spectral limbs announce their fall is
> in Johannes Bolte und George Polívka,
> Anmerkungen żu den Kinder- u. Haus-
> märchen der Bruder Grimm, vol. I
> (Leipzig, 1913), p. 30, n. 1. A good text
> is in the Southern Workman, XXVII, no.
> 3 (March 1898), p. 57, "The Boy and the
> Ghost." A poor boy stays in a haunted
> house, which is offered to anyone who

passes the night there. He cooks his supper,
and a leg up the chimney says, "I am going
to drop." "I don't keer jes' so's you don'
drap in my soup." The whole man finally
drops; the boy goes to bed, legs pull him
under the house and show him money. A
very close text is in A. M. Bacon and E.
C. Parsons, "Folk-Lore from Elizabeth
City County, Virginia," JAF XXV (1922),
no. 50, p. 290, "The Dismembered Ghost."
     A variation of Type 326 from a Por-
tuguese Negro living on the New England
coast, interestingly localized, and with
the present episode, is in Elsie C. Parsons,
Folk-Lore from the Cape Verde Islands,
Part I, MAFLS XV (1923), no. 81, pp.
241-244, "As Broad as He Was Long."

Some travelers in olden time traveled with a yoke
of oxen. So they come to this old house. So they
'cided they'd put up for the night there. They took out
everything and got the cook vessels, 'cided they would
cook them something to eat. So they cooked the bread.
Then John put his meat on. Just about time his meat
begin to cook, something holler,

          "I'm going to fall." [Very high]

     They looked around, looked at one another. Say,
"What was that?" He just kept hollering,

          "I'm going to fall."

     So John thought it was some of the boys trying to
kid him, said, "That's not none of us, that's up high,
whatsever it is." So he hollered again,

          "I'm going to fall."

So that made John mad. John hollered back, "Fall then."

That-time down he come into that skillet, and down went the skillet, and knocked his meat and fire and everything, and out went the boys. John whirled and got away from there.

41. Waiting for Martin (Julia Courtney)

> Variations on this comic tale of frights
> that scare a man from a haunted house cir-
> culate widely in American white and Negro
> tradition. I collected ten Negro versions in
> Michigan, of which one is in NFIM 128-129,
> "Rufus in the Hanted House," from Joe D.
> Heardley; another from John Blackamore
> is in "Negro Tales," Western Folklore,
> XIII (July 1954), pp. 167-168, "The Hanted
> House"; and a third from Suggs is post,
> no. 100, p. 264, "Wait till Martin Comes."
> References are given in note 85, p. 220
> in NFIM. See also William A. Percy,
> Lanterns on the Levee (New York, 1941),
> pp. 293-294. Baughman classifies the
> story under Motif J1499.19.2, "Man at-
> tempts to stay in haunted house all night.
> One cat after another enters. . . ." Like
> the preceding tale, this one represents a
> humorous outgrowth from Type 326, "The
> Youth Who Wanted to Learn What Fear Is."
> Other Märchen likewise require the hero
> to endure horrors in an enchanted dwell-
> ing (Motif D758.1); see e.g. Types 400, 401,
> 402; an example of Type 402, "The Mouse
> . . . as Bride" is in my "Polish Wonder
> Tales of Joe Woods," Western Folklore,
> VIII (Jan. 1949), pp. 33-37, no. 2, "The
> Black Kitty."

You see that ghost was named Martin. See it was
a hanted house, could no one stay there. And so they
put up money to see could they find someone to stay
in the house. And so everyone would go to stay in that
house couldn't stay there. And so one of the mens
went in town, quite natchally was telling about the
hanted house. And so the preacher came along. The
man said to himself, if anyone could stay in the hanted
house, it should be a preacher. So he saw the preacher,
and he axed the preacher, was he afraid of a hanted
house. And the preacher says, "Why no, everywhere I
go I reads my Bible." So this man takes him on back
there to this man what owned this house. So when they
got there the man told him how much money he had for
everyone that stayed in the hanted house. So that
night the preacher got his grip and his Bible and went
on over to the hanted house. He went on in and he
sat down. He opened his Bible, and the preacher began to read. And the verse he was reading was very
familiar to everybody. The preacher said, "In those
days came John the Baptist preaching in the wilderness
of Judea. Repent for the Kingdom of Heaven is at
hand." So he read it for a long time. After a while he
heard a door squeak. He kept reading his Bible. He
read it, "In those days come John the Baptist preaching in the wilderness of Judey."

The spook come on by and just said, "How de do."
He kept reading and he never looked up. Way after a
while he heard another door open. That spook come
on by. The preacher began reading just a little bit
faster.

"In those days come John the Baptist preaching
in the wilderness of Judey."

After a while he heard another one. This time

didn't no door open, but he heard footsteps. He began
reading just a little bit faster.

"In those days come John the Baptist preaching in
the wilderness of Judey."

This spook got even with him and stopped. He said,
"Mister," he said, "will you be here when Martin
come?" The preacher kept reading.

"In those days come John the Baptist preaching in
the wilderness of Judey."

He's getting scared.

So way after a while the hant touched him again.
He said, "Will you be here when Martin comes?"

The preacher kind of looked up slyly and axed,
"Who Martin? Sure I'll be here when he comes." (He's
trying to bluff this spook you see.)

Way after while the preacher began to read faster
an' faster. This time he heard the turriblest noises
of all. This was Martin. Martin dug on up to the
preacher he did. This time the preacher put his finger
on the Bible.

"In those days come John the Baptist preaching
in the wilderness of Judey."

(See he didn't want to look up.)

Martin stood there and listened at him read. After a while Martin shook him. Preacher kept reading.
He wouldn't look up. He kept tetching the preacher on
the shoulder, and arter a while Martin wouldn't go
away, the preacher looked up. And when he looked
and saw Martin's face, instead of reading "In those
days come John the Baptist," the preacher begin to
tremble. And every which a way he turn Martin was
there. The preacher finally couldn't get out the room.
The preacher says, "Oh mama." Way arter a while,
he was so scared, he hollered, "Oh papa." Martin was
chasing the preacher so bad till when he did get a

chance he grabbed his Bible and grip and got going.
And no one ever saw the preacher again.

(He figgered he'd just take a gait he could hold that
was familiar to the spirits.)

42. Hardheaded Ghost

Similar texts occur in Ray B. Browne,
"Negro Folktales from Alabama," Southern
Folklore Quarterly, XVIII (June 1954), p.
130, no. 1, "The Hard Headed Ghost" (living brother pretends he is dead twin's
ghost to pacify grieving father); item 8,
reel 167 in the University of Arkansas
Folklore Archives, told by Mrs. Theresa
Warren, Brinkley, Arkansas, 14 Nov. 1953,
collected by Mary Celestia Parler (prank-
ster pretends to be ghost of grieving father's dead son); Arthur H. Fauset, "Negro Folk Tales from the South," JAF XL
(1927), p. 270 (text 2 of "The Ghost Walks,"
which Fauset has mistakenly associated
with a text of Big Fraid and Little Fraid).

42a. Hardheaded Son (John Courtney)

They say if your people die while you're young and
can't remember, after you get up some size you go to
a two-headed woman and she'll call 'em up and let you
talk with them. And so fellow by the name of Joe
wanted to see his mother and father, had never seen
them. So they went to this old lady and told her to call
up his father, he wanted to talk with him. So she called
him up, and in a few minutes up come his father. So
when he got pretty close to her Joe commenced looking
at him. So Joe kept looking at him. After a while Joe

begin to back up. Joe said, "That's enough, that's
enough, I just wanted to see you." So he kept coming
you know. Joe say, "I told you to go back, I told you to
go back. That's the reason you're dead now, your head
is hard."

(Head hard or head long means you go looking for
trouble.)

42b. Hardheaded Brother (Tobe Courtney)

Brother died and he was away, and he told them to
hold the burying till he got there. But they couldn't
wait, they had to bury him. So when he come and they
done bury him, he went to praying to the Lord, "Lord,
let me see my brother." He hadn't seen him in a long
time. And he'd go out to the grave every morning and
evening, where he was buried at, praying to see him.
At last one evening he went out, and met his brother.
He just looked and peeped—it was dusk dark you know
—said, "Brother is that you?" [Gesture of looking
hard, first on one side then on other.] He said that two
or three times. Brother just kept a-coming. He said,
"Go back brother, I done seed you now." Brother kept
coming. Said, "Brother that's how come you dead now,
you so hard-headed."

(A schoolteacher told that during the service.
Everybody in church just looked like they'd fall out.)

43. On the Cooling Board

Other Negro cooling-board stories were told
me in Michigan by Mary Richardson (see "Negro
Tales of Mary Richardson," no. 21, pp. 18-19),
Willie Sewall, J. D. Suggs (see post, no. 50,

p. 217, and Walter Winfrey. All the Michigan and Arkansas texts in common derive
from the old custom, explained by the storytellers, of shrouding the corpse and laying
it on the cooling board all night, while the
family sits around, sings, prays, and drinks
coffee till daybreak. Richardson and Suggs
both lay the tale in their home state, Missi-
sippi, and tell it as truth, although Richardson
has the apparently dead man revive from a
trance, while with Suggs a trickster stands
the dead man up in a corner. Winfrey's
corpse is a hunchback, who is tied down
with string to make him lay flat. When the
string around his neck breaks, he sits up-
right, and the praying mourners gradually
ease out until only the preacher is left;
after his Amen he looks up straight in the
hunchback's face, grabs his pistol and
says, "Lay down or I'll kill you again."
Sewall has a seemingly dead man come to,
while the family are eating baked potatoes,
and say, "I'll take one if it's soft." He was
an old man without teeth.

Baughman's Motif J1769.8*, "Dead man
is thought to be alive," is applicable here,
although extracted from a different complex.

43a. On the Cooling Board (Tobe Courtney)

It was at the church at a wake. In them days they'd
have a prayer meeting in the night. Long about the turn
of the night John was praying—he was the last of 'em
that prayed that night. John you know was in a big way
of praying.

"O Lord, have mercy tonight." [High]

John when he was praying kept his eyes shut all
the time.

"O Lord, bless the relatives of this bereaved family." [High]

John heard a little rumbling but he thought it was shouting. So after a while he heard a door open, so John when he hollered again he opened his eyes, and there was a fellow sitting up on the cooling board. John looked up and saw him. Everybody done gone but John on his knees. John said, "Hah, hah (say) don't you move, hah hah (say) don't you move, if you ain't dead you will die."

He's moving toward the door all the time, and when he got a space to move he went on outa there.

43b. On the Cooling Board (John Courtney)

There was two fellows setting up with the dead. And in the olden times people would go off in a trance and finally come to. So Sam had went off in trance that evening, and had been quite a few people there sitting up. So after a while pretty well all the people had gone, and left nobody there but John and Ike. So John and Ike they slept together; it was round about three o'clock Ike woke up. Sam was setting up on the cooling board. Ike wanted to hunch John but John was little too far from him. So Ike say, "Sam, Sam." [High] (He was trying to get away all the time.)

Sam was setting there looking at him. So after a while Sam said, "Wake John up."

Ike kept reaching for the door. Ike said, "I'm damn if that's so, I'm going to leave you and John right here."

So when Sam made all that racket, that woke John up. When John woke up, Sam straightened up on the cooling board, and he laid hands on John. And John carried him straight up to the Boss's house.

(John left there like a hurrycane.)

43c. On the Cooling Board (Julia Courtney)

Back in the olden times when anyone died there wasn't any embalming then. They kept the bodies at home. After they bathed them and dress 'em, they lay on the cooling board. And that's why they would stay until they got the casket to put 'em in.

So that night all the people went to the wake. And they sit up until late that night. There was one man there was very sleepyheaded. He slept from the time he get there until everybody was about gone. And he still was 'sleep. So it was two of the mens left there wasn't fraid of dead people. So they 'cided that they would scare this sleepyhead man. They had a few baked potatoes, so they stood the dead man up, peeled a pota- toe, and put it in his mouth. And then they went outside and called this sleepy man. He was pretty hard to wake up. Then they knocked on the wall. That time he heard the noise. He woke up and looked all round and wasn't anyone in the room but him and the dead man. So when he saw the dead man he knew he was dead, and he was 'fraid of dead people.

He looked at the dead man and kind of laughed, and said, "You eating 'tater." He looked at him again and backed up.

And this time he said again, "You eating 'tater." This time he got the door open, and was a cotton patch all around the house.

He broke out in the field and begin to say,

"You eating 'tater."

And fur as they heard him he kept saying,

"You eating 'tater."

until he got home.

44. Ketch Me John (John Courtney)

Paul climbed up a great tall pole, and had to climb
up there to do some work. John told him, say, "Hell I
wouldn't go up there." John kept prevailing with him
not to go. So Paul climbed to just about the top of it,
and he lost his holt.
And Paul lost his holt, he commenced to hollering
to John,

"Ketch me John. [Very high]
Ketch me John, ketch me."

So John wasn't paying no attention. After a while
John looked up, and Paul was pretty close to the ground
then. John grabbed the rake, said, "I'll just level a
place for this son-of-a-bitch, 'cause I see he's going
splatter all over everything."

45. A Is-er (Oliver E. Jackson)

A man going around saying he's looking for a good
mule. And the dealer says, "Here's a little mule that's
going to be a very fine worker some day." A little piece

farther he says, "Now here's a mule that used to be one
of the best in the country."

And after he'd shown him all the mules, the pur-
chaser said, "Hey mister, we're not looking for any has-
beener, and we don't want no will-be-er. What we wants
is a is-er.

46. What Darkens the Hole?

> This is Motif X911.3, "If the wolf's
> tail breaks." Halpert appends to a non-
> Negro text in Folktales and Legends from
> the New Jersey Pines, no. 187, p. 669, ref-
> erences from Alabama, Georgia, North
> Carolina, South Carolina, Texas, and Vir-
> ginia (all Negro), and Newfoundland, Nova
> Scotia, Ontario, and Scotland. See Bacon
> and Parsons, "Folk-Lore from Elizabeth
> City County, Virginia," no. 54, p. 292,
> "What Darkens the Hole?", for a text
> and two references. Suggs tells the
> tale with a different ending, post, no.
> 89, pp. 253-254.

46a. What Darken de Hole? (E. M. Moore)

Two fellows were out in the woods. They could
catch any animal they wanted for the zoo, so they decided to go out where there some bear. And they laid
away and watched the den of the mama bear until she
left, going to get food. So when they got to the den they
decided one better stay on the outside and watch for the
mama bear, and not catch both of them in there. While
John was in the den, Tom fell asleep, who was the watch-
man. And when Tom woke up, the mama bear had

passed by him and was entering the den. And he jumped
and grabbed her by the tail, trying to hold her.

John yelled out, "Hey Tom, what darken de hole?"

Tom was pulling the bear's tail trying to keep her
from going in there on John. Tom said, "If this tailbone
break you'll find out what darken de hole."

46b. Who Darket de Hole? (Silas Altheimer)

Sambo and Jim Bungum were straggling through
the woods one day looking for muscadines and wild
grapes. And finally they came upon an embankment
with a ditch below and a large stump up above, where
there was high ground, which went down into the hole.
And the stump was hollow at the top. So Jim Bungum
went down and peeped into the big hole below, and saw
some bear cubs. So he decided to go in, to get him one
of the cubs. In the meantime the bear at some distance
had seen them. The bear came in great haste, and she
chased Sambo round and round a good while. And finally the bear quit chasing Sambo, and stuck her head
in the stump on the high ground. And she started down
the hole from the embankment. And so when she got
part way down Sambo grabbed her by the tail and held
her.

And so Jim Bungum down below said, "Sambo, who
darket de hole?"

Sambo says, "If tail hold slip you'll see who darket
de hole?"

47. Preachers at the Fish Fry (Ben Jones)

Negro jokes about the rival denominations,

particularly Methodists and Baptists, are
popular. See "Methodists and Baptists" in
NFIM 174, and note 136 on p. 228 for four
references.

They were having a community fish fry, and some
of the boys wanted to play a joke on the denominations.
They had the Campbellite, Methodist, Baptist. So the
first fish they caught was a grinner. The boys said,
"That's a Campbellite fish."
So the Campbellite preacher wanted to know why.
Said, "He's a grinner, can't stand much when you get
him out the water."
The next one they caught was a fish-eel. So he
said, "That's a Methodist fish."
So the Methodist preacher he wanted to know why
he called him a Methodist fish.
So he said he was so slick you couldn't do nothing
with him when you got him outa the water. (Methodists
are very slick in the Bible and all.)
So they caught two more and they didn't name them.
So the Baptist preacher wanted to know did they ever
catch any Baptist fish.
He told them, "Not yet, we catch them at the still-
ery."

48. White Man, Jew, Colored Man (Ben Jones)

Cf. the variants from John Blackamore
in my "Negro Tales," Western Folklore,
XIII (April 1954), pp. 96-97, "Colored Man,
Jew, and White Man," reprinted in NFIM
77; and J. Mason Brewer, The Word on the
Brazos (Austin, Texas, 1953), pp. 88-89,
"Good Friday in Hell" (the Jew tries to

bargain the devil down from the ten dollar
fee, and the Negro offers to pay eleven dollars the coming Saturday).

The white man, Jew and colored man died and went
to hell. And the Devil he had so many souls he was
crowded out, and he told them if they would give him
five dollars apiece, they could go back to yonder world.
So the white man he give him his five dollars and left.
So he came on back, and when the people seen him they
said, "We thought you three fellows had died and gone
to hell together."

"Yes but it was so crowded the Devil said we could
give him five dollars and come on back."

They wanted to know where the other two fellows
were.

"When I left the Jew was offering him $4.98 and
the colored man said he would pay him on Saturday."

49. Hunting Partners (Grace Bedford)

Baughman under Motif X584.2* sum-
marizes this episode, and gives three references, two from Texas (Negro) and one
from Canada. See the Fables of Aesop, trans.
S. A. Handford (Penguin Books: Melbourne,
London, Baltimore, 1954), no. 177, p. 181,
"Share and Share Alike."

My uncle used to tell a tale about the fellows going
hunting. (Guess this was back in the times of slavery.)

There were two fellows hunting, one could shoot
very well, the other one couldn't. The bears were bad
in that locality, and everybody was encouraged to shoot
the bears. The one who could shoot well shot the bear.

The other fellow who couldn't shoot so well said, "Oh look what we've done, we've killed the bear."

The good shooter said, "We nothing, I killed that bear, and that's the way it's going to be."

So old Marster had a big fine horse in the pea patch. He was trigger happy, and shot the horse, thinking it was a bear. When he see what he had done, he said, "Look what we done."

The little one said, "We nothing. You did it, and that's the way it's going to be."

50a. Little Boy Sees Lion (Harrison Stanfill)

This little boy, his family didn't have but one kid, and every Saturday they would let him go to the show, and give him enough money to carry the little boy's friend with him. Every time he come back he have such a big lie to tell, his mother said she wouldn't let him go any more. So she told him, "If you come back with a lie today I'll give you the worst whipping you ever had." When he was downtown the boy saw a little old pug dog shaved like a lion, his hair clipped off from shoulder to the head. So when he came back that evening he told his ma he'd seen a lion in the street. She told him if he didn't go upstairs and ask the Lord forgiveness for that lie she'd give him one of the worst whippings he ever had. So he went upstairs and prayed the Lord forgiveness, and when he came downstairs he was crying. She asked him, "Did you get on your knees and pray the Lord forgiveness?"

He said, "Yes I did." He said, "The Lord forgive me, 'cause he thought that was a lion too."

50b. Little Boy Sees Lion (Ben Jones)

There was a widow woman that preacher loved to go home with him. And she was boasting to him how truthful her Johnny was, and smart, and never told a lie. So it was a fellow by the name of Sam Jones had a big shepherd dog, and had sheared him and left a switch in his tail. So Johnny he walks out on the porch, and seen this dog walking down the street, and he said, "Look mama, there's a lion coming down the street."

So his mother walked out, and she recognized the dog and said, "Johnny, shame on you, I just told the preacher you never told a lie. Now you come and told a lie in front of him, and you must go up and pray and ask the Lord to forgive you."

So Johnny went upstairs and prayed and asked the Lord to forgive him for that lie. So he stayed awhile and said, "Mama, can I come down now?" Says, "The Lord done heard me pray."

So she said, "Come down and tell us what the Lord said to you."

So he said, "The Lord said, when he first seed that dog he thought he was a lion too."

51. Irishman at the Dance (Silas Altheimer)

Irishmen noodle jests remain a vigorous tradition in various pockets of the United States. For Irish jokes from White sources see Herbert Halpert, "Aggressive Humor on the East Branch," New York Folklore Quarterly, II (May 1946), pp. 86-97; and Leonard Roberts, Eastern Kentucky Folktales: A Collection and a Study (University of Kentucky doctoral dissertation, 1953), nos. 42-55. A large Negro collection is in A. M.

Bacon and E. C. Parsons, "Folk-lore from
Elizabeth City County, Virginia," JAF XXXV
(1922), nos. 72-108, pp. 300-310; and see
also NFIM 182-185.
    A number of common Irishmen num-
skull tales were told me in Pine Bluff, but
I give here only two unusual texts. A re-
semblance to the present one occurs in
Roberts no. 52, "Irishman and the Fiddler,"
where the dunce thinks the fiddle is a cat
being tortured by the fiddler.

    A slave from the Old States (Carolina and Virginia)
told me this when I was a child, when the railroads
first began to build, sixty years ago.
    There were building a road through Virginia and
the Carolinas, and the contractor had many slaves and
some white men, Irishmen. And there was one Irishman, Pat, had recently come from Ireland, and never
seen a colored man. A dance was given in the area,
and the white men were invited to the dance. They had
to go through a bottom and across a creek to reach the
seat of the dance. And of course when they arrived
Pat went in and took his seat, and stood very still in
one place, and the other boys began to talk to the many
beautiful girls at the dance, and choosing their partners.
    There was a big black man sitting in the corner,
with red eyes, and he was tuning his fiddle. And after
a while when the dancers were ready, they were all
assembled on the floor. The fiddler began to play and
the dancers began to move around the room, promenad-
ing we'd call it. Pat sat there and all at once he
jumped up, he couldn't stand it any longer, and so he
ran out. He got lost, and he tramped around the whole
night in the mud, and fell in the lagoon. So he pulled
himself out, and next morning, just before day, when

the train was heating up to go out, Pat coursed in, all
muddy and wet, about seven o'clock. So the boys began to laugh and tease him about leaving the dance.
"Well Pat, how did you enjoy the dance?" They didn't
know what had become of him.

When they asked him, Pat gave his conception of
the dance. He said, "When I got there, there were
many beautiful girls there. And the boys began to enjoy theirselves, chatting with the young ladies. But the
Devil was sitting in one corner, and he had a little red
babe in his arms. And he pulled its ears, and it was
all I could do to sit there. And finally he picked up a
stick and whaled the baby across the back, and of all
the racket I ever heard, there it was. And the people
were flying around, hunting the door. And no one could
find it but me."

52. Irishman on the Job (Tobe Courtney)

Motif J246.1, "Literal following of
instructions," applies here. E. L. Smith
in Calvin, Michigan, told me a longer hired-
man noodle story, "The Slowboy," using
this motif.

Farmer hired the Irishman to work, had a little
laying by to do. So he hired him you know and asked
him could he do the work. And he told him, "Yeah."

So he carried him out there and showed him what
was to be done. So every morning he's asked him,
"Tom, how you getting on?"

"Just fine." (It was chopping through the cotton
the last time, they call it laying by.) So finally next
morning he thought Tom was about through you know,

and he went out there to see. And he asked Tom,
"What have you done?"

"Boss, I done just what you told me to do."

Says, "Well what did I tell you to do?"

"Well you told me to lay by, and that's what I done,
lay by it."

And that's what he done, hadn't done a lick of work.

53. Dreaming Contest (Harold Lee)

> Baughman gives the Motif K66* as
> "Dream Contests," and lists one Master
> and Negro and four Indian and white man
> examples. The Negro variant in J. Mason
> Brewer, "How John Stopped His Boss-man
> from Dreaming," Mexican Border Ballads
> and Other Lore, Publications of the Texas
> Folklore Society XXI (1946), pp. 89-90,
> has John get the best of the officious
> planter. Usually the white man outdreams
> the Indian; the original version involves
> Sir William Johnson and Hendrick, king of
> the Mohawk nation. See my "Comic In-
> dian Anecdotes," Southern Folklore Quar-
> terly, X (June 1946), p. 122, quoting from
> The Merry Fellow's Companion; or Ameri-
> can Jest Book (Harrisburgh, 1797); and
> Harold W. Thompson, Body, Boots and
> Britches (Philadelphia, 1940), p. 177,
> who takes the tale from Funny Stories:
> or the American Jester (New York, 1804),
> and gives variants attached to other per-
> sons.

Dreams is very significant with us you know. We
both were farmers, wealthy, and I had a piece of property you wanted, and you were figuring how to outwit
me out of it. You figured I like to dream, and my

dreams were so insignificant and minor, you thought you'd make my dreams come true if I made your dreams come true.

I would have such unsignificant dreams as about hunting and fishing and how many chickens I had and all. About three or four weeks I was just dreaming about how many fish I'd caught, and ducks I'd shot, and snakes I'd killed. And all that time you wasn't dreaming nothing. So it comes the time you dreamed that all my children was working for you, had left school, all my money was yours, and property, live-stock, feedstuff, my wife was working for you and I your horseman.

I had to make that dream true. In the course of time you noticed me not dreaming no more. About six months I was quiet, singing my songs, doing my work. Finally one morning I woke you up, telling you I had a dream. I dreamed that my kids were back in school, that I had all my money back, my property, livestock, foodstuff, and everything you owned was mine, and I dreamed that I ain't going dream no more.

54. The Fool Discovered (Julia Courtney)

The only printed analogue besides my own three texts seems to be in Straight Texas, ed. J. F. Dobie and M. C. Boatright, Publications of the Texas Folklore Society XIII (1937), "A Still Tongue Makes a Wise Head," from A. W. Eddins, and condensed in Boatright, Folk Laughter on the American Frontier (New York, 1949), p. 107. A variant told me by Mrs. E. L. Smith of Calvin, Michigan, appears in NFIM 194, and one from Suggs is post, no. 94, p. 260. The general Motif J2460, "Literal obedience,"

in the section of the Motif-Index on Literal
Fools, applies here.

His father didn't have but just that one little boy,
and he raised him up in the country. And everything
the little boy done, everybody said he was a fool. So
his daddy 'cided to take him to town. So he taken him
to town and left him on the corner, Main Street, and
told the boy, "Speak to everybody."
 The people begin to come to town slowly. The boy
began to speak slowly. He said, "Good mo'ning. Good
mo'ning. Good mo'ning." Begin to be more and more
people. He began to speak "Good mo'ning," little
faster. Begin to get so many of 'em on the streets, he
begin to speak faster and faster, all day long.
 That evening two ladies come by and said, "He
been standing there all day saying 'Good mo'ning,' and
this is evening. He ain't nothing but a fool."
 The little boy heard what they said about him. So
when his daddy come, he told his daddy, "They found
out I was a fool." His daddy taken him home.
 Next day his daddy brought him back to town again.
In the part of town he put him in they had a little pea-
nut stand. Was a mighty few people in that end of town,
but they were friendly. So they begin to speak to the
little boy, "Hi little boy." Little boy didn't say anything.
 So some little children went where he was and
they spoke to him. So one of the kids axed the little
boy, "Do you want some peanuts?" The little boy still
didn't say anything. He stayed there all day.
 More and more people spoke to him. "Hi little
boy." [Cutely] He still didn't say anything.
 Way after while some of the same people come
along that evening that had passed that morning. They

spoke again to the little boy. "Hi little boy." The little boy still didn't say anything. So they said that he
wasn't nothing but a fool because he wouldn't talk to
anyone.

So his father come after him. When the little boy
saw his father coming he runned and met his daddy
and said, "Daddy, daddy, they found out I was a fool
after all."

55. Nearsighted Old Lady

This is Type 1456, "The Blind Fian-
cée," and Motif K1984.5, "Blind Fiancée
betrays self." See E. C. Parsons, Folk-
Lore of the Sea Islands, South Carolina,
MAFLS XVI (1923), no. 117, p. 114, "The
Blind Old Woman," and note summarizing
a variant in the records of the Hampton
Folk-Lore Society, and referring to another published in JAF by Portia Smiley,
"Folk-Lore from Virginia, South Carolina,
Georgia, Alabama, and Florida," XXXII
(1919), no. 17, p. 365 (same title). In the
Ozark text of Vance Randolph, who says
the tale is known throughout the region
(note, p. 206, in Who Blowed Up the
Church House?; see pp. 86-87 for "The
Pin in the Gatepost"), a nearsighted but
goodlooking young girl sets her cap for
a rich old man. Negro variants I col-
lected appear in NFIM 192, "The Old
Lady with Poor Eyesight," from Mary
Richardson; and in "Negro Tales from
Bolivar County, Mississippi," Southern
Folklore Quarterly, no. 15, p. 113, "Old
Lady Who Couldn't See Well," from Rev.
J. H. Lee.

55a. Nearsighted Old Lady (Julia Courtney)

A man wanted to marry a woman that could see
real good. So he started to cou'ting on her. (You
know how it is some old people want to be real young.)
He done cou'ted all around and every time he come on
one she couldn't see like she oughta. That was his
idea y'see. So someone was telling him about this
wealthy woman. So he 'cided he'd go and see her.
When he got to her home he introduced hisself to her.
She introduced herself to him, and axed him in. They
made good friends, and from time to time he would go
and see her. He cou'ted her for a long time, until at
last one time he went to her home, she invited him
over one night. So when he got there, she had a maid
to fix him some tea. They drank tea together, laughed
and talked. And so she had a maid to understand you
know, to stick a needle up in the gatepost. So 'bout
time she figgered she had the needle out there, she got
up an' stretched, "Ho ho, let's walk out on the porch
and set in the cool." So when they gotten out there and
set down, they had no more than gotten out there and
sit down good when she played like, "Look like to me
I see something out there on that gatepost." And she
called to her maid and said, "Go out there and look on
that gatepost." Said, "Look like to me I see something
out there shining."
So her maid went on out there and played like
she's looking for it. But she knew it was there. After
while the maid said, "It's a needle." So the maid
brought it to her.
The man began to like her better. He says,
"You're the very one I want, someone can see real
good."
That night he axed her to marry. The next day,

she had plenty money, boy she put a wedding out, because she wanted a husband badder than he wanted a
wife. The night of the wedding come. She had her
maid just to cook up much food. And they prepared a
big dining room table. Unbeknownst to her mistress
she set a great big old white pitcher of milk on the corner of the table betweenst the bride and groom. And
Ol' Mistress had a big white cat too. Everyone circled
around the table and sit down and began to eat. They
had been eating a good while, when suddenly she happened to kinda glaze around and see this pitcher a
milk. She slapped the pitcher of milk off the table, and
says, "Get off from here, you nasty stinking cat you."

So he found out then she couldn't see at all. So he
had married her then, but that was the separation. So
she still didn't have her husband.

(I thought that was one of the most precious stories
when I heard it. When we were cou'ting we told sweet
stories, no nasty ones.)

I just know how that dining room floor was messed,
and all them guests.

55b. Nearsighted Old Lady (Tobe Courtney)

There was a young man courting this old lady, and
she wanted to show him she had good sight. She could
'cern anything but she couldn't see good. In all of
them's absence she took a needle and carried it out
and stick it in the gatepost. And when the young man
come back y'see, they sat there talking, she says to
him says, "I see a needle sticking in the gatepost."
Says, "Go get it." So he went and got the needle and
give it to her y'know.

And so he came back on Sunday, and they fixed a

big dinner. They had a big pitcher of milk on the table.
So they all got around the table y'know, and they had a
big white cat. And as they setting on the table she
spied that cat and said, "Scat you bitch you." And
slapped at it with her hand and spilt that pitcher of
milk over everything.

Daughter said, "You done ruined it all now."

56. Three More Bigger Fools (Julia Courtney)

This tale includes Types 1450, "Clever
Elsie," 1384, "The Husband Hunts Three
Persons as Stupid as His Wife"; 1210, "The
Cow is Taken to the Roof to Graze"; 1245,
"Sunlight carried in a bag into the Window-
less House," and 1286, "Jumping into the
Breeches," which are often joined. Baughman
reports these as among the most popular
folktales in England and the United States.
Three characteristic Negro examples of
this combination are in Parsons, Folk-Lore
of the Sea Islands, South Carolina, no. 87,
pp. 94-97, "Three More Damn Fools," who
gives further references. Emelyn E.
Gardner notes these Negro variants at the
end of her extended commentary on a text,
"The Four Fools," in Folklore from the
Schoharie Hills, New York (Ann Arbor,
1937), pp. 163-172. West Indies texts of
Type 1450 from Andros Island, Barbados,
Guadaloupe, Jamaica, and Puerto Rico
are cited in Flowers. A version close to
the present one is in "Negro Tales of
Mary Richardson," no. 29, pp. 23-24.
Mrs. E. L. Smith told me Type 1450
by itself. An engaged couple goes down
to the spring to get water, and falls to
studying what to name the first baby;
each successive member of the family

asks "What's the matter with yourance?"
and joins the brown study, until a neigh-
bor man says, "That's easy, if it's a girl
name it Puss, and if it's a boy name it
Dick." Suggs has a tale of three fools,
post, no. 95, pp. 260-261. The Courtney text
differs from those of Richardson and
Smith, and falls closer to Grimm no.
34, "Clever Elsie," in that the silly
woman worries about an overhead object falling down, rather than about
the name of her baby.

Two old peoples had young daughter. So the one
daughter had a boy friend whom was co'ting her, name
was John. So John one day axed the girl to marry him.
So the girl come home and told her mother and father,
"I and John is going to get married." The next day her
mother was fixing to cook dinner. She sent the girl
down to the next house to draw some molasses. (They
had sorghum molasses in sixty gallon barrels in those
days. We had a sharecropper house didn't no one stay
in it, and we kept things in it.)
　　So when she got there she set her bucket down under the barrel and poured the stopper out the barrel,
and the molasses begin to run slowly. So she sit down
and begin to think about her marriage. She said, "If
John and I marry, who will be the father of our first
two children?" So she sit down and begin to cry.
　　She stayed down there so long until her mother
thought she'd go and see her daughter. When she got
there she saw the girl was crying. So she axed the
girl, "Honey, what you crying for?"
　　And the girl told her, "I was just studying, mother:
if John and I marry, who would be the father of our
first two children?"
　　Her mother said, "Well, that's something to think

about." And the old lady sit down and begin to think
too. "If my daughter marry, who would be the father
of the first two children?"

Twelve o'clock come, the old man come home
from work, father's gone out in the store, and wasn't
nothing done. He said, "Mhm, wonder what happened
to the old lady?" He decided that he would go and see.
When he got there the molasses had run the bucket
over, all over the floor, and running off the porch. He
went on in, and when he got in there he axed what was
the matter.

And so the old lady told him, "I sent the baby
down here to get some molasses to make molasses
bread for dinner. And when she got in here, and
turned the 'lasses on, she said she sit down and begin
to think if her and John marry who would be the father
of their first two children."

So the old man said, "That's something to think
about." He sit down and begin to think too. So all
three of 'em was sitting down thinking about the same
thing.

Way after while salesman come along. He stopped
at the house and honked his horn. No one come to the
door, but he knew someone was there by seeing the
'lasses running out the house, into the road. So he decided he'd go and see where the molasses was coming
from ('cause the people wasn't saying anything). So
he saw the three of 'em sitting down, not either one of
them saying a word. So he axed 'em, "What's the matter with you-all?"

So the old man told him, "We was all thinking, if
our daughter would marry John, who would be the father of her first two children?"

So the man said, "I'm going on down the road a

little further, and if I find three more fools, bigger than
your daughter, I'll come back and marry her."

So he left and went on down the road about a mile
further. And the first thing he saw was a old raggedy
shangle-topped house with long moss on top. One of
the boys was in front had a long rope, the other one
was behind the house with a stick beating the cow, trying to make her climb up upon the house and eat the
moss off. The man said, "That ain't the way to do that."
Said, "Take the rope off the cow, and put her back in
the lot and cut the moss off the top of the house, and
carry to the cow."

So then he went back and got in his car, and drove
down the road just a little further. This time this old
lady had scrubbed her house, and the way she scrubbed
her house, she took the bucket and went to the pump,
and pumped it full of water, and just dosled it in there.
She put so much water in her house, until she couldn't
sweep it all out. So the old man 'cided he would get
the wheelbarrow and roll the sun in to dry it. This
time the man told him, "Let you h'ist your windows,
that's the way to dry your house."

So then he got on his journey again, and went 'bout
a mile further. And before he gotten there, he saw a
man standing way by. And then he'd run and jump.
When he gotten there, he saw the man had his pants
with a rope tied on each side of 'em. So he told the
man, "That ain't the way to put no pants on. Take the
ropes off of it, and put one foot in each leg." This
time the salesman thought about the pretty girl that
was studying, if her and John marry, who would be the
father of their first two children.

So he went back there and told the girl that "I have
found three more bigger fools than you was. So now I
come back to marry you."

57. The Silly Girl (Grace Bedford)

Here the previous tale-types are combined (save for the two forgotten episodes of
Types 1245 and 1286) with Type 1541, "For
the Long Winter" (Motif K362.1) and Type
1653A, "Guarding the Door" (Motif K335.1.1,
"Door falls on robbers from tree"). The 1541-
1653A combination appears in Parsons, Folk-
Lore of the Sea Islands, South Carolina, no.
147, p. 132, "Mr. Hard-Times," text 1; and
in Halpert, Folktales and Legends from the
New Jersey Pines, no. 178, "Mr. Time-of-
Need; Above the Robbers," who gives full references (vol. II, pp. 661-663). A text of "Mr.
Hard Times" I collected from Archie Tyler appears in "Negro Tales from Bolivar County,
Mississippi," no. 19, pp. 114-115. Mrs. E. L.
Smith in Calvin told me a variant of "Mr.
Hard Times" in which the child of a "widder
woman" gives the money she had saved in her
old black stocking to the stranger. Grimm no.
59, "Frederick and Catherine," contains pretty
much the 1541-1653A story, with a foolish
wife giving her husband's money away and then
luckily rescuing it from the robbers with the
aid of the house-door. Flowers reports eleven
variants of Type 1653 from the West Indies,
and five of Type 1541; two of the latter, from
Andros Island and Antigua, have the 1653 ending of the robbers under the tree.

(I heard this from my mother and father. They
were both very good storytellers. My mother's people
came from South Carolina and my father's from Georgia. They were born in Arkansas. Doesn't it sound
like a mountain story?)

A traveling salesman was going around from house
to house in the country. And come dinner time he
asked this lady to prepare him some food. She

consented to fix him a ham dinner, and sent the girl to
the smokehouse for the ham. Lena was twenty-five
years old and she'd never been married. She was
called an old maid, back there then. Out in the smokehouse were great big hams and they were hanging from
the rafters. Lena stared up at the hams and said to herself, "If those hams would fall on me I'd never get a
chance to marry." And she stayed so long her mother
she came out to see.

And when the daughter told the mother what de-
tained her, her mother said the same thing, "If one of
those hams would fall on you, you'd never get a chance
to marry."

And the father gets alarmed on the front porch, so
he goes around the back to see what's the trouble, and
he agrees with them.

"Oh yes, that's true, if one of those hams should
fall on you, you'd never get a chance to marry."

And that's the way the salesman finds them, all
three of them staring at the ham, saying "Oh yes, if
the ham should fall you'd never get a chance to marry."

So he tells them, "Well if I can find two other people as silly as you, I'll come back and marry the girl."

Finally he comes to a house where a handful of
green grass is growing in the eaves, and the people are
trying to pull the cow on top of the house to eat the
sprig, or bunch, of green grass. (Make it very small.)

(I can't recall the second one.)

After he finds the two other silly incidents, he
goes back and marries the girl. But her silliness pays
off—have you heard that?

Every so often he would bring her a few coins of
money and tell her to keep it for Mr. Hard Times. She,
thinking it was a person, a man, was very anxious for
Mr. Hard Times to come, so she could give him the

money. Finally one day a hobo passed, begging for food. He asked her, he was hungry, could she give him some bread and he would cut her some wood. And she asked him if he was Mr. Hard Times. He said, "I surely am."

So she said (You notice each part of the story seems to belong to a different age. Each one adds his part as he tells it. I'm trying to tell it as it was told to me), "I have something better for you than just a piece of bread. My husband has been saving for you." She goes inside, gets the coins and gives them to him.

Soon after her husband comes home, and she tells him, "Oh, Mr. Hard Times came, and I gave him the coins." He was startled. And so he asked her which way he went, and started down the road after him. And he told her to come on with him and "pull the door to behind you." (In those days they hooked it on.) She was coming along so slowly behind him he looked back and saw her carrying the door on her back. Then he took the door so they could go faster.

Night came and they had to stop. It was in the woods, and he put the door up in the tree and they lay down on it. It was a shiny new door, because it came from a new house—they were just married. Some robbers came and settled under this tree to count their money. And they got so loud and quarreling over the money the girl was wakened, and she became frightened and screaming. She began twisting, and the door lost its balance and fell down on them. Just as they looked up, the white skirt and apron looked ghostly, and the shiny door, and she screaming, and they just left.

So they got more money than they lost.

V I

PROTEST TALES

While the term "protest song" has entered the vo-
cabulary of folklorists, an equivalent phrase for the
folktale remains to be coined. I submit that numerous
traditional tales, involving the grievances of minority
groups and the lower classes, might well be designated
"protest tales." Sometimes these narratives center
about proletarian heroes, who champion the cause of
peasant and crofter against an overweeening aristoc-
racy. Often they take the form of grim jests, as in the
body of Jewish folk humor growing around Russian and
Nazi persecutions.[1] In the richly diversified story lore
of American Negroes, certain tales inevitably reflect
their racial humiliations. These too appear in comic
garb, and sometimes are told by white men, just as
non-Jews have adopted Jewish stories.

The note of protest may be directly sounded with
sharp and bitter irony. My leading informant of protest tales, E. M. Moore, a building contractor in Pine
Bluff, regarded his narrations as a true expression of

---

[1]See such collections as Here's A Good One: Stor-
ies of Jewish Wit and Wisdom, ed. S. Felix Mendelsohn
(New York, 1947), "Hitleria," pp. 77-91; Jewish Wit and
Wisdom, ed. Jacob Richman (New York, 1952), "A Stone
on Hitler's Grave," pp. 362-370; Let Laughter Ring, ed.
S. Felix Mendelsohn (New York, 1948), "Third Reich,"
pp. 107-146; A Treasury of Jewish Folklore, ed. Nathan
Ausubel (New York, 1948), "Bitter Jests," pp. 439-443.

108

Southern Negro suffering. A discrimination incident, where I was refused curb service for having colored people in my car, suggested to John Courtney the fearful yarn of John fighting the bulldogs (text 58 below). In other tales a gentle humor cushions the ugly facts, and pictures ignorant country Negroes who cannot recognize a bathtub, or a train, or a traffic light. Here the protest sounds more faintly, but such episodes pass comment on the society that denies learning and opportunity to some its members. Sometimes this ignorance is feigned, to avoid penalties. "Those white folks made us lie. We had to lie to live," one descendant of a slave remarked to me. My new acquaintances fully understood the ironies of the American dilemma, and revealed to me amazing instances of how Bilbo and Huey Long befriended their people, in the midst of savagely anti-Negro public utterances.

A shift in stereotypes emerges in this group of stories. First comes the naive and gullible rural Negro, then the knowing and crafty city boy, who outwits the white man by playing dumb, and finally the proud self-supporting "new Negro," who tells his former boss "I'm sopping my own gravy now." This change in plot mirrors the gradual ascent of the colored man in American society. A similar pattern appears in comic anecdotes Indians have told about their relations with white men.[2]

Few variants as yet can be found for these protest tales among the numerous printed examples of Negro folkstories. Collectors avoid them, or fail to inquire for them, or do not know of them, and continue to gather texts about Brer Rabbit and graveyard hants. But these serio-comic yarns of protest enjoy wide oral currency,

[2]Described in my article "Comic Indian Anecdotes," Southern Folklore Quarterly, X (June 1946), pp. 113-128.

and deserve attention both as folklore and as documents
of social protest.

58. John In Alabama (John Courtney)

     John went to Alabama for a vacation. And while he
was there he got into some trouble with a white man.
John was telling his friends how they do over here in
Arkansas, how they treat the colored better. So this
white fellow was passing by, and he taken it up, and he
wanted to know where John was from. So John told
him he wasn't speaking to him.
     So he said, "You know who you speaking to, nig-
ger?"
     So John told him he didn't care. He stepped right
up to John and knocked him down. John knocked his
leg out from under him and crawled over under him.
So they seed John was going to win that fight. Up came
the laws. They arrested John. Then they carried him
to the place to punish. Buried him in the ground up to
his shoulder. Got two bulldogs and turned them loose
on John. John was nodding his head so fast they
stopped those dogs, called John, told John to fight those
two bulldogs fair.

59. John Dodges White Man (Tobe Courtney)

          Although this tale contains the same mo-
     tif of the skillful dodger as the preceding, it
     is I believe a separate type. Two close vari-
     ants were told me in Michigan, by Walter
     Winfrey and J. D. Suggs (for whose text see
     post, no. 19, pp. 182-183). In Winfrey's text the

Negro dodges the fists of Bob Fitzsimmons, former world's heavyweight champion.

Two men were traveling, John and his partner. And they got loud-talking, stiff-talking you know, after they had some drinks—John was a wise-head, say things he had no business. So a white man heard him and took it up, jumped on John and beat him up a little. His partner said, "Say listen, there ain't a man in the world can beat me up that way."

So the white man asked him, "Say, what you got to do with it?"

John told him, "I got nothing to do with it, but there ain't a man in the world can beat me up that way, nobody."

So the white man jumped on him and commenced hitting at him. And John commenced a-dodging. The white man hit at him till he got tired, he said, "Hold your head still, nigger."

John said, "Boss, I'm a dodging son-of-a-bitch, ain't I?"

60. Fast Departure (E. M. Moore)

This happened up at Corning, Arkansas. At that time Corning didn't allow Negroes in the little town. This colored man was walking up the railroad track. Some white man caught him and held him until the gang came. They first thought they would whip him, but then later decided to make him dance. When the Negro had danced until he was just about out of breath, one big-hat-wearing white man said, "Nigger, if we don't whip you, will you catch the next train coming through here, and leave and never be caught here again?"

He said, "Boss, if you just don't whip me, and let
me go, I'll catch that train that's already done gone."

61. Chastising the Negro (E. M. Moore)

That the following fantasy may have a basis in fact appears in the realistic account by
Suggs, "The New Dance Step," post, no. 67,
pp. 234-235, in which white men make colored boys
dance.

This also happened up at Corning, Arkansas. A
Negro was passing through there. It was cotton picking
time, but no Negroes lived there, and weren't allowed
there. They didn't want to pick this Negro up and make
him go to picking cotton. So one big white man walked
out to the railroad as he was walking by, with a pistol
in one hand and a quirt in the other. So he called him
over, told him to come over. Said, "Don't you know we
don't allow no niggers through here?"
     He said, "No, Boss, I didn't know it."
     He said, "I'm not going to kill you, I'm just going
to whip you, and make you remember this place, so you
don't ever come through here again." And he said,
"Well, before I whip you, I'm going to see if you can
jump this fence." He had a six foot fence there, and he
told the Negro, he says, "Now when I tell you to go over
this fence," he say, "you go over. And when I say 'Back
again,' you jump back on this side." He said, "Now if
you attempt to run, I'm going to kill you." So he drilled
him on it. "Have you got it now? When I say 'Over,'
you jump over. And when I say 'Back again,' you come
back and don't touch that fence. And when I say 'Halt,'
you stop."
     So they got started. He said, "Over." The Negro

jumped over. He said, "Back again." The Negro jumped
back. "Over. Back again. Over. Back again." And as
the Negro was jumping back again he hollered "Halt,"
and caught him right up over the fence. So the Negro
knew the white man meant for him to do what he had
told him to do. The poor Negro just had to hang up there
in the air over the fence.

62. Its and Ifs (Harold Lee)

Two colored men were talking to themselves. One
was a farmer, the other had quit. He said he wasn't going to farm any more, there were too many its and ifs.
The ifs were, if the boll weevils don't eat it up, if the
worms don't eat it up, if the drouth don't come, he'll
make a good crop, for the man to take with the pencil
and pad.
The its were: to plow it, to plant it, to chop it, to
poison it, to pick it, to weigh it, haul it to the gin, sell it,
and the man behind the desk take it.

63. Gifts from Heaven (Harold Lee)

Cf. Hurston, Mules and Men, p. 102, "De
Reason Niggers Is Working So Hard"; and NFIM
76, "Colored Man, Jew and White Man," the
first text by Tommy Carter.

It was raining, and after the rains subsided two
packages was seen. Two men ran to see what it was.
After discovering a plow and a hoe in one package, one
exclamored real loud, "This is a gift from heaven."
The other fellow said, "Look what I have, a pencil
and a scratch pad and a cushion."

So the retired farmer says, "That's why I stopped
farming. After all my hard work, the fellow behind the
desk gets it all."

64. Grass Eater (E. M. Moore)

For a similar text I collected in Benton
Harbor, Michigan, see my "More Tales of
John Blackamore," Western Folklore, XIII
(Oct. 1954), pp. 258-259, "The Hobo's Experi-
ence," reprinted in NFIM 81.

A hungry colored man was passing through a rural
area in Mississippi. He hadn't had any food for four
days, and he happened to be in an all-white community, and
he didn't want to stop and ask for food. He decided to
stop at a white residence and ask for salt, thinking that
if he would sprinkle the salt on the grass and pretend
that he was eating the grass, that they would give him
some food to eat. So the white lady brought the salt to
the gate, poured it in his hand, and he started sprinkling
the salt on the grass just outside the front gate, which
had recently been mowed. The lady asked what he was
doing that for. He said, "Oh miss, I'm so hungry I
thought I'd eat some of this grass, and the salt makes it
taste better."
    The white lady said, "Poor old thing, come on
around the house to the back." And going around the
house he thought his trick had worked. The lady went
through the house and met him at the back door with the
salt box. She said, "Go over to this corner of the yard
near the peach tree. There's some taller grass over
there."

65. I'm Glad I'm Back Home (Billy Jack Tyler)

This story and no. 76, also from Archie
"Billy Jack" Tyler, were collected in Cleve-
land, Mississippi, July 2, 1953, and are in-
cluded here because of their appropriateness.
Billy Jack was a nineteen-year-old Negro por-
ter in a second-rate hotel where I stayed in
Cleveland my first night after leaving Pine
Bluff. He proved an excellent narrator; and I
printed a number of his stories in "Negro
Tales from Bolivar County, Mississippi,"
Southern Folklore Quarterly, XIX (June 1955),
pp. 104-116.
The present tale is told by both Southern
Whites and Negroes. Professor Thelma James
of Wayne University informs me that Senator
Tom Connally of Texas tells it for political
purposes, and has had it printed in the Congres-
sional Record. A similar text appears in Fred
W. Allsopp, Folklore of Romantic Arkansas, 2
vols., The Grolier Society, 1931, II, 184-185,
"Dat Sho' Sounded Good to Dis Ole Nigger,"
told on a newly freed plantation darky.

There was a boy and he had a brother that had been
in Chicago for a period of about five years. And he kept
on writing to his brother and telling him that when he
made enough money he would send for him, for he was
doing fine. In about a month after that his brother send
him a ticket. And he went on up and got him a job. He
had been working for about three months, when work got
short on the job and they turned him off. So he went to
his brother's house, and axed him could he stay with
him until he was able to get another job. His brother
told him he just had enough room and enough food for
his wife and family. And he told him to get farther.
The reason he had wanted to go to the North in the first
place was because the discrimination down South. He

had heard that when you in the North, everybody's created equal. As he was walking down the alley he knocked on the front door of the house. A white lady came to the door and said, "Good morning, sir. Something I can do for you?"

He said, "Yes mam. I'm hongry and I wonder would you give me something to eat."

And she said, "No, because I just do have enough for my husband and my kids."

He walked on and he passed several houses through St. Louis, and he come to a house and knocked on the door. And he never noticed the sign up on the wall, that read like this: "If you have lost your way this is not a information bureau."

He kept on walking until he came to the Mason-Dixie line. And he came up to a house in Tennessee. And he noticed he had crossed the state line, and he said, "Tennessee's the place for me." He knocked on the door.

A big fat white man came to the door and said, "What can I do for you, nigger?"

Said, "Boss-man, I'm hongry."

Said, "Bring your black self to the back door and I'll give you something to eat."

Said, "Thanks God, I'm back home."

(In the South they'll always feed the colored people if they're hungry. Up North it's each for himself.)

66. The Light Child (E. M. Moore)

Another ending was given me by Jesse Burnett at Sodus, Michigan; the Boss assures John his wife must have got scared by a white cow, which marked her baby so that it was born white.

A farmer on a Mississippi plantation had thirteen children. He and his wife both were very dark. The thirteen children were between their colors and the fourteenth child was very light. The father was very disturbed about the color of his child, so much so he wasn't pleasant with the Boss on the place. So the Boss decided he'd go out and talk with him about it. He told him, said, "John, I've discovered you just aren't the same John you've been for the last twenty years. I want you to tell me what's wrong."

He said, "Well, you know all my thirteen children are of the same color, and the fourteenth child came up half white." And he said, "I just can't understand it."

"I don't think you ought to let that worry you, John." He said, "You know I have a herd of sheep, to be exact four hundred. They all are supposed to be white, but every now and then one comes up black. But I don't worry about it. They're my sheep and these are your children. So I don't think you ought to worry about your children. I want you to make me a promise, that you don't worry about them. Now will you make me that promise?"

"Yes, under one condition. If you stay out of my house, I'll stay out of your pasture."

67. Mule, Buggy, and Harness (John Courtney)

White lady in the state of Georgia (we give Georgia a hard name here), went to a livery stable and rented a black mule and a black buggy. She went out for a drive, round the skirts of town. Mule seed a book of paper and he ran away, broke her leg and arm. They executed the mule, sentenced the buggy to lifetime in the state penitentiary, bind the harness over to circuit court.

68. White Man's Ice (Edna Nelson)

This-colored man had worked up a nice trade selling ice in a community. And all the people in that community, both white and colored, was buying from him. The white man began selling ice too, since the colored man doing so well he thought he would go in there and get him some customers.

So when the white woman saw the colored woman had changed to the white man—the white woman was still buying from the colored man—she said, "Now why did you stop buying from John, he was so courteous and nice, and we did business with him a long time?"

"Well I tell you truth Miz George, I tell you just why I changed—that white man's ice is just colder than that nigger's ice."

(They told that tale to try to get colored people to patronize each other, when their things were just as good as the white man's.)

69. Running the Red Light (Tilman C. Cothran)

E. M. Moore has the arrested Negro tell the judge, "Boss, I thought the red light was a Christmas bell."

The colored man was arrested in a town in Mississippi for crossing a red light. He explained, "I saw all the white folks going on the green light, I thought the red light was for us colored folks." The judge let him off.

(Frequently educated Negroes will pretend to be ignorant to fool the white man.)

70. Educating the White Folk (Tilman C. Cothran)

The appropriation for the Negro school was used for the White school. The superintendent explained this to the Negro principal, who of course couldn't make a direct protest. So he said, "The one thing we need most of all is educated white folk."

71. Measles (Edna G. Nelson)

Crime and disease has no respect of persons. The cook was coming in, so the white woman told her, "Don't come in this morning, Sally, the children all got the measles."

"Oh Miz George, don't worry about that, my children done had it down at the house the last six weeks."

(You've got to make the whole town safe.)

72. Mistake in Account (E. M. Moore)

A similar theme appears in J. Mason Brewer, The Word on the Brazos (Austin, Texas, 1953), pp. 92-93, "Uncle Si, His Boss-man, and Hell," but in that case the deluded slave emerges on top.

It was on a large plantation in Mississippi, all Negro tenants. This man would settle with them seven or eight years. And one Negro, George Jackson, couldn't read or write. Neither could his wife. But they lived on the main road that led from where most tenants on the place lived, up to the headquarters. So this year the Boss decided to settle. And this particular man, the

Boss gave him a statement and a check pinned to the statement for $750. He carried his statement and his check home. He and his wife looked over it. With that being the first settlement they had had in seven years they didn't know what to do with it. Living on the main road where all the Negroes had to pass his house to go down to the headquarters or the office, some of the Negroes could read or write, or could figure. After going home with their statements, several of them found mistakes. They passed back by George Jackson's house going back to have their mistakes corrected. George Jackson being one of the busybodies, he asked everyone that came by, "Hey buddy, where you gwine?"

So they would all tell him, "Well I found a mistake in my account, and I'm going back to have it corrected."

And after so many of them had found mistakes, something just told him that there was a mistake in his account. So he went in and told his wife Mandy, said, "Do you know, I believe there is a mistake in our account. You give it here." And he went back to the office to talk to the Boss.

When he walked in the office the Boss said, "Well Uncle George, what's your trouble?"

And he says, "I think there is a mistake in my account."

The Boss knew George Jackson couldn't read or figure. He was just coming back because others were saying they were coming back. He decided to have some fun off him. He took the statement and looked over it for a little while. Called George Jackson over to the desk. He said, "Well Uncle George, I did discover a mistake here." He said, "I find here that I paid you $250 too much."

George said, "I knowed it, I knowed it, I knowed it."

73. Never Seen a Bathtub (E. M. Moore)

A Negro in Mississippi had lived on a plantation all
his life, had reached the age of seventy-five. So the
Boss called him in and told him, says, "John, you've
been on this farm all your life, even before I was born."
Says, "I'm going to stop you from work now. I'm going
to build you a little house in town, you and your wife, and
take care of you the rest of your life."
So he did build the house and move them to town,
but he moved them in before the house was completed.
A day or two after they moved in, the Boss just called
one of the plumbing companies and told them to take a
bathtub out there, and to leave it on the front porch. So
a day or two later the truck driver from the plantation
went by the man's house to take something. And he told
the truck driver to tell the Boss that the white man
brought that boat out there, but he didn't bring the oars
to it.

74. Po' Thing (John Courtney)

See the similar text of Suggs, post, no. 69,
pp. 237-238, and headnote.

Old man Sam and his wife he was the father of four-
teen children. And he had never carried his wife and
children to town. So in the spring of the year he loaded
them all up in the wagon and 'cided to take them to town.
When they all reached town, he unloaded them outa the
wagon, and begin walking around showing them. So after they'd looked the town over, he 'cided to take them
round to the station. That was to let them see the train
—they had never seed a train. Pretty soon after they

got around there, the train showed up in sight. So when the train showed up in sight, when the train blowed the stop whistle, wasn't no one standing there but he and his wife. His children done scattered all over town. Some was going and meeting the people, shaking hands you know, glad to see each other. She done backed up again the station as far back as she could go. When the train run up and stop, it say, "Choo, choo, choo, choo."

She say, "Po' thing. Done run so much, so tired, hot and sweating. Won't anybody pay it no 'tention." And she take off her big old straw hat, her Bill Bailey, and commenced fanning it. "Po' thing, I know she's tired."

75. The Governor's Convention (Rev. Mrs. L. R. Toler)

The governor of Mississippi called a convention of all the governors. And he wanted to show them the colored people were treated all right in the South. So he called the old colored man over and said, "Sam, when you're hongry we take care of you, don't we?"

"Yessuh, Boss."

"And when you need a new suit, we give you one, don't we?"

"Yessuh, Boss."

"And if you need some money, we'll put some in your pocket, won't we?"

"Yessuh, Boss."

"All right now Sam, just step up to this mike here and tell all the people how we take care of you."

Sam he goes to the mike, and he says, "Who am I talking to, Boss?"

And the governor says, "You're talking to Washington, D. C., and New York, and the high country up north."

"You mean I'm not talking to Alabama, Georgia, Mississippi?"

"No, Sam."

So Sam hollers into the mike, "HELP! HELP! HELP!"

76. Bill Adams and Georgia the Peach State (Billy Jack Tyler)

Bill Adams he was born and reared in Illinois. He was eighteen years old then, and he thought it was about time for him to travel some. And he had read about Georgia in his school books, so he thought he would go to Georgia. So he got his little clothes together and put them in a paper bag. He got on a train and hoboed to Albany, Georgia. And he didn't like it there so he went on further, hoboed to Atlanta. He hitchhiked a ride from out of Atlanta, about eight miles out in the rural to a little old country town that had a few little junk stores. And he had got lonesome so he thought he would sing a song. Before he begin singing he saw a tall rednecked man coming down the streets. And he began singing,

> "Just Molly and me
> And baby makes three.
> We're happy as we
> In our blue heaven."

And the rednecked with a strong expression, "What did you say, nigger?"

"I didn't say nothing, white folks."

He called out again in a harsh voice, "What did you say, nigger?"

"All I said, white folks,

"Just Molly and you-all
No niggers at all.
You-all happy as you-all
In you-all's blue heaven."

(I heard it in several different arrangements but
that's the only one I remember.)

77. Our Father (Dan Holmes)

Colored man was hungry, he asked for something to
eat. But the white man was religious and he attempted
to teach him the Lord's prayer. He said, "Say, Our Father."

But the colored man said, "You-all's father."

The white man said, "Why don't you say Our Father?"

"Well, the word Our would mean your father and
my father and that would make us brothers."

The white man says, "That's right." (He hadn't
thought of it that way.)

Colored man said, "Well, give me a bigger sandwich
then and don't make it look like you-all's father."

78. John and the Twelve Jews (John Courtney)

Surprisingly my fellow-folklorist D. K.
Wilgus gave me a variant to this one, when I
passed through Bowling Green, Kentucky, one
day in August, 1954. His shortened version has
only two Jewish business men; each thinks the
other has tipped George who, when he finally
gets the twenty-five dollars, says, "Now I know
that you Jews didn't crucify Christ, you just
scared him to death."

The present text is transcribed from a
tape recording.

Once upon a time there was twelve Jews and they
had a porter boy. His name was John. John had been
traveling all over the United States with those Jews, and
everywhere they go you know, where they get off y'know,
they tip John you know. And John would have something
to help support hisself in the place y'know while he was
there. So they went to Chicago y'know. They came
from New York to Chicago. They give John, oh, a big
pocket of money. John had a big time y'know. And they
all got ready to go y'know, he'd go get all of 'em their
grips y'know, and he'd put 'em, load 'em all on the train
y'know. And then John he'd be standing there when
they'd get on y'know. And when the last one get on, why
John he get right on up behind the boss, y'know. And he
say, "Okay John, you all loaded and ready to go?"
So John traveled with them y'know for quite a bit of
time, like he'd been with 'em for years. So they left
Chicago for Los Angeles, California. And so John
loaded their things. So when they got to Los Angeles,
the train pulled up, the porter put the box down. John
got off y'know, and John took all their grips off y'know
and set 'em down, taken 'em off. John got all their grips
sorted out y'know before they came out. Okay. The
first big boss came out y'know, he came right down
y'know, his coat fastened, picks his two grips y'know,
and never looked back. John looked at him y'know.
Okay. Here comes the other, the second one. He come
down, he picks up his two grips y'know, never looked
back, steps right on.
John said, "Well, maybe the other one's got the
money." So here come the third one down. He picks up
his grips, step down, and never looked back. So John

still thought about it y'know, getting worried about the
money. And so here come the fourth one. The fourth
one picked up his grips, and he never looked back. Fifth
one came down and picked up his grips. He never looked
back. John ain't got nothing. So here come the sixth
man. The sixth man come down, he picks up his grips,
never looked back. So John begin to frown, "That's half
of 'em y'know." So John looked all around y'know at the
porter and the porter looked at him y'know. And so
John looked, "Here come the seventh one down." And he
done the same thing, the seventh. He picked up his
grips. The eighth one, he picked up his, and he ain't
looked back. John just kept frowning. So the ninth one
he picked up his ones. He never looked back. The tenth
one did the same. The eleventh man he was a big, heavy-
sot, great big feller. He wagged down, he got his grips
y'know, and he looked back at John. John he never said
a word. John all frowned up. "That's the eleventh man
y'know." John said, "Well maybe Old Boss is got the last
one." Old Boss is long, tall. He come down y'know,
he's <u>tall</u>. He picks up his grips. John looks at him. So
he picks up his grips and set 'em over there on the side,
y'know, and he turned around to John. Run his hand in
his pocket, got his billfold out y'know.

    John says, "Cap'n," says, "let me tell you some-
thing." Says, "Y'know they just telling a damn lie on
you-all." Say, "I..I..I thought that like hell y'know, for
a long time. I'se been thinking it like hell." Said, "But
I'm going to tell you," said, "they sure told a damn lie.
They say you-all killed Christ. But you didn't kill him."

    He said, "What's the matter, John?"

    He said, "You-all just worried hell out of him."

79. Eating Farther Down the Hog (Rev. Mrs. L. R. Toler)

Two other texts were given me by Michigan Negroes, J. D. Suggs (printed in NFIM 67) and Lulu Powell, both of Calvin. These variants have the colored man eating further up the hog. Lulu Powell heard the tale from her minister in the First Baptist Church in Vandalia. "He was making the point how we had progressed in our church work."

There was a man named John Ashe, cut wood for a living, usually would accept just a hog head—raised in a country where they grew hogs. So one day somebody gave him a piece of shoulder—tasted pretty good to him, never tasted it before. Passed by one of his old friends, she'd killed a couple of hogs. Children called out, "Mammy, here comes Uncle John."

She called out, "Children, tell Uncle John I'll give him a hog head to cut a load of wood."

Children said, "Uncle John."

He just throwed up the back of his hand, wouldn't stop. Finally their mother came out, called "John, John —give you two hog heads for the one load of wood."

He kept on going, said, "Children, tell your mammy I'm eating further down the hog now."

80. I'm Sopping My Own Gravy Now (E. M. Moore)

The Negro worked for the Southern doctor. The doctor would leave home before breakfast every morning and the Negro would carry breakfast to the office. One morning the doctor was sitting looking out the window from his upstairs office. He saw the Negro coming down the street with his breakfast. He took a biscuit

from the plate and sopped the biscuit in the doctor's
gravy and ate it. When he reached the office, the doctor
whipped him, told him he was fired. "I don't allow a nigger to sop out of my gravy. Get out and get you some
gravy of your own to sop."

The Negro left and moved to Arkansas (from Mississippi). The first year he was in Arkansas, farming was
good. He made money, he bought a pair of mules and
some plow tools. The next year farming was good. He
started buying forty acres of land, paid for his mules,
his forty acres of land, bought a horse and buggy and
nice clothes. The next year he drove back to the same
town in Mississippi. He saw the doctor he had worked
for when he lived in Mississippi. The doctor wanted to
know who he was driving for when he saw him in the new
buggy with the nice horse.

He said, "I'm driving for myself."
He said, "What are you doing now, John?"
He said, "I'm farming."
He said, "Who for, John?"
He said, "Myself."
He said, "Whose buggy and horse is that?"
He said, "They belong to me."
"And you're farming for yourself?"
"Yessir."
"Own your own mules?"
"Yessir."
"Own your own land?"
"Yessir."
"Well John, tell me, what are you doing in Arkan-
sas?"
"Sir, I'm sopping my own gravy."

INFORMANTS

Altheimer, Rev. Silas Jenkins. Born in Toledo, Cleveland County, Arkansas, 21 August 1870. His father was a German immigrant, his mother was born a slave. He was a pastor of the African Methodist Episcopal Church in Pine Bluff, and spent 54 years teaching, 13 at Alcorn A. & M. in Mississippi and 8 at the A. M. & N. College in Pine Bluff. He heard many stories from his grandmother, a runaway slave.

Bedford, Mrs. Grace Raspberry. Born in Warren, Arkansas, 23 January 1907. Her mother's people came from South Carolina and her father's from Georgia. She is an elementary school teacher, married to a horse trader, whom I was originally introduced to, but she turned out to be the storyteller.

Cothran, Dr. Tilman C. Born in Hope, Arkansas, 17 November 1917. Professor of Sociology at the A. M. & N. College, with a Ph.D. from the University of Chicago.

Courtney, John. Born 1907, in Drew County, Arkansas. "I used to be a showboy—that Sugarfoot Green Show—from 1925 to 1927. I was a tapdancer, I was pretty good at the foots." Due to heavy injuries received on the job, John now does only light work.

Courtney, Julia. Born in Drew County, between Helena and McGeehee. Married John Courtney in 1931. "My grandfather on my mother's side was mixed with Indian and Creole. I never saw my father but once, when I was seventeen."

Courtney, Sally. Born in Drew County, Arkansas, in 1895, as Martha May Stevenson. Married Tobe Courtney in 1906. Works in the cotton fields.

Courtney, Tobe. Born in Drew County, Arkansas,

17 December 1879, between Collins and Monticello. "I
made ties for the railroad, cut timber for sawmills,
herded cattle, chopped, picked, ploughed cotton." Like
his son John, he went up North when he was young, just
gallivanting. Came to Pine Bluff in 1944.

Heard, James. Born in Teller, Arkansas, 1 January
1868. Blind, an inmate in Mrs. Toler's Old Folks Home.

Holmes, Dan. Born in Monroe, Louisiana, in 1879.
An interior decorator in Pine Bluff. I met him through
E. M. Moore at a Methodist service.

Jackson, Oliver E. Born in 1906 in Asheville,
North Carolina. Professor of Modern Foreign Languages at the A. M. & N. College.

Jones, Ben. Born in Altheimer, Arkansas, 31
March 1886. Now a farmer in nearby Gethsemane. His
dad came from Alabama, was born a slave and died at
ninety-two, in 1942. "My mother was real bright, and
had red hair."

Jones, Emma. Born in Gould, Arkansas, in 1932.
A student in Professor Jackson's class.

King, A. J., Jr. Born in Little Rock, Arkansas, on
25 June 1920. Both his parents came from Trinidad.
Head teacher at Barnes Elementary School, outside
Pine Bluff, a graduate of the A. M. & N. College. Se-
verely wounded in World War II, but now fully re-
covered.

Lee, Harold. Born in Louisville, Kentucky, in 1920.
Has lived in Arkansas about fifteen years. I met him
in the Lion's Inn.

Mazique, A. A. Born in Natchez, Mississippi, in
1907. His family moved to Wildsville, Louisiana, in
1912. Owner of the Lion's Inn, on the campus of the A.
M. & N. College. Has French, Indian, and Irish as well
as Negro blood.

Moore, E. M. Born in Utica, Mississippi, 23 November 1907. Spent 23 years up and down the levees,
excavating and landscaping. Built the football stadium

for the A. M. & N. College. His mother was an Indian, his paternal grandfather a white man.

Moore, Roscoe. Born in Hope, Arkansas, 24 April 1886. A legless but active inmate of Mrs. Toler's Old Folks Home.

Nelson, Edna G. Born in Pine Bluff in 1884. She formerly lived with a "fortune-teller," who operated in cahoots with a white insurance man.

Parker, Clara. Born in West, Mississippi, 11 May 1909. A student in Professor Jackson's class.

Stanfill, Harrison. Born in Columbus, Tennessee, 30 November 1894. Blind veteran of World War II, living in a rooming hotel apparently with aid of a pension.

Summers, Maria. Born in Columbia, South Carolina, in 1864. Lives in Barnes Settlement nine miles outside Pine Bluff; still active in church work.

Toler, Rev. Mrs. L. R. Born in Macon, Noxubee County, Mississippi, in 1896. Taught school in Mississippi, Louisiana, and Alabama, was ordained in the African Methodist Episcopal Church, and felt the call for her mission to found a colored Old Folks Home in Pine Bluff in 1942.

Tyler, Archie "Billy Jack." Born in Cleveland, Mississippi, in 1934. Has picked cotton, worked in restaurants, and was employed as a hotel bellboy, about to enter the Navy, when I met him in Cleveland.

White, Bertha. Born in Little Rock, Arkansas, 12 March 1906. A student in Professor Jackson's class.

INDEX OF MOTIFS

References are keyed to Thompson's index, except those
marked (*) which refer to Baughman's index. (See
p. 289)

B. Animals

B81.13.4* "Mermaid gives mortals gold from sea bottom." P. 73

B210.2 "Talking animal or object refuses to talk on
demand. Discoverer is unable to prove his
claims, is beaten." P. 50

D. Magic

D758.1 "Disenchantment by three nights' silence under
punishment." P. 78

J. The Wise and the Foolish

J17 "Animal learns through experience to fear man." P. 34

J217.0.1.1 "Trickster overhears man praying for death
to overtake him." P. 52

J246.1 "Literal following of instructions." P. 94

J551.5 "Magpie tells man that his wife has eaten an eel." P

J955.1 "Frog tries in vain to be as big as ox." P. 33

J1499.19.2 "Man attempts to stay in haunted house all
night: one cat after another enters. . . ."
(Thompson rev. ed. makes this J1495.2,
"When Caleb comes.") P. 78

X. Humor

X424 "The sexton carries the parson." P. 49

X459.2* (b) "Fowls hide when preacher comes to visit."
(Not in Thompson rev. ed.) P. 38

X584.2* "Man without gun accompanies hunter. Every
time hunter kills an animal, man without gun
says, "We killed a (rabbit)." This goes on until the hunter kills a mule thinking it a deer.
He says, "We killed a mule." The other says,
"We nothing; you killed that mule." (Not in
Thompson rev. ed.) P. 90

X911.3 "If the wolf's tail breaks." P. 87

INDEX OF TALE TYPES

According to Aarne-Thompson index. (See p. 289)

I. Animal Tales

II. Ordinary Folktales

III. Jokes and Anecdotes

PART II.

NEGRO TALES FROM CALVIN, MICHIGAN

I

THE ASTONISHING REPERTOIRE

OF JAMES DOUGLAS SUGGS

In Europe, where folklore rests on systematic and organized field collecting, storytellers with vast repertories do not astound the collector. In a fine article on Scottish Gaelic folktales, Kenneth Jackson tells us of an Irish woman who yielded 375 stories, of which forty were long wonder tales; of a Lochaber man with five hundred shorter type anecdotes; of a single tale written down by the great Campbell of Islay that occupies eighty pages in print; of a West Kerry beggar who spent seven nights relating one narrative.* Alongside such feats the 175 assorted yarns and the score of songs given me by James Douglas Suggs may well seem modest. But for the United States, lacking the medieval heritage of hero-traditions and Märchen, and the static peasant culture that still obtains in the Highlands, and much of the Old World, this figure does startle. More than mere volume is involved, however, for Suggs narrates with art and relish, and his agile, retentive mind mirrors the ample folk traditions of the Southern Negro.

James Douglas Suggs was born March 10, 1887, in Kosciusko, Attala County, Mississippi, the second child and oldest boy of five children. All his grandparents

* "The Folktale in Gaelic Scotland," in the Proceedings of the Scottish Anthropological and Folklore Society, IV (Edinburgh, 1952), p. 136.

grew up as slaves. He said: "I knew them as well as
my own folks; they lived not far apart. Their Marster,
old man Suggs [whose slaves of course bore his name],
he treated 'em good. He let them make crops themselves, let them clear a few acres in the woods and
plant corn or cotton. He'd give them everything they
made on it. They could work Saturday evenings and
moonshiny nights, in the early part of the night. They
stayed on there after freedom. They was raised up with
the young Marsters and stayed with them as sharecroppers and tenants." (20 March 1952.)

Like all my other Negro informants in Michigan,
Suggs came from a mixed ancestry. He himself was
very dark, but his father, who was half Indian, and one
sister were light. Both his parents were born in Mississippi, his mother (Isabella Cottrell), in Artibashaw
County (?) and his father in Goodman, where he worked
as carpenter, janitor and handyman; in later life he
turned preacher. Kosciusko, the county seat, contained
five thousand people, mostly colored, and there Suggs
went to school from his fifth to his fifteenth year, getting through the twelfth grade. "I went all the year
round, and made two grades some years." Once he began steady work, Suggs entered a variety of occupations
that took him into thirty-nine states. His first "public
working job" was guard on a county prison farm at Itta
Bena, Mississippi, in his twentieth year. In 1907 he
joined the Rabbit Foot Minstrel Show, and traveled from
New Mexico to North Dakota, singing, dancing, and telling jokes in a troupe of twenty-eight Negro entertainers.
He turned to professional baseball in 1908 and 1909,
pitching and catching for the Sliding Delta team spon-
sored by a Negro friend of Theodore Roosevelt who
owned a big farm near Indianola, Mississippi. The
team played exhibitions in Greenville, Memphis, Helena,

Vicksburg, and Little Rock. For three of the next four
years Suggs worked out of Memphis as a brakeman for
the I. C. (Illinois Central). "The men who were turned
down were all dolled up; I was dressed for the job." He
switched to a sand hog in 1912 while the Harland Bridge
was building across the Mississippi River.

Returning to Mississippi he worked for a wealthy
white planter, Dave Bishop, as cook and nurse. With
Mr. and Mrs. Bishop he visited Quebec, Florida, Texas,
Salt Lake City, and Newport News. The boss would give
him money and he would go to the colored section. He
voluntarily entered the army in September, 1917; fought
in France with the Ninety-Second Illinois, a light infan-
try division; and was discharged in April, 1919. Next
Suggs worked on a dredge boat around Carrothersville,
Missouri, for the MacWilliam Drainage Company, which
built ditches to drain the county of flood water. From
1920 to 1922 he cooked short orders in a "vanold" in the
depot at Popular Bluffs, Missouri, where he had pre-
viously visited a cousin. Crossing the line to Arkansas,
he worked for a big oil man named Lattimore at Jonesboro, making mortar and cleaning his stores. In 1924
and 1925 he made molds in a steel foundry in St. Louis,
and the two following years hung around Chicago with
his brothers, "just spo'ting."

In 1928 he married, at the age of forty-two, a part
Indian girl he had met in Bono, Arkansas. For the next
dozen years he headquartered in Arkansas: farming,
fishing, cooking in private homes and for hunting parties, and acting as handyman, "like a good old hunting
dog." The hunting trips organized by wealthy doctors,
rice growers, and syrup makers, which he accompanied
as camp cook and general factotum, earned him up to
$150 in ten days; Suggs, apparently a fixture and come-
dian on these excursions, cut off a hunter's shirttail

when one missed a deer. On one such trip in 1939 he
worked seventy-two hours straight without sleep, and
then drank some wine, which affected his already high
blood pressure; he blacked out, and spent four months
in the hospital at Hot Springs. He now brought his family back to Chicago, where his brother ran a rooming
house, and from 1940 to 1947 helped him renting flats.
When his brother bought a home in Vandalia, a village
of mixed population some five miles east of Cassopolis,
the county seat of Cass County in southwestern Michigan, Suggs followed him, like many Chicago Negroes
fanning out into the countryside during the last two de-
cades. After three years at Vandalia he shifted to the
next township, Calvin, a unique all-colored pre-Civil
War farming community, where I met him in March,
1952.

A chance conversation at the tavern in Calvin led
me to Suggs, when the proprietress gave me his name
as a likely person fitting my model: Southern born, a
good talker, and with time on his hands. He was dirt
poor too, she added, and could use any help I might give
him. She had taken old clothes over to his family when
they were living in a converted chickenhouse in Vandalia; the mother was subnormal, and had recently lost a
child through improper care.

I drove down to Suggs' house, close by the four corners known as Calvin Center, and found his shabby dwelling faced with cheap brick siding, just beyond the impos-
ing Community Church. Suggs himself answered my
knock, and stood expectantly in the grimy eating and
cooking room, various of his ten children peering
around his ankles, barefooted in spite of the cold and
the dirty wooden floor. "Edith from the tavern sent me
down," I said. "She tells me you know lots of stories."
His grin broke out at once, and he promptly declared,

"I know a million of them." We matched yarns for two hours, standing all the while, with mounting excitement. That first evening I simply jotted down titles or themes of his narratives, and returned later to write them out at dictation for entire days.

On subsequent visits, in June, September, and November, 1952, and February, March, July, and August, 1953, I recorded his stories and songs in notebooks and on tapes, finding him always an effortless and inexhaustible talker. In the summer of 1953 the Suggses moved to a smaller and even more derelict structure, on the other side of the Four Corners, a one-story affair with perhaps three rooms; they had to leave extra beds outside, and that so large a family lived and cooked in such quarters seemed physically impossible, especially during the winter months when they must be so closely confined. A well supplied water and gas lamps light. Actually, apart from the house, their situation had advantages over city living, since the children could see open fields and sky and breathe clean air. Mrs. Suggs appeared indeed non compos mentis; for all the tens of words her husband delivered to me, she scarcely vouchsafed a dozen. One time she called out to me, "Hey Mister," as I was leaving, greatly to my wonder; Suggs hushed her and I learned no more about the matter until my next visit when he replied to my query with his usual candor. The boys had been kidding his wife. They had told her that when Suggs said he was going to Cassopolis to make a recording with me, he was really playing around with a girl in town. A small, frozen-faced woman, she showed traces of earlier good looks, reflected in her budding daughters, but a dozen years of childbearing and childcaring had drained her. When I saw her, in February, 1953, she was swollen with a twelfth pregnancy, and was momentarily expecting.

I give these details about Suggs's history and circumstances for the light they may throw on the human channels of folklore. Suggs rose supreme above his poverty and faced the world with indomitable good will. At sixty-five he had nothing to show materially for his varied life but a parcel of young mouths to feed, the price of his late and prolific marriage; he worked as a laborer for construction companies in South Bend, hitching rides since his own jalopy had finally gasped out, and when snow interrupted work, he drew compensation. Yet a smile, laugh, or joke always hid near his surface, and he once said to me: "I was born lucky. It's lucky if you are born with a veil over your face. Well, I've never had to go on relief." And he looked confidently at the field across the way, and talked of building on it next year. Well built, unwrinkled, pleasant featured, Suggs showed little trace of age and none of care; he exuded high spirits, as if all the world were a minstrel show, and he the chief performer. His expressive eyes, wide-breaking grin, and fluent, melodious tongue equipped him well for his self-appointed role. He joked with the boys, on the job or in the tavern, with wholehearted delight, and in the course of his varied career had soaked up a mass of fraternal jests and tales. A sober supernatural strain tempered his jocularity however, for he believed in spirits, hoodoos, and the dark powers of the universe, and regularly quoted Scripture to document their reality. Like other Southern Negroes I met in Michigan and Arkansas, he devoutly accepted the literal word of the Bible, and constantly recited, within his own vernacular, its miraculous passages.

Suggs's story repertoire falls for the most part into definite categories. The largest group, some twenty-three, deals with talking animals, followed by experiences (16), spirits and hants (15), miscellaneous

folktales (15), tall tales (15), Biblical and moral tales
(14), preachers (13), hoodoo and fortune-telling (11),
Old Marsters (10), humorous anecdotes (10), beliefs (9),
Irishmen (5), colored man (5). (I omit from this count
some narratives not strictly classifiable as folktales or
folk history.) All these divisions reflect major patterns
of Negro tradition in the United States, as indicated
from the literature and from my own collecting. Except
for the one text of "The Animals in Night Quarters"
(Type 130), no complex tale suggesting a straight European influence appears, and no Märchen with aristocra-
tic characters occur. Some tales that seem intruders,
like "The Devil's Daughter" (Type 313A), or "The Mermaid," or "The King of the Beasts Meeting Man" (Type
157), are nonetheless well established in Afroamerican
storylore. Suggs faithfully represents his enthnocul-
tural group, in the inclusion of American whoppers and
Irish noodles, the limitation of wonder tales, the rein-
terpretation of Christian lore, the contrast of preacher
jokes and spectral experiences, and the recognition ac-
corded two tricksters, Mr. Rabbit in the animal cycle
and the crafty slave in the Old Marster cycle.

Looking first at the animal stories, one finds about
half of them falling within the Uncle Remus framework
of the rabbit outwitting the bear, panther, fox, and other
members of the forest family. Where well-known New
World Negro types appear, like "Playing Godfather,"
"Rabbit Makes Bear his Riding Horse," and "Playing
Dead in the Road," Suggs invests them with freshness
and color. Thus in "Playing Godfather," which merges
into the "Grease Test," as this plot generally does,
Suggs gives a novel twist to the final episode. Usually
the animals sleep by the fire, to discover the culprit
when the stolen butter runs out his pores. Suggs has
them jump over the fire instead, on the rabbit's theory

that the guilty one will fall in. The terrapin avoids the
trap on the first jump by running around the fire when
the wind blows a smoke screen for him, and on the return jump by flattering the bear that he can stop in midair, cross his legs, and pull out his back titty for the
crowd. Pleased, the bear tries this, and falls smack
into the fire. The familiar tale of the Southern buzzard
flying north for a change of scene, to return when he
finds that carrion is buried there, Suggs modernized
with a World War I locale; the buzzard and his young
ones fly to Europe, but come back on learning that the
war dead are burned. Going outside the Uncle Remus
animals, we see a good illustration of Suggs's technique
in his tri-episodic narrative of "The Monkey Who 'Im-
pitated' His Master." The first act simply follows the
popular anecdote of "Big 'Fraid and Little 'Fraid," with
the monkey in a white sheet frightening his master who
had put on a white sheet to scare some boys. Suggs
builds up a dramatic sequel. The monkey copies his
master, who is an engineer, so effectively that he runs
away with the train while the crew is in the station; the
operator telegraphs ahead, "All trains take the side
track, for the monkey has the main line." Not wishing
to sell, give away, or kill his pet, the engineer shaves
next morning and pretends to cut his throat with the razor; the monkey "impitates" him, and kills himself.
The third episode is rare and the second appears unique.

Another group of fictional narratives widespread in
Negro tradition involves the master (Old Marster) and
the slave, who outwit and support each other in a shift-
ing relationship. Suggs called the cunning slave Efan,
a name signifying a schemer; only one other of my informants, also from Mississippi, uses Efan instead of
the customary John. Efan performs such generic ex-
ploits as praying to the Lord to take him away, and

reneging when Marster appears in heavenly guise; and
guessing the coon hidden under the pot, by referring to
himself as "the old coon" caught at last. More novel
are his feats of stuffing himself with dumplings, in a
wager with his Marster, until they protrude from his
throat and he can't swallow any medicine to cure himself; and pretending to catch a live panther in whose
cage he is thrust, by the lucky accident of stepping on a
loose board in his pell-mell flight, which breaks the
panther's neck. A characteristic yarn with a new twist
has rascally old Bill (the equivalent of Efan) caught
stealing a hog, but his Marster forgives him for admit-
ting that he stole just this one. Marster then finds
about five hundred pounds of hog jowls in Bill's quarters. "To tell the truth, Marster," explains Bill, "I like
jowls so much I cut this one hog up into nothing but
jowls." So Bill triumphs.

The Old Marster cycle draws close to the tart humor of protest tales, and Suggs possessed his share of
these. Sometimes they take the guise of an innocuous
tall tale, as in the windy about the speedy colored man,
who struck a white man in Arkansas, and then outraced
a train, a plane, and finally a buck whom he mistook for
a comrade in a similar fix, running from the law with
a rocking chair on his head. The protest note sounds
more shrilly in the account of the white man who shot
and killed two Negroes but missed the third who hid behind a mule; the court fined him five dollars for killing
the mule and five cents for killing the colored men.
Outright retaliation appears in the happening at More-
house, Missouri, where a gang of white youths made all
colored travelers dance their feet off. One pair of Negro lads volunteered to do a step called "Get Your Gun";
they reached in their suitcase, pulled out their guns,

and pointing them at their tormentors commanded them
to dance in turn.

Humor bulks large in Negro storytelling, and while
the animal and Marster series provide laughter, the tall
tales, noodles and jokes constitute the most risible fare.
Like many Negro humorists, Suggs makes preachers
and deacons the butt of frequent jests. Sometimes the
joke turns on the preacher's text, in such rhetorical
questions as "What did Paul say?" or "Abraham, what
hast thou got in thy bosom?" to which a member of the
congregation replies literally. In these jests Suggs in-
tones snatches of sermons and shrills the audience re-
sponses with eerie simulation.

Tall tales are liberally strewn through Suggs's narratives. Among the common extravagances in American white collections, he knew such classic whoppers
as the great bag of game procured with one shot, and
the stretching buckskin harness, which he joins in one
adventure, and he told, too, of giant punkins, cabbages,
and watermelons; of the gallinipper so large its bones
were used to fence in a forty acre field; and of the clever chinch bugs who dropped on their victim from the
ceiling when he lay down on the floor in a ring of molasses. More unusual is the colored cowboy, Brother
Bill of Texas, who rode to town on a panther with barbed
wire for reins and a rattlesnake for a whip, and drank a gallon of nitroglycerine and dynamite at the tavern. Although
Suggs related this as a prose tale, which he heard when traveling to Texas in 1910, it also takes the form of a rhymed
"toast," of the kind prevalent among Negro funsters.
Brother Bill foreshadows Pecos Bill.

Along with the jocular, gregarious, and joke-swap-
ping strain in Suggs courses a grim and sober, God- and
devil-fearing mood, that evoked his most awesome
tales. These reveal a universe peopled with spectral

shapes, two-headed fortune-tellers, violent white men, and malevolent hoodoos. The realities of racial tension and the mysteries of supernatural phenomena converge toward a dark and bloody ground, where death takes cruel forms and the dead haunt the living. Suggs saw the spirits himself, because he was born with a veil, although in later years they did not bother him very much. If the veil is lifted over the baby's face backwards, and hung to dry until it rots, he said the baby will speak with an educated tongue. His grandmother, Clara Suggs, who died at the age of 117, in 1927, could heal headache with a stroke of her hand, remove warts by saying "Who told you I could cure them?" and dispel toothache with a splinter from a lightning-struck tree. His nine-year-old daughter Beatrice was born with a ghost-hole in her ear, which enabled her to see and hear spirits. "She used to see babies on the wall terrible." Signs spoke to Suggs; when his right eye quivered he would rejoice, when his left eye quivered it would rain or he would get mad; itching in his right hand signified money coming, in his left hand the advent of a letter. If he cut his finger- or toe-nails on Sunday, he took sick before Monday.

From this belief-system grows an intriguing set of experiences. Some describe simple incidents where Suggs or his family or acquaintances saw spirits; others deal with complex situations rich in details both physical and spectral. A median example, perhaps akin to the Ghostly Hitchhiker, came to Suggs from a brother in Willis, Ohio, who heard it from the man involved. A hobo (a white man) looking for shelter on a rainy night, found a friendly stranger who conducted him to his home, but disappeared when a woman opened the door. The woman explained that her dead husband habitually led benighted travelers to her door, since his death in a train accident some years before. Besides this conventional

type of ghostlore, Suggs related powerful individualized
ghost-dramas. One concerns a spectral train he en-
countered when serving as brakeman on the Yazoo and
Mississippi Valley railroad. Taking it for a real train,
the engineer dropped Suggs off to flag it, and backed up
to Cleveland. But inquiry proved that the tracks were
clear, save for this unreal engine often sighted on the
spot where a wreck had occurred a dozen years before.
Suggs sat down and cried and cried, thinking of his nar-
row escape from a lonely encounter with an immaterial
train.

A few years before this he stopped late at night at
a hotel room in Greenville, Mississippi, and took the
only remaining room, despite the warning of the girl
clerk. But he found no rest that night, for a weird noise
kept him crouched on his feet, razor in hand, until morning. Then Suggs learned a jealous lover had shot his
sweetheart in that room and killed six policemen who
attempted to enter, an affair that had received statewide
notoriety. In a melodrama laid in the Mississippi Delta,
where Suggs was working on railroad construction with
hundreds of other laborers, a Negro and a white man
conspired to murder the proprietor of a nearby gambling
house. The colored killer was found and burned alive.
The twin brother of the murdered man passed Suggs and
his work gang in the woods, on his way to visit the scene
of the murder. He reappeared some time later, stagger-
ing and bloody. Suggs at first believed that as a twin he
had suffered his brother's pains, but later conceived
from the movies that he might have been attacked by
someone hidden in the trees. All these episodes Suggs
described with photographic precision and intense emotional conviction.

In the adjacent area of hoodooing, fortune-telling,
and other occult matters, Suggs proved equally fecund.

Curiously, while he believed in these black arts, he also realized they involved deceit and imposition. So he pictured Uncle John, a "two-head," ejecting lizards from a patient by dosing her with butterfly root to make her heave, and John the Conquer to quiet her; then he clubs to death a lizard, pretending she had vomited it up, to fix the evil hoodoo who had planted it in her stomach. (Another Mississippi Negro, Mrs. E. L. Smith of Calvin, informed me that she had seen a hoodoo doctor cut lizards out of an invalid's swollen leg.) Suggs also told how a hoodoo charlatan in Poplar Bluff, Missouri, fled town on meeting a "feather-breasted" rival, none other than the local garbage collector who glued chicken feathers onto his chest.

In spite of these impostures, Suggs credited the power of genuine "two-heads." Jack Farmer killed his white boss for beating his sick daughter, and then eluded hundreds of searchers who had him surrounded in the woods; he ran to his daddy, a hoodoo, and they could never after lay a finger on Jack, although they would see him in the distance. Some "two-heads" specialized in fortune-telling, such as Aunt Carolyn Dye, a famous consultant from Newport, Arkansas, whom Suggs celebrated in the "Yellow Dog Blues" in the lines

> I'm going to Newport
> To see Aunt Carolyn Dye,
> For she's a fortune-telling woman,
> She never told a lie.

A white man who doubted Aunt Carolyn's talents hid seventy-five cents in a stump to test her, but she revealed its whereabouts before he could even ask the question. At Algey (Algiers), across the bay from New Orleans, congregated a whole community of fortune-tellers, whom Suggs visited on occasion, and saw perform marvelous

divinations. One showed his buddy a flash of his missing
wife in Kosciusko, and forecast their speedy reconcilia-
tion. A "magikin" trained in Bombay impressed Suggs
mightily, in Lumford, Arkansas, in 1920, with his ability
to shoot blindfolded a block of wood off his wife's head,
provided a person born between June 29 and July 2
placed two fingers behind his neck. "Magicking" or
"vanquilling" once prevented Suggs's Uncle Jack from se-
curing buried treasure his dip-needle had located. A
Civil War colonel on a snorting horse appeared before
Jack, deep in his treasure hole, and frightened him off;
but Jack later learned this was not the dead owner's
ghost but his own white partner's hypnotic conjuration.
Professional magicking slides down the scale to secret
spells and formulas and lucky talismans and mojos possessed by the rank and file. A proprietary lover can
immunize his lady against all other comers by rubbing
her vitals with the forked tongue of a snake. Suggs believed that a willing girl he once made fruitless love to
had been so treated by her boy friend.

Behind these malignant and transcendent forces
stands always the Christian myth, designating Christ
and the Devil as their fountain-heads. "All witchcraft
is from the Devil—mi'acles, hyp'tizing, seeing things.
That always has been, and is going on today." Biblical
folk tales and folk allusions cropped up persistently in
Suggs's talk, to explain the evil ways of men and the
swift punishments of heaven. He used the term "man-
gelizing" to describe the visits of good angels to the
earth before the coming of Christ in the guise of aged
beggars. Knocking on doors, the beggar asks for food,
which he hits with his staff, and sends to heaven as a
burnt offering; then he too vanishes like smoke. Later
bad angels came down, who liked the good-looking daughters of man and remained on earth, to become mighty

and wicked giants. "Norah" alone remained pure in blood, but after the flood mankind no longer possessed angel blood.

Separate little episodes from the folk Bible stand by themselves. Some are common in Negro circles, such as how the Devil coined the word Mhm; or the way Christ fooled Peter by changing his stone to bread one day and deciding to build his church upon it the next; or the reason the Jews don't eat hog. A nice example of folk-Biblical synthesis occurs in the anecdote of Samson and the anvil, where Samson pretends to hurl the anvil toward the clouds and the blacksmith begs him to desist—a regular incident in the Märchen contest between the giant and the little hero. The story of Moses defeating the Pharoah's wizards, when his staff-turned-serpent eats up theirs, Suggs calls "How Hoodoo Lost His Hand." He commonly made such mergers and cross-references between Christianity and occult forces.

An allied narrative type takes its facts from contemporary life but its moral from Scripture. Suggs illustrated God's vengeance on sinners from personal knowledge. Ben Weatherby cursed God and drowned desperately in a Mississippi flood. A hunter in Mississippi kept missing church because he started out Saturday night and stayed in the woods till Sunday morning. Returning from one such hunt, he saw a woman in white silk stretched out against the side of the house; the vision struck him dumb for twenty-four hours, and he never hunted on Sunday again. Suggs interpreted this as a divine token, like God's striking John the Baptist dumb for doubting the angel who told him of Christ's coming.

Another grouping covers realistic stories, that Suggs knew from his own experience or from local report. Often highly dramatic but lacking a supernatural element, they verge toward the local legend and folk

history. Suggs of course garnishes these accounts with
vivid particulars and a full sweep of the social context,
and they provide some of his meatiest offerings. Several involve race friction, and portray the terrorism of
the white man over the Négro, with perhaps the stoic
resistance of the colored man as climax. (Suggs himself displayed no emotional resentment over race relations, and told these tales quite dispassionately.) In
one long and graphic history Suggs chronicled a con-
certed murder plan against Negro brakemen during the
hard times of 1908, that drove him and three hundred
colleagues from their jobs, until a white conductor was
shot by mistake. In the saga of Will Kimbro, who taught
Suggs in school, a valiant colored man singlehanded de-
fies a mob surrounding his house, and kills sixteen men
from the woods. He was acquitted in Circuit Court and
ended up as a Federal detective. Suggs's stark account
of this action reads like a movie script. Other more-or-
less true stories deal with such matters as Jesse
James's tunnel from his home near Cairo, Missouri, to
the banks of the Mississippi; a bandit disguised as a
woman who is foiled in his attempted holdup of a wealthy
planter; a bear hunt that nearly ends fatally for the celebrated bear-killer John Hugens, when he lost his nerve
upon being surprised from behind. Even the strange re-
conciliation of Suggs with his own lost son, whom he had
never seen from the age of six months to that of thirty-
two years, makes wondrous telling.

A thin line divides these memorable occurrences
from the body of floating folktales which constitute a final category. These migratory tales sometimes assume
the guise of realistic events, and may be told for true,
but are widely distributed. Two ubiquitous witch legends
—of the witch caught by salting and peppering her dis-
carded skin, and the witch detected when a severed cat's

claw turns into her finger—take on local coloring in
some variants. The tales of the snake who plays with
and becomes the life partner of the baby, and of the bear
who abducts and brings up the baby, are customarily
presented as truth. Even the account of mermaids, who
stop ships and call for persons whose names they have
heard, Suggs and other informants offer as reliable data.
On the other hand the highly popular tale of the haunted
house, where a series of scary sights eventually drive
out the daredevil, generally gets told as a laughable
spook story, and the equally well-liked narrative of
"The Devil's Daughter" seems recognized as fiction.
In this last division, then, the narrators waver between
belief and fancy.

What made Suggs an outstanding storyteller? The
circumstances of his varied and mobile life clearly expanded his repertoire, by enlarging his experience and
contacts. His own gregarious and congenial nature led
him easily into social groups and friendly talk. He related tales with mnemonic authority and contagious en-
thusiasm, customarily repeating his narrative in a swift
recap as soon as he finished it, with high excitement.
Once having heard a story he never forgot it, so he
claimed, and his narrative powers bore out the boast.
Whatever he described, whether the technology of his
jobs, the local color of Bible plays and election fights
in the deep South, or actual folktales, he etched fully
with myriad details and hues. He did not simply tell the
story but acted it out and dressed it up with sounds, ges-
tures, and tumbling words. He reproduced the snorting
of a steam engine with intensifying chugs, when the monkey runs away with the train; if the deer sings to the fox,
or the bee chants to the dirtdauber, or the rabbit exhorts
the animals to pull the bear out of the mudhole, he
faithfully performed their parts. Even in ordinary

conversation his range of inflection and musical timbre
enriched his speech, while certain vagaries of his vo-
cabulary—"impitate" for imitate, "minister" for minstrel, "Sinus and Arts" for the School of Science and
Arts on my letterhead—added to its flavor.

One distinctive feature in Suggs's narrative technique
heightens interest in his stories. He frequently supple-
mented the text with a moralizing comment or an apt
illustration from life. The tale of Old Missy, who had
the mule and buggy from which she was thrown sentenced
to whipping and death, reflects the supreme authority of
the white mistress in slavery times; "The Farmer and
the Snake" suggested to him the case of a thorough in-
grate, Dan Sprowell, who abused all those who trusted
him; Nicodemus fibbing in Heaven about his birthplace
prompted him to remark how often Negroes pretend to
a higher station; "The Bee and the Dirtdauber" called
to his mind the impatient person who goes ahead without waiting for instructions; and the Buzzard flying to
Europe reminded him of discontented people looking for
greener pastures and better jobs and finding themselves
worse off after the change.

Luckily Suggs proved as cooperative an informant
as he was skilled a raconteur. He took considerable
satisfaction in the visits and attention of the professor,
talked freely to all his tavern cronies about our recording and dictating sessions, and even exhibited proudly a
photograph I sent him of the two of us standing before
his house. He confided to me that certain persons in
Vandalia and Calvin resented Edith's giving me his name
in preference to theirs. Several times he asked if anyone had ever told me as many stories as he had, and appeared greatly pleased to learn that he far outdistanced
my other informants.

Two years passed after August, 1953, without my

getting to Calvin. When I returned, it was to learn that
Suggs had moved to South Bend the previous fall, to be
near his work, and died there in March, 1955, as he entered his sixty-eighth year. He never lived to see the
books of Michigan Negro folklore to which he contributed
so substantially. It is consoling to know that the spirit
and salt and kindly humor of Suggs will not completely
vanish with his death.

*

NOTE: In Negro Folktales in Michigan
(Harvard University Press, 1956), I published
sixty of his tales. Although he monopolized
one-third of the book, many good tales could
not be included, and remained in my notebooks.
These narratives are here given for the benefit
of folktale students who wish to consider the
full repertoire of a gifted raconteur. (One further text from Suggs, a variant of Type 157,
"Learning to Fear Men," appears in my article
in the Southern Folklore Quarterly, "King Beast
of the Forest Meets Man," XVIII, June 1954, p.
122.) I hope to publish his songs later.

II

ANIMAL   AND   BIRD   STORIES

1. Why the Buzzard is Bald

A similar well-contrived text is in NFIM
41-42, "The Reason the Buzzard is Got a Bald
Head," from Sarah Hall, where the fox trapped
in a hollow tree by the buzzard plays dead and
then claws off the buzzard's feathers. See also
note 9, p. 206, for five Southern Negro references. The distinctive feature of this tale is
the cante-fable element in the chanted conversation between the buzzard and his captive.
The aetiological motif explaining the buzzard's
baldness may become attached to other Negro
tales, as "Learning to Fear Men," Type 157
(see text N, "Buzzard and Rabbit," in Dorson,
"King Beast of the Forest Meets Man," Southern Folklore Quarterly, XVII, June 1954, p.
127); or the crow duping the buzzard into peck-
ing at the buttocks of a supposedly dead mule
(see "Negro Tales of Mary Richardson," no. 4,
pp. 8-9. "How the Buzzard got his Bald Head");
or the man holding the bear's paws around a
tree (see ante, Pine Bluff no. 11, pp. 32-33, "Bear
and Buzzard"). Albert H. Stoddard has recorded
a Gullah text, "How Buh Buzzut Lost de Fedder
on a Head," Library of Congress Record L44
A4, Booklet pp. 7-10, which involves the rabbit,
fox, buzzard, and a hollow tree.

The Buzzard seen a mink runnin' a Rabbit. And so
a man shot the mink—he didn't see the Rabbit. The

Buzzard seen the Rabbit go into the hollow log. So he
flew down and got him a chunk and stuffed him up in
there. Said, "When he die I'll have something to eat."
And every other day he'd go back. He called to Brother
Rabbit,

> "Bum-bee." [Chanted]

Rabbit said,

> "Pullin' pegs." [Chanted]

He goes off and stays three more days. He come
back, say,

> "Bum-bee."

Rabbit getting weak now. Say,

> "Pullin' pegs." [Faintly]

He stayed six days this time, know he'd be dead
when he get back. He says again,

> "Bum-bee."

No answer from the Rabbit. "Well, I guess I'll go
in get my dinner now." He reached in and got one chunk
and pulled it out. Out come a swarm of green flies.
   Brother Buzzard said, "Rabbit sperrits, Rabbit sperrits, Rabbit sperrits!" And up he goes. He flew into a
hickory limb and knocked all the skin off his head. Now
he has no feathers atall on his skin and his head is just
as red.
   (Just like we are punished because Adam sinned.

The Buzzard was punished for shutting in the Rabbit.

One fly musta got in and laid his eggs. The flies turn to maggots and ate the Rabbit and got fat and turned back to flies, and when he pulled out the chunks they swarmed right out.)

2. Rabbit Fool the Panther

> Suggs uses a similar jumping incident in
> his text of Type 15, "The Theft of Butter by
> Playing Godfather," where the Terrapin saves
> himself by getting the Bear to cross his legs
> in midair as he jumps over the fire; see NFIM
> 35.

Brother Rabbit and Brother Turtle were trapping. So they goes to the trap one morning. There was Mr. Panther in the trap. Mr. Rabbit says, "Oh, we've caught Mr. Panter. Won't we have lotsa meat!" So they goes and gets 'em a stick, puts it across Mr. Panter's neck. Each one put a foot on each side of the stick. Mr. Rabbit said, "You get one hind leg and I'll get the other." They began to pull. Just in a little while Mr. Panter begin to roll and kick as though his neck was broke. So they taken him out the trap, began to drag the panter home.

Mr. Panter was afraid to reach up and grab the Rabbit for he was afraid he would miss him. So to get rid of Mr. Terr'pin he would scratch him every once in a while. But Mr. Terr'pin said he felt superstitious about the dead panter scratching him. He says, "Ooh, let's change sides, this hand is tired on this side." So he said, "We'll go again." So Mr. Panter scratched him on that side, after he changed sides. Mr. Terrapin said, "Whoo. I'm tired. I'll go out here in the shade and rest while

you watch Mr. Panter." So off he goes to the shade. Instead of going to the shade as he said, he went and dug
him a hole side of a log. And he got in it. Then he
called to Mr. Rabbit. Says "I don't care what you say,
Mr. Panter's not dead."

So off goes Mr. Rabbit running as fast as he could.
Mr. Panter was up and right after him. So he outran Mr.
Rabbit and caught him. As soon as he had caught him,
Mr. Rabbit said, "Oh Mr. Panter, I heard that you was
one of the greatest jumpers in the world. Anyone could
take a apple and th'ow it, and you could jump and cross
your legs and catch it before it hit the ground." So Mr.
Rabbit out with a red apple.

Mr. Panter said, "Oh yes, I can do that."

Mr. Rabbit said, "We'll see." So he th'ew the apple
with all his might. So while he was jumping and trying
to cross his leg and catch the apple, Mr. Rabbit had ran-
ned away. So Dr. Panter didn't get any dinner.

(Mr. Panter got in the trap on purpose to catch the
Rabbit. He couldn't tackle both; he was afraid they would
whup him. That's why he kept tickling the Terr'pin—
he couldn't eat the Terr'pin.)

3. Riding-Horse

   This well-known tale is Type 72. "Rabbit
Rides Fox A-courting," and Motif K1241,
"Trickster rides dupe horseback." I have a
text in Pine Bluff, ante, no. 7, pp. 26-28, "Mr. Rabbit
and Mr. Frog Make Mr. Fox and Mr. Bear their
Riding-Horses," unusual in having a pair of
mounted deceivers. The Joel Chandler Harris
version is in Uncle Remus, His Songs and His
Sayings, no. 6, "Mr. Rabbit Grossly Deceives
Mr. Fox." Full references can be found in
Parsons, Antilles, no. 47, pp. 73-76, "Riding-

Horse." Stoddard has recently recorded a Gullah text, Library of Congress Record 46 A3,
Booklet pp. 9-11.

Brother Bear had a girl and he'd always carry
Brother Rabbit with him, for company. After Brother
Bear leave he slip back to his girl's house, tells her,
"Don't you know Mr. Bear's my riding horse?"
        She says, "No, he's not your riding horse."
        Brother Rabbit says, "Well I'll show you one of
these days." So one day here come Brother Bear along.
        "Brother Rabbit, why don't you go with me over to
my girl's house?"
        "Oh, I'm sick I can't go, I'm sick."
        "Come on and go, I'll carry you over there."
        "I wouldn't mind going but I'd need a bridle, I never
could ride without a bridle. You'se never seen me ride
without a bridle, Brother Bear."
        "Yeah that's all right, git it, git it."
        "And I got to have a saddle too, you knowed I never
could ride without a saddle."
        Mr. Bear says, "Yeah that's all right, get it."
        Says "I want to get my spurs, you know we cowboys
always wear 'em for style, we don't hardly ever use 'em."
        "Yeah that's all right, get 'em, yeah that's right."
        Mr. Rabbit climbs up and off they go, to see Brother
Bear's girl. He got near the house and said, "Get down,
Brother Rabbit."
        Brother Rabbit says, "Go on up there." So he
wouldn't go and Brother Rabbit stuck the spurs into him
both sides, run him right up to the girl's porch. Brother
Rabbit says, "Look, I told you Brother Bear's my riding
horse." So he rode Brother Bear away from the house,
and returned back and taken Brother Bear's girl from
him.

4. Playing Dead in the Road

> See the note, ante, to Pine Bluff no. 8,
> pp. 28-30, "Rabbit and Fox Go Fishing," from Maria
> Summers. A recent variant from Richard
> Smith is in Publications of the Texas Folklore
> Society XXV, pp. 233-235, "Mr. Wolf Goes A-
> Fishing." Rabbit's escape from the animals in
> the text below forms a second, separate episode.

Ber Rabbit didn't like to fish. So Brother Bear
come along, say, "Ber Rabbit, come along get your hunting pole let's go fishing."

Say, "No it's too hot, I don't like to fish."

So Mr. Bear he goes on down to the lake and commence to fish. Brother Rabbit he follows him down
there but lays upon the hill in the shade watching him in
the hot sun. Well about three o'clock Brother Bear had
caught enough fish, decided he'd go home. He reached
down in the water and pulled up this long string of fish,
about three feet long. Brother Rabbit was up on the hill
watching him. "Phew, I sure want some of them fish."
So Brother Rabbit lit out back to the road, lay down acting like he was dead.

Brother Bear said, "Why here Mr. Rabbit dead." He
retched [reached] down and felt Brother Rabbit—"Hm
he ain't been dead long, he's warm and just as fat as he
can be." Says, "Aw I don't need him, I got plenty of fish."
Just left him stretched there alongside the road. Lays
him down, says, "Well, I'll go on home."

At that point Brother Rabbit jumped up, run around
about fifty yards and lay down again by the side of the
road. So Mr. Bear lays his fish down and feels Brother
Rabbit. "Sure he good and fat, something must have hit
him like it did Brother Rabbit back there, and he just as
fat as he can be. Oh well, I'll just lay him right alongside

the road so won't nothing run over him." He wasn't aiming to go back but he hated to see the meat destroyed.
So he picked up his fish, went on. Same thing again.
"Well here's another Rabbit—that makes three—big
snowshoe rabbits." Says, "Well, I'll just lay my fish
down here and go back and get the other two." (It was
worthwhile now.) When he got back there was no rabbit
there. He goes back and the fish and the rabbit are gone.
Then he knows Brother Rabbit had tricked him.

So Brother Bear goes around and gets up the crowd,
Mr. Wolf and Mr. Panter and Mr. Fox—Brother Rabbit
had been tricking lots of people. They were going to fix
him now sure enough. So Brother Rabbit had cooked his
fish and was sitting down eating it. He looks out the window and seed them—so out the window he goes. Mr.
Bear say, "Yon go Brother Rabbit, yon he go," and they
all taken after him. Brother Fox and Brother Deer was
gaining on him—they could catch him if he didn't go in
a hole.

Brother Rabbit thought of another trick on them.
He looked up and seen a tall cypress tree. He run to the
tree and grabbed it and tell them to run quick, the world
was falling. Say, "All of you run and hold it while I go
get an ax to cut a prop and hold it." They look up and
see the tree wiggling against the clouds, looked as if it
was falling—the world done mashed it over—low clouds
made it look like the world was falling. He going to get
a prop to keep it up on that side. (I've seen it with the
skyscrapers—it look like it just weaving. Fellow never
seen a skyscraper would think it was falling—"Looky
yonder, building swaying.")

He run to get the ax and never did come back.

(Rabbit is a smart fellow—he'll stop dead in his
track, let the dog run over him, then double back. You've
got to use all the senses God gave you in this world.)

5. The Rabbit and the Dog

This is a form of Type 62, "Peace among
the Animals." An abbreviated variant I heard
in Mound Bayou is in "Negro Tales of Bolivar
County, Mississippi," no. 5, p. 107, "The Convention," from Rev. J. H. Lee. Walter Winfrey
of Inkster, Michigan, also told me the story.
Hurston, Mules and Men, has the tale, pp. 146-
147, "What the Rabbit Learned." Stoddard has
recorded a Gullah form on Record L46 A4,
Booklet p. 11, "E Might Ober Run De Law."
The Fox tells the Turkey about the new law that
all creatures are friends, but then runs from
the hounds; such long-legged devils might run
over the law. Thompson has added a Joel
Chandler Harris reference to Motif A2494.4.4,
"Enmity between dog and rabbit," in Vol. I of
his revised Motif-Index, Bloomington, Indiana,
1955, but it belongs to a different plot.

Well the animals all met, and called a meeting at
the hall. "We want every animal to meet, to get together
and be as one." Mr. Bear was the moderator. So he
gets up, he began to speak to them, "Now listen gentlemens, we wants to live peaceable, and we all'll be as one.
Mr. Hound won't bother Mr. Rabbit, Mr. Panter won't
bother Mr. Fox." Says, "Well you know who all has been
enemies to each other."
Well all the animals had got in but Mr. Rabbit— he
was kinda late. There was just one vacant seat next to
Mr. Hound Dog. So he had to sit down by Mr. Hound Dog.
Mr. Hound Dog had fleas on him and the mange awful bad.
So the fleas begin to bite Mr. Hound, and the mange begin to eetch [itch] him. So he begin to retch [reach] up
and want to scratch what's biting him. Mr. Rabbit he's
superstitious. Mr. Rabbit he's scared, up he jumped and
began to run around in the hall.

Mr. Deer says, "Brother Moderator, we's here on business and Brother Rabbit keeps jumping around. Now I motions we fine him five dollars. We's here on business, we ain't got time for that." So they fine him five dollars. He pays his fine and goes back to his seat again.

Brother Bear says, "Now ladies and gentlemens, I'll start the p'ceedings where I left off at. We all must live together in harmony."

About that time the fleas begin to bite Brother Hound again, the mange begin to eetch. He go to scratching, up go Brother Rabbit again, running all around the hall.

Brother Bear say, "Order, Brother Rabbit, order, Brother Rabbit. We's here on business, we don't want this running around."

Brother Deer say, "Brother Moderator, I motion we fine him fifteen dollars — might keep him quiet." So he paid his fine, went back and taken his seat.

Brother Bear say, "Well I'll p'ceed again, on my subject." Says "Ladies and gentlemen, I'll p'ceed where I left off at. We got to live together in harmony and peace with each other."

Fleas begin to bite Brother Hound again, mange begin to eetch him, and he goes to scratch again. Rabbit superstitious, up he go again. He makes straight for the door this time — he going outa there. Brother Bulldog was the inner guard. He grabbed him and th'owed him back in there, said "Sit down and be still."

Mr. Deer says, "Mr. Moderator, we'll have to fine Brother Rabbit twenty-five dollars."

Brother Bear says, "It has been motioned and seconded that Brother Rabbit would pay the sum of twenty-five dollars for jumping up and running around in the time of business." Brother Bear say, "Are you ready for the question?"

Brother Rabbit say, "Not ready."

Brother Bear say, "Then state your unreadiness, Brother Rabbit."

"My unreadiness is, the way Brother Bulldog he grab people and th'ow 'em around, somebody going get hurt. I was only going out the door."

(Old Bulldog he's powerful you know, that's why they want him for the inner guard.) [Suggs hereupon went into a description of a bulldog grabbing a horse by the nose and throwing him.]

6. Fox and Rabbit in the Well

Motif K651, "Wolf descends into well in one bucket and rescues fox in the other," gives four American Negro references, including one from Joel Chandler Harris, Uncle Remus, His Songs and His Sayings, no. 16, "Old Mr. Rabbit, He's a Good Fisherman." Suggs's text is close to Harris's, even to the mocking verse the rabbit sings to the fox as he passes him in the buckets; Harris's analogous lines are "Fer dis is de way de worril goes; Some goes up en some goes down." Type 32, corresponding to the motif, gives only European references.

The Fox was after the Rabbit to kill him. So Ber Fox was about to catch Brother Rabbit. There was a well down in the flat between the two hills. It had two water buckets, one on each end of the rope. When you let one down, you'd be pulling one bucket of water up. Brother Rabbit jumped in the bucket was up. Down he went, the other bucket come up. The moon was shining right in the well. It looked like a round hoop of cheese.

Ber Rabbit didn't know how he was goin' git back up after he was down there. He commenced hollering for Mr. Fox to come here quick.

Mr. Fox goes up to the well and looked down in there, says "What you want, Brother Rabbit?"

"See this big old hoop of cheese I got down in here?" Says "Man, it sure is good."

Ber Fox says, "How did you get down in there?"

Says "Git in that bucket up there," says "That's the way I come down." Mr. Fox jumped in that bucket was up, Brother Rabbit jumped in the one was down. Down goes Mr. Fox, up come Brother Rabbit. Brother Rabbit passed Brother Fox. "Hey Brother Fox, this the way the world goes, some going and some coming."

My sister'd been watching round that well and she left a bar of soap. I stepped on it, and I skated on back home.

7. Why the Cat Won't Fish

One time the cat went fishing with a hook and pole. He baited his hook and threw it in the water. A big cypress trout (they call 'em dogfishes here) grabbed it and lit out with it. Brother Tom he throws the fish out of the water, over his shoulder. He was setting on a log in the water. When he went to pull the fish back, the cypress grab his tail—he's got teeth you know—and that made Brother Tom fall back into the water—he was pulling on himself. So he managed to git to shore, and said he'd never go fishing again unless he catch him out of a plate or a dish.

(And you know a cat never will go around the water, though he's crazy about fish. He'll climb up and take it out of your hand—he go crazy when he smell a fish.)

8. Crane and Eel

Randolph in <u>Who Blowed Up the Church</u>
<u>House?</u> gives the tale with the same proverbial
saying at the end, in "The Heron and The Eel,"
pp. 20-21, and he cites European and Indiana
variants in his note, p. 186.

A Crane has just one straight gut. He was fishing,
and he seed an Eel, and swallowed it. Then he turned
around and the Eel had slipped out his backside. So he
swallowed him again, and he slipped out again. The
Crane goes over and sits on a dead log. "I got the dead
wood on you this time." He had him till he died.
They say that in the Southern part: "You can't beat
me if I got the dead wood on you."

9. The Bull and the Elephant

Once there was a Bull that roamed the woods. He
weighed about twelve hundred pounds. He was crossed
with buffalo (he's of the cow tribe), and the longhorn
whiteface of Texas. He'd whipped every animal, beast
he'd met—he was king of the forest. He couldn't find
nothing to whip him. He's going through the woods, talking to hisself, mumbling,

"I'm the best man of the woods,
I'm the best man of the woods."

He seen an Elephant walking along through the woods,
looking sleepy and clumsy. He said to the Elephant,

"I'm the best man of the woods."

So Mr. Elephant reached out with his trunk, lift him
up from the ground, carried him around two or three
times in the air, then threw him down on the ground.
The Bull gets up, goes to hopping off, saying to himself,

> "A man don't know, he just don't know.
> A man don't know, he just don't know."

(A bull got to be particular about what he charges
ever since. He don't hardly ever charge anything except
a man or another horse. He won't charge a horse, without you try to rope him.)

10.   Fowls at the Crap Game

> The present text varies the popular South-
> ern Negro tale of fowls who utter human cries
> of warning and alarm on seeing the chicken-
> loving preacher. Standard variants I collected
> are Suggs's own text in NFIM, "The Preacher
> and the Guinea," pp. 47-48, and see note 17, p.
> 208; "Negro Tales of Bolivar County, Missis-
> sippi," no. 6, pp. 107-108, "Preacher and Fowls,"
> from Rev. J. H. Lee; Pine Bluff ante, no. 16, p.
> 38, "Preacher and Fowls," from Tobe Courtney;
> and "Negro Tales of Mary Richardson," no. 8ab,
> pp. 10-11, "Preacher and the Fowls."

The farmer had four pets, a duck, goose, and a
guinea, and a rooster. So the preacher came to take dinner. They didn't know which one they wanted to kill, they loved
'em all. And the farmer say, "I know what I'll do. I'll
get a pair of dice and let 'em shoot, and the first one
th'ows the lowest on the dice, that's the one we'll kill."
So the farmer gave them the dice. The goose shot first.
    The Rooster says,

"What did he thro-o-ow?" [Very high]
The Duck says,
    "'Leven." [Short]
Then it was the Turkey's shot, Mr. Turkey's shot
with the dice. Turkey shook 'em, and rolled 'em out.
The Rooster said,
    "What did he thro-o-w?"
The Duck says,
    "Craps, craps, craps." [Short]
The Guinea says,
    "That's his neck, that's his neck." [Short]
So they killed the Turkey for the preacher's dinner.

III

WHITE MAN AND COLORED MAN

11. The Old Coon

For this well known Old Marster story see note 20, p. 209, to the text in NFIM, "Coon in the Box," pp. 51-53, from John Blackamore. Baughman gives eight references, seven being Southern Negro, to this episode, which comes from Type 1641, "Doctor Know-All," and is placed as Motif N688, "What is in the dish: 'Poor Crab.'" The general motif K1956, "Sham wise man," applies to the character of Efan. Randolph gives a Negro form, with the pun on "coon," from Ozark white tradition in The Devil's Pretty Daughter, pp. 133-135, "Second Sight." The popularity of the tale in the West Indies appears in the twenty variants listed by Flowers, eight from Puerto Rico.

Suggs uses the name Efan in place of the customary John for the roguish slave who pits his wits against Old Marster. Only one other informant of mine, Lee Curtis, originally from Paris, Tennessee, also used Efan.

Efan was a fortune-teller. Told Old Marster he dreamed last night that Sambo and his wife had stole his hog, and he had him in the bedtick in the bed. Old Marster goes down, says "Where's my hog?" Says "I know you stole it, what's come up with it?" Old Marster goes in the house, th'ows the cover back off the bed, there was the whole hog in the bed. He taken the hog, give them a whipping, go back and tell Efan, "Your dream was true,

you sure can tell fortunes." So he's talking to Mr. Jones
how Efan was on telling fortunes. "Tell anything you
want to know."

Mr. Jones says, "Sure, there ain't nothing to no for-
tunetelling."

"I bet you five thousand dollars you can get anything
and hide it and he can tell you what it is, and not see
what it is."

"Okay, I'll take that bet."

"Well, when you be ready?"

"Well come down Thursday—tell everybody to come
—bring all your friends. Then we'll have witnesses that
Efan did tell what was in the box."

On Thursday all of them was there, a hundred or a
hundred and fifty peoples together. "All right, Efan.
Now tell the people what's in that box. Don't tetch it—
don't get close to it—but you can walk a distance around
it, and look."

Efan begin to walk around and scratch his head, look
at the box, and then at the people. At last Efan said, "I
guess you've caught de ole coon at last."

Mr. Jones said, "Well he got it."

12. Efan and the Dumplings

Efan told Old Marster he could eat more dumplings
than anybody. So Old Marster made the bet.

Mr. Johnson said, "No, I got a man could eat more
than he can."

Said, "Okay we'll have a contest."

Efan said, "Put on me about twenty gallons of dumplings." Said, "I don't want no bread, we'se just betting
on eating dumplings."

So him and Sam begin to eat. When Sam had eaten

about five gallons, he quit. Said, "Sho, I thought you was
going to eat some dumplings."

So Efan said, "I'll clean the pot." Well, Old Marster gets the money, wins the bet.

So Efan goes home, lies down. "Phew, my stomach
hurt." He say, "I feel like I got a cramp. Get a horse
and carry me to the doctor." Efan go all the way "Mmh,
mmh" [sound of distress].

When he gets to the doctor, doctor says, "Come in,
Efan, come in. What seems to be the trouble?"

"Oh Doc, gimme something quick."

So doctor begin to give Efan medicine and shots. After a while doctor says, "Open your mouth, Efan." So
Efan opened his mouth, doctor looks in. Says "Great Sho,
you got the dumplings, I can see them."

(They were right up level with his th'oat. No medicine couldn't go down, so he died.)

13. Efan and the Padderolls

Suggs in the first paragraph below gives
accurate historical tradition, as a setting for
the anecdote that follows. For the system of
patrols or "padderolls" see Botkin, Burden, pp.
6-7, "What the Pass Said"; John Hope Franklin,
From Freedom to Slavery, New York, 1952, p.
188.

The slaves would slip out from one plantation to another when they wanted to go to prayer meeting. They
could get passes from Old Marster to visit, but not to go
to meeting. If they got caught by the padderolls without
a pass they got a beating. (The padderolls were poor
white folk who didn't farm, and that was the only way
they had to make money.) When they had the meeting

they would turn the iron pot over to keep the sound in.
Servants like surrey-drivers would hear what the
preacher been saying, and he'd get behind a table and
make out like he was reading, from an old alamack.

Efan was preaching at the meeting. The padderolls
came in and began to holler for passes. Efan jumped up
and said, "Get going, get going. [Very loud] Old Marster give me the privilege to carry on this meeting.
Don't touch Sambo or you'll get in trouble."

So out go the padderolls—they all know how Efan
stands with his Old Marster. "We can't bother him."

14. Fooling the Padderoll

The popularity of "Run, Nigger, Run," one
of the oldest plantation songs, which Suggs al-
ludes to below, is mentioned in Miles M.
Fisher, Negro Slave Songs in the United States,
Ithaca, New York, p. 81. Fisher quotes Dorothy
Scarborough that "The darkies sang many amus-
ing songs about the patrols and their experiences in eluding them." E. L. Smith tells a
graphic account of his grandfather escaping
from the patrols, in NFIM, "Outrunning the
Patterolls," pp. 85-86.

Old man told me a tale about slavery times. The
padderolls caught a slave and was going to whip him.
That night it was a cloudy night, and the moon would
come out from under the cloud every once in a while.
They made him stretch out on top of a log, where they
could whip him good. So they got to him one lick, with
the strap, when the moon came out. So he just whirled
under the log—he could go plumb under it, just has his
legs and his arms around it, and they hit him so hard it
spun him plumb around. (The log was propped up about

two feet, that was the whipping post; they make you lock
your legs and arms to it and then pour it on you.)

So he stayed under the log and every time they hit
the log, bam—he'd holler,

"Ohh, Marster, Ohh, Mr. Padderoll." [Chanted]

They give him twenty or thirty licks, but when he
got home he only had one lick on him.

(Mr. Suggs never let his slaves get whipped, my
grandfather and grandmother told me. I used to hear
them say,

"Run nigger run,
The padderolls'll ketch you."

They'd practice running you know.)

15. Old Marster and the Hant

This suggests Type 1318*, Motif J1782.1,
"Robber or dog in church thought to be a ghost,"
although the plot is more elaborately developed.

Jim had been telling Old Marster about hants. Old
Marster told him, "Well you ketch a hant and I'll set you
free, and give you five acres of land and a mule."

Jim knowed there was a cemetery right at the
church, and that would be a good place to ketch one, because they had all the funes [funerals] in the church, and
they'd be coming in backwards and forwards. After supper every night when it got dark he'd disappear, every
night for three weeks, waiting in the church. One night
at the end of three weeks it began to rain while Jim was
in the church—started about eleven o'clock I guess. Old
Marster had been off to a party that night on the other
side of the church, and Jim didn't know he'd gone because

he'd left right after supper. And Marster didn't know
he was in the church, because he knew Jim p'posed to
ketch a hant, but he didn't know where or how. About the
time Old Marster got even with the church it begin to
rain.

"Lord," Old Marster said, "I'll just stop in here till
the rain's over." Jim was in the church waiting for his
hant. So he sees something coming in the door. So he
grabbed him—didn't know it was Old Marster he was
grabbing. Old Marster was struggling, trying to get
loose. Jim was holding onto him, thought he had his hant.
Out the door they went. They'd fall down, Marster was
struggling to get away, but Jim was holding on to him.
When they'd gone about three hundred yards, Jim fell in
the tussle. Old Marster got loose from him. It was so
dark he couldn't see to tell which way he went—up the
road, down the road, cross the field or where. He was
so tired he went back home and went to bed.

Early in the next morning he was down there knocking on Old Marster's door. Says "Say Old Marster, git
up. I got some news to tell you. I caught you that hant
last night, but he got away from me."

Says, "No [deep], you ain't caught no hant."

Jim says, "Come Old Marster, I'll show you where
I caught him, and how far we got before he got loose
from me." Old Marster goes on with him. They went
about four hundred yards. Says "Marster, you see that
big tree there, you wait till we get there, that's where
we was at."

So Old Marster looked down, there was his watch.
Says "Looky here, this is my watch. I thought a hant had
me, and had taken my watch off me. That was you had
me in that church, instead of a hant. And you had caught
me, instead of ketching a hant. I won't give you that five
acres and mule, but I will give you one acre of land and

a good hoe, and then you can raise you some watermelon and peanuts, and sleep one hour each day, for trying to ketch me a hant. So you see there's no hants, and so do I."

(Each was afraid to holler. Wasn't no use to holler if it was a hant.)

16. Colored Man in Heaven

The accidents caused by the overenthusiastic colored angel comprise a Negro tale-type I have heard in seven variants, although it is seldom reported. See NFIM note 48, p. 216. A detailed text in NFIM, from Tommy Carter, with the above title, pp. 79-81, explains the mishaps as the result of drunkenness, which ends with the colored angel losing his wings. Suggs's brief text lacks this customary ending, but contains the motif Baughman lists for K237.1, "Heaven entered by a trick." A text in "Negro Tales of Mary Richardson," no. 24, p. 20, "Cropped Angel," has the colored angel cropped in one wing to slow him down, while in K. Leroy Irvis, "Negro Tales from Eastern New York" (New York Folklore Quarterly, XI, Autumn 1955), p. 171, he has two left wings. Irvis gives a related variant, pp. 171-172, where God tells John not to wake up the colored people as they will break up the place.

Jim's Old Marster was on his way to heaven, and Jim was carrying his suitcase for him. They went up to the front gate. Marster was checking in with the head betterman (that's where the bellhop picks up your suitcase), that was St. Peter. And Jim set down the case while the Marster was registering. It looked so good he just broke in and kept on running all through Heaven.

Gabel and Rafel—them the great archangels—they was
running after him trying to ketch him to throw him out.
He was running down them golden streets, and out on the
Sea of Glass all mingled with fire.

Good Lord said, "Let that nigger alone, he'll tear
up all the furniture if you keep chasing him."

So that's the way the first one got there, and they
been going ever since.

17. Jake in Heaven

> Suggs heard this tale from his cousin Ike
> Shaw, also from Mississippi, but who had lived
> in Vandalia, Michigan, next to Calvin, for
> twenty-four years. Apparently Suggs merged
> it with the previous story.

Well Old Marster he told us if we would be good we
would all go to heaven. Be obedients unto him like his
father's slave was unto him—they all went to heaven.
So week later Jake decided he was going on up first.
Well he went up to heaven and knocks on the door.

St. Peter come to the door. Say "Who is that?"
"Jake."

Say "Wait a minute, Jake." Says "I got to see if
your name on the book." In a couple of minutes he's
back. Says "No, no such name as that on the book." So
he closed the door in Jake's face and Jake going on back
home. He's awful heartbroken with his head down because he couldn't get into heaven.

So when he'd walked about six miles he met his Marster with a great big heavy suitcase and a small briefcase
in his hand. Jake said, "Hello Marster, where you going?"

"I'm going to heaven, Jake. Here take this suitcase.
I want you to go back and carry it for me."

Jake was so glad, he said, "Yes sir, Marster, I'll
carry it, yessir." In a couple of hours he was at the
door. Old Marster knocks.

Says "Who is that?"

"This is Old Man Craft from Shaw, Mississippi."

St. Peter said, "Come right in, Mr. Craft, right over
this table here is where you sign up."

Jake, when he turned around to go signing up, dropped the suitcase and [gesture to indicate speed] through
the door to Heaven he went. Rafel and Gabel taken right
after him. Down the golden streets Jake went, crost a
sea of glass, Rafel and Gabel right after him.

The Lord said, "Let him alone, he'll break up all the
furniture up here." [Loud]

Mr. Craft he rushes right in, up to the altar where
they had Jake. Says "He's a good worker, he's a good
worker at home. If you got anything that he can do I'll
be glad if you give him a job."

Said "Well, we have the moon to put out every night,
and the sun to take in. And then we have the sun to put
out and the moon to take in—that's all he'll have to do."

So he made a trade with Gabel, if all his servants be
good he give them a job, of hanging out all the stars and
taking them in. So that was the way the colored man
first got to Heaven, by being good, and the colored men
been going ever since.

(So that made whole lots of them got a job up there.
Like the fellow who said, "How many stars are there up
there?" And the other one answered, "Eleven billion,
seven hundred and eighty-two thousand, eight hundred and
fifty-one, and if you don't believe it go and count it for
yourself.")

18. Nicodemus from Detroit

> Here Suggs characteristically illustrates
> from real life the folktale he has just told. An-
> other good example of this trait is in NFIM,
> "The Farmer and the Snake," pp. 196-197.

Well, Nicodemus went up to the Golden Gate and
knocked. St. Peter was the doorkeeper—you had to see
him to get registered. So he walks up to the door and he
knocks. St. Peter says, "Who is you?"
    Says "Nicodemus from South Bend."
    "Wait a minute." Looks over his record. Said "No,
there ain't no such name as that from South Bend."
    So he goes on off a little piece. He got to studying.
Goes back and knocks on the door again. St. Peter come
to the door. Says "Who is you?"
    Says "Nicodemus."
    Says "Where are you from?"
    Says "Chicago."
    Says "Wait a minute." St. Peter goes in looks over
the register. Says "No, there's no such name as that
from Chicago here."
    Nicodemus begin to get worried bad, he don't know
what to do. Said to himself, "I'll make one more try."
Goes back and knocks on the door again. Feeling awfully
downhearted then, he was.
    St. Peter come to the door. Says "Who is you?
What's your name?"
    Says "Nicodemus."
    Says "Where are you from?"
    "Detroit."
    He shuts the door, says "Wait a minute." He goes in
looks over the register—comes back and throws the door

wide open. Says "Come right in Nicodemus, for you are
the first Negro ever come to heaven from Detroit."

(That was his native home. I know a colored fellow
did that from Clarksdale, Mississippi. He had his leg
broke, and they had him laid on his back in a plaster
cast in the station ready to be shipped out, in Ioway or
Nebraska—he'd put that down on his card. About five
minutes before the train come in—he was a section
hand, knew the train times—he commenced to hollering,
"I want to go home, I want to go home."

They told him, "Well, you're going home. We're
going to send you home." They had a pass for him. Finally they got mad and stopped pitying him, and asked
him, "Well, where is your home at?"

He said, "Dublin." It was just five miles away from
there, could have pushed him down in a pushcart.

Lots of people around here won't own they're from
Arkansas, or Georgia. Say they was raised in Chicago.)

19. The Dodger

A close variant is in Pine Bluff, ante, no.
59, p. 110, John Dodges White Man," by Tobe
Courtney. In Pine Bluff no. 58, "John in Alabama," by John Courtney, the colored man
packed in a hole in the ground expertly dodges
bulldogs.

Pete he was in town, him and a white merchant got
to arguing. So the merchant begin to hit Pete in the face
and the side of the head with his fists. John was standing
by looking. He said, "I wouldn't let no white men do me
that way."

Mr. Bill says, "How come I won't?" And he swung
at him with his fists, missed, swung, missed again.

John says, "I'm a dodging son of a gun, that's why
you can't hit me."

20. Monkey and the Cadillac

> Irvis has a similar text, pp. 170-171,
> where the monkey plays the part of a beggar
> and is run over by a Negro who takes away his
> dime. The monkey then says, "Our race won't
> do." Suggs brings me into his moralizing com-
> ment here, to show that the white man proves a
> better friend to the Negro than one of his own
> race.

Well, the monkey you know he'd been working hard,
and he come to town and he got tired and set down right
on the intersection. And along come a great big fellow
in a Cadillac. He drove around him. Here come along a
fellow in a Rocket 8. And he drove around him. Here
come one in a Studebaker, going to turn to his right.
Here come along a colored fellow in a Model T Ford. It
was hitting and missing—"Spit, bang, boow." It runs
square over the monkey and knocked him over and
knocked his hip out of place—he could just barely hobble
over to the curb. He set down on the side of the curb,
and his wound was hurting. He shook his head, and he
said,
      "My peoples, my peoples won't do."
   (Anywhere you go colored people will tell you, we do
each other more harm than anyone. Like when I told this
colored fellow about you, on the job. He was a mudmaker,
getting $2.10 an hour. I was getting $2.00, so he went
and told the foreman, 'cause he thought I was getting superior, saying you would write my stories.
   A white fellow will pick up a colored fellow, but not

a white fellow. And a colored fellow will pick up a white
fellow. All nationalities work against each other.)

21. How the Negro Got His Hair

> In NFIM, "Why the Negro has Curly Hair,"
> pp. 78-79, from Newton Curry, the colored peo-
> ple are too busy eating watermelon to come
> for their hair. Joel Chandler Harris gives a
> form where the Negroes are last in getting to
> the pond, and find no water left to unkink their
> hair: "Why the Negro is Black," no. 33 in
> Uncle Remus, His Songs and His Sayings.
> Irvis gives two tales, pp. 173, 174, which ex-
> plain why the Negro is black, and has big feet.

When the Lord was makin' 'em, he made the colored
man big and strong, and he told 'em, "Now go look in the
glass and see how you look." He [colored man] started
walkin' on off, leaving him. Says "Wait, y'ain't got no
hair yet."
So he retch over and grabbed 'em some kinky hair.
Lord said, "No, reach over and get you some of that
good hair."
So he said, "This all right, I'm going to keep it cut
off anyway." He was in too big a hurry and he thought he
looked all right without the hair.
So now most older colored persons keep their hair
cut off. The whites look funny with their hair cut off—it
stands up straight like porc'pine.

IV

SUPERNATURAL EXPERIENCES

22. Devil's Imps

This and the following ten accounts all involve spectral appearances, usually referred
to as "spirits" by Southern Negroes. Ch. 8 in
NFIM, "Spirits and Hants," contains some
similar experiences, and see also "Negro
Tales of Mary Richardson," no. 11, pp. 12-13,
"Spirit of Grandmother." A spirit is a recog-
nizable person, where a hant is usually a fright-
ful sight or sound. A spirit differs from a
ghost in coming from a live person, where a
ghost is the spirit of the dead. The best collection of spirit stories is in <u>Drums and Shadows,</u>
whose index refers to forty examples under
"Spirits." Motifs F400-499, "Spirits and De-
mons," apply to the present group, and F402.1.1,
"Spirit leads person astray," to the present
story. Mary Richardson told me, September
13, 1952, "The witch is the Devil's imps, or
part of the Devil. They come from the Devil,
or some of the Devil's kinfolks."

I don't believe in no dead travelin', but there is
something else, the Devil's imps, spirits of the Devil.
They can come in any shape or form that they want to.
The Devil tried to tempt Christ when he went on the
mountain—he came in the shape of a King—he was the
leading singer in heaven, the bright morning star, one of
the prettiest of the angels—Luceefus they called him.

185

And when he left they called him Serpent, or Devil. He
could change into anything—he came to Eve like a serpent.

All witchcraft is from the Devil—mi'acles, hyp'tizing, seeing things. They always has been and is going
on today.

My grandmother, Francis Henry, was coming down
the lane (betwixt Silas and Durant, in Mississippi—we
was living in the country at the time—they was about
ten miles apart). My mama seed her going by (east) to
her home, so she went out to try to catch up with her—
she was going to work. She commenced gaining on her,
till she came to a little dry ditch, with a high bridge running over it. And grandma got off the road—it was a
public highway—and walked under the bridge. My
mother sat there about ten minutes, thought she'd be
right back. Then she went down and looked, there wasn't
a thing under there, not a bush or anything. She went on
to grandma's house, about a quarter of a mile from there.
Said "Mama, how did you get here so quick, I didn't see
you come out from under there?"

She says, "What bridge?"

"The bridge right out under there in that lane."

She says, "I haven't been out of the house this morning." It was about seven-thirty (my mother was going
to wash at Dr. Henry Smith's).

Grandma was carrying a pair of pants over her back,
and mama wanted to ask her what she was doing with
those pants. She was a widow, and wasn't nobody around
the house big enough to wear pants. She was about sev-
enty-eight, eighty years at the time.

My mother didn't drink, use tobacco, drink coffee,
no bad words, never called one of us a fool or a liar,
prayed three times a day. Maybe the Devil was trying
to make her think her mother was a witch—there was so

much talk of hoodoo and witchcraft. If she had thought
that, she would have sinned, and once she started the
Devil would have had her tilted, and keep her a-falling.
He don't never work on no one that's already doing wrong.

23. A Steamboat Ghost

> Motifs G273.4, "Witch powerless to cross
> stream," and E530, "Ghosts of objects," are in-
> dicated here. The "hant train" that Suggs re-
> fers to is in NFIM 126-127.

You never see a spirit crossing a bridge—they
can't cross water. I believe in spirits 'cause I seen
them. I guess they can't hurt you, like shadows. They
thought Christ was a spirit when they saw him walking
on the water, so they must have seen spirits. Peter
asked him, "If you're Christ let me come to you."

So Christ let him come on the water, but Peter
doubted him so much he started sinking, so Christ took
him by the hand and led him back to the ship. But he
didn't say there wasn't no such thing as a spirit. He
said, "Feel my flesh and bones; a spirit doesn't have
flesh and bones."

There are ship-ghos'es. I heard of a steamboat
ghost once. Everybody got killed on the steamboat and
there was a lot of treasure on it, and they said you could
see it at certain time of night, when you weren't expecting it. Like that hant train I told you about. When it get
to a certain place it disappear. That was on Little River,
ran into Clarktree, Arkansas. It was a robbery. The
captain sunk the ship to keep the raiding crew from getting the gold. He could have torpedoed it, or opened the
hatchholds. That was way before the Civil War.

24. Born With a Veil

The belief in the powers of a person born
with a caul or veil is widespread; informants
of Puckett say that only such persons can see
spirits, under " 'Doublesighted' Folks, " pp.
137-138, and see the similar statements in
Drums and Shadows, pp. 5, 15, 24, 29, 39, 69,
76, 77, 123, 127, 128. See also "Negro Tales
of Mary Richardson, " no. 10, p. 12, same title
as above, where she says a person not born
with a veil can see spirits by looking over the
left shoulder of a person who is born with one.

When the baby is born with a veil, if it is lifted off
over the front of the head, the baby won't be bothered,
but if it is lifted off backwards, it will be bothered until
manhood. It sees things. That happened with my father
and with me. Doctors don't believe in nothing like that.
I've seen men come [become] like dogs, just the flick of
your eyes and you look back and it be something else.
About twelve years ago I was going up to Mrs. Cook's
and I saw a dog sitting on the bank and I swung at him
with an empty bucket and the bucket went right through
him—and the moon was shining just as bright. One
thing, they can't harm you.

At Itta Bena, Mississippi, Willie Squale was coming
from a picnic with a gang of boys. They passed the picnic grounds where a boy got killed a year before. He
used to ride behind Willie all the time, doubling up—
even the night he got killed when a fellow shot him. The
other boys, Willie Howard and the rest, six or eight, saw
the same boy come out and get behind Willie Squale.
None of them would let Willie ride alongside him, and he
didn't know what was the matter with them. So when
they got up the graveyard where he was buried he got off
and went right back into the graveyard. Nobody said

nothing all the way home. They must all have been born
with veils. Willie tried to get a conversation but couldn't.
He never did ride that horse no more, and they never did
go by there no more.

25. Sees Own Self

   Two cases of a man meeting his own
ghostly double, from New England, are reported
in my Jonathan Draws the Long Bow, Cambridge, Mass., 1946, pp. 62-63. One of them
proved a death token, whereas in the present
account the vision boded good. Motif T589.4,
"Birth with veil brings luck," does not occur
frequently among Southern Negroes, although
the veil does bring wisdom; see Drums and Shadows, p. 15. Treating the veil is described in
Vance Randolph, Ozark Superstitions, New York,
1949, p. 203, as a means to avoid misfortune.

Joe Kratoff was telling me how his uncle Thomas
met his own self in a public road. Joe lives down the
road [in Calvin, Michigan]. He's a little old mulatto,
rides with me every day.

His uncle was living about three miles from Columbus, Ohio—he was a country farmer. And he was coming down the road and he seen a man coming. And he
wasn't studying about hisself or anything. And he looked
up, on his way to work, and seed that man. The closer
he gets, he says, "That man looks like me." He was
dressed just like him. When he got close enough to look
in his face he said, "That's Me." He knew it was him.
And when he walked right up to him he was going to
speak—and then there wasn't no man. And he looked
down the road and he seed nobody. It was just like looking in a mirror. Before he spoke, he was gone.

Joe's daughter was born with a veil, like me. A
colored boy in Chicago was born educated with a veil,
but his people knew what to do. He could read or write
or figure or tell the comets or anything. You don't destroy that veil, just put it up in a place to dry, and when
the baby gets old enough let him tie it up and destroy it
himself. Then he's born educated. If Joe had known
that at the time, his daughter could of been born educated. But she married wealthy. And I reckon that's
why I'm lucky. I was never on relief in my life, even in
the depression. When I've been down to half a dollar,
people I've never seen before have come to me and ask
me to take a job. And other fellows had been out looking
for jobs. My brother tells me I make friends easy and
get along.

After he met his double he became lucky. He didn't
have nothing at all, he was working by the day, till he
met himself. He was around fifty-five, sixty some odd
years along. He never told funny jokes or stories.

26. Spirit of Ella Eptings

The familiar Motif E275, "Ghost haunts
place of great accident or misfortune," applies
here.

My father was coming from one of them dances like
I was telling you about. He was about thirty year old
then. He'd seen Billy Buford snapping a pistol at the
other boys there that night. After the party was over,
my father and his brother-in-law and Ella Eptings and a
crowd of others were on their way home, and they got to
playing with each other, and running each other with

switches. So Domp Lee ran to Billy Buford and said, "Give me your gun, I'm going shoot Ella."

He handed to him and she say, "Come on, I ain't scared of that gun. I know it won't shoot, for I seen Billy snap it tonight on the boys." That time the gun went off and shot her between the eyes, killed her instantly.

So my father's brother-in-law was arrested for the shooting, Domp Lee was, and my papa deputized to turn him over to the court the next day. So Billy Buford he run away, and Domp was given two years in the penitentiary for playing with the pistol, and saying, "I'll kill ye."

So he served his time out, come home. Two years after that, they was holding a convention at New Bannion Church (Baptist). My father was the moderator. His name was Reverend L. S. Suggs. So he gets sick about eight o'clock in the night. He begged to be excused, and the assistant moderator taken his place. So he got his horse and was going home. He rode up to the bars, which was crost the road, and there Ella was a-setting there, right on the fence. And so he turned and went on another road, about a mile out of the way. And he stayed sick a year, just lost his appetite, wouldn't eat nothing, kept getting smaller and smaller, taking medicine every day.

So Dr. Brumber says, "Lee, damn if I'm coming here any more." Say "If you don't eat something, you sure going die." Didn't leave him no medicine. So my father started to eat, and in two months he was well, weighed two hundred like he used to.

He could see things like I did. He was born with a veil, too, grandma said. 'Nother fellow may not see them but I know I do. Used to be I couldn't sleep when I was little. As you get up in age you stop seeing them. I ain't seed spirits in eight or ten years, since I been married.

Last one I saw was a dog, in Arkansas, a great big old
dog.

27. Spirit Dog

Motif E423.1.1, "Revenant as dog," is rele-
vant, and Motif E423.3.6, "Revenant as hen,"
is the closest to a spectral rooster.

In Bono, Arkansas, 1930, I was living next to Mrs.
C. W. Cook—I was working for her, cooking, tending
cattle, hogs—and I was going round to her house to get
some water, first part of the night. I was walking along
the road, and saw a great big old dog sitting on the bank
—the grading had made kind of a bank alongside the
road. He just sat there, and I wanted to hit him. I made
a sweep at him with the water bucket— "flookit"— the
handle made a noise against the pail, but didn't tetch him
no way. First I tried to hit him sideways, then I come
down on top of him, but that big old dog just kept a-sit-
ting there. So I walked on to the well, and when I came
back the dog was gone.

Other people had seen it in that same spot, but in
different forms, like cats. Mildred Smith, a white girl
there, said she seen it look like the biggest rooster she
ever seen in her life, just about dusk dark, about a foot
and a half high. But Mrs. Cook didn't have no rooster,
neither did we. I hadn't seen that dog then, so I said
she must have seen it.

On the other side of the house the Yankees had killed
old man Cook. That was the old Jackson trail, going to
the county seat, which was Jacksonport then, by the
river. (But since they got the railroad they moved it to

Newport.) The spirit was right on the old trail from Little Rock to Jacksonport.

28. Henry Allen Sees a Spirit

Henry Allen and I sleep together in the same bed in South Bend—that's why I don't come home during the week [to Calvin]. He was telling me about this thing he saw. He was rooming with Mrs. White, summer before last. So he came in about eight o'clock, in the summer. So the light was on, he goes in the house. So she's sitting in the living room, and he speaks to her and goes on upstairs. But she didn't speak. So he pulls off his coat and hat, says "I'm going back and see what's the matter, she didn't say anything." So he sat down, wondered where she's at—she was there a few minutes ago. Say he set there till near ten o'clock. So she came in.

She say, "Hello."

So he says, "Where you been?"

Say "I've been to the show."

"Well you was here at eight o'clock when I come here."

At that time her husband come in. He axed him where she at. He says, "We was at the seven o'clock first show."

He said after he seen her and she wasn't there he didn't want to stay there, so he moved over to Johnson Street.

(Peter see Christ walking on the water and got scared. He told Peter, "Feel me, I'm flesh and blood, spirits don't have no flesh and blood." So Peter walked out to him, and when he saw what he had done, he got scared and fell to sinking and Christ lifted him up.)

29. Mother Sees Dead Son

> E320, "Dead relative's friendly return,"
> is the closest motif.

Henry Allen's brother died, and he'd been buried three weeks. For four days straight hand-running his mother'd hear that beat of the clothes wire— "bam— bam-bebam—bam—bam" [Soft]. So the fourth day she went to the door and looked out there at the clothes line to see what it was, and there was her son and he had on the clothes that he was buried in. She looked at him 'bout three or four minutes, and when she looked back he'd gone, and there wasn't no place for him to go. He'd been beating on the line with a stick.

He was calling her I guess, wanted to see her. She never saw him again. She wasn't the kind to see things either, but the Lord had it for her to see him.

30. Hunting on Sunday

> Three comparable hant warnings experi-
> enced by persons who hunt or fish on Sunday
> are in NFIM 164-166, and Mr. and Mrs. E. L.
> Smith of Calvin have told me other instances.
> Baughman assigns the motif Q223.6.2*, "Per-
> son is punished for hunting on Sunday," and
> gives five American references, two Negro.

Ernest Russell, a colored fellow in Mississippi out from Indianola, he belonged to the church, but he would go out hunting every Saturday night until about nine o'clock Sunday morning; that was the usual time he would come in. He said that was his lucky time, which he did really catch more game than on Saturday night. So he

quit going to church, because he'd be sleepy on Sunday.
So this Saturday night he hunted up till four o'clock and
he hadn't struck a thing—had a good coon dog, never
knowed him not to strike a trail in that length of time before. Believe he'd gone home, quit hunting.

When he got within half a mile of the house the dogs
hit a trail. It was going direct to the house for about
one quarter of a mile. Then it turned and goes back
southwest. So he stops there. Then it made a circle and
went straight to his house. Well he knowed then it was
his house cat the dog had treed— something he'd never
done. So he has a headlight on his head, and he walked
on ahead to the porch and looked back to where the dog
was barking (the old Southern houses were T shaped with
double wings), and he saw a woman standing up against
the wall with both arms stretched out, all white, everything she had on was silk.

He flopped in the door, groaning, and his wife said,
"What's the matter?"

But he couldn't say a word—he could hear people
but he couldn't talk—and he sat all day rocking in the
chair, never went to sleep, rocked all day, Sunday night,
until Monday morning. He just went "Mmmmm." And
he never went hunting again.

(I think it was a token God had sent to scare him
back to the Church, and I can prove it by the Bible. The
angel told John he should never speak until the child was
born, because he didn't speak. That's why I believe if
God can do it one time he can do it another.)

31. Shep's Two Spirit Experiences

Shep Turner lives in a two-story house on the main
road in Calvin. Moved out here from Chicago about ten

years. He was telling me about this spirit he saw in Indianola, Mississippi. He had been over to Hatfield Jackson's, courting his girl. And it was a dark night, like
you could feel the darkness. He was about two hundred
feet from home, and he seed this man about twenty-five
feet from him. And he had to go a mile back to the nearest house. Says, "Well, it's too far to go back, but I'll
bear around the edge of the lake—the wire fence has
me barred on the other side, I can always swim." He
could see the white shirt bosom, and had on a black suit
of clothes, plumb black. And it seemed like he was
smoking, but he still didn't have no head. He thought it
was Reverend Payton, he was a big old bishop had just
died, and he just knew it was him, he'd just been to the
burying. And he just kept easing along and looking, said
"Well I'm going to see." So he stooped down low to the
ground—you can see better that way in the dark. The
cow seed him stooping down and she blowed. It was old
Doc Edwards' cow. He seed that white spot on the head
but couldn't see no head above. And the cow blowing he
thought was smoke. He said, "If I could have run I would
have, but it was too far back." He was half an hour
studying how to pass that hant. So after that he didn't believe in hants no more. (That was in '08.)

But he got believing again in '12, when he was driving a buggy. He was carrying his mother off to the station, and was driving fast to get back to a Mount Zion
Church festival. He seen an old lady walking down the
road—it was a moonlight night. She wouldn't get out the
road, and she checks up. She stepped between the hose
and the axle, and the axle went right through her. And
when he looked back she was just walking right on, and
never jarred the buggy. But the horse began snorting
and rearing, and Shep commenced whipping the horse after he seen the woman.

32. A Hant in France

My cousin, Walter Suggs, from Indianola (he lives in
Saginaw now) he was in the army too, in the heavy artil-
lery. And he got cut off from his company, just him
alone. So he's about three miles from his regiment before day, trying to find his way back. Said he passed by
a house. Old man was in the door. He said he spoke
French.

Say "Hey G.I."; say "gimme a franc or two."

So he gives him two francs. So when he gets to the
camp, to his regiment, after he taken his sleep and woke
up that day, about three or four o'clock, somewhere
along in there, he told them about the old Frenchman
asked him for two francs. Say he give it to him, and
axed him which direction from there. He told him,
"About two miles south."

They told him there weren't no house there. He told
them there were. So he bet them all the cognac they
could drink there was a house there. They said no,
'cause several of them had given that old man money,
and there wasn't no house there. So they went down
there. "There's my francs laying on the ground and no
house there at all, just ashes where a house had been."

They said that man had been murdered and the house
burnt, and several of them had seen him. He said he just
knowed he give that man that money.

33. Conversion

Compare the experience of Mary
Richardson in NFIM, "My Conversion," p. 132.
Puckett, pp. 540-542, discusses Negro visions.

Time I was cooking at the vanold in Poplar Bluff, Missouri, every night after the last train run at two-thirty A.M., we used to have a big crap game in the kitchen. The main hasher always wanted to be in the game, and if somebody came in to be served he wanted us to wait for him. One night I told him he shouldn't play. I quit myself. Next night they asked me to drink whiskey and I said no. I wasn't thinking about religion. About three weeks after I was in Lumford, Arkansas, they were carrying on a revival, and I went to the mourner's bench. I prayed and asked the Lord if he had made a change in me, and to let the sun quit shining. When I went outside I stayed out about ten minutes and I didn't see no sun at all, couldn't see anything, just like dark, like Joshua. And then suddenly it passed, and the sun shot out. I knew that God had fixed it to make that film over my eyes.

34. Catching the Witch

> Suggs with his trace of rationalism tells
> this as a fictional tale, but Leozie Smith gives
> a detailed account of catching the witch with a
> sifter, as literal truth, in NFIM 142-144.

People used to say witches rode them all night; then they called them nightmares; then the doctors found it was the blood stopped circulating.

Hoodoo doctor—he was a two-headed man— told them how to catch the witch. He said, "Get a sifter (not like the ones with the crank now, but the big ones you'd sift the meal with your hands—pit-a-patter, pit-a-patter), and put it about a foot from your bed. And when the witch begin to ride, tell your husband (he'd awake up from the noise she made, and then the witch would just

ease on out of the house) to shake her. Then the witch
would slide out the bed into the sifter—head first. They
couldn't back up when they start, and she couldn't go
through that thin sifter.

When he heard the noise on the floor he lit the lamp
and there it was Grandma Jane from next door on the
hill. She was going bump, bump against the floor trying
to get through that sieve.

35. Treasure Hunt

Other Negro accounts I collected of searching for Confederate treasure guarded by hants
are in NFIM, "Buried Treasure and Hants," pp.
133-135, by Mary Richardson, and see note 92,
p. 221, and Pine Bluff ante, no. 37, pp. 70-72, "Treasure Dream" by John Courtney and see headnote. South Carolina Folk Tales has three personal reports of digging for supernaturally pro-
tected treasure, "Hidden Treasure," pp. 51-57.
The widespread practice of "Searching for Hidden Treasure" in the South, often with expen-
sive finding instruments and associated superstitions, is discussed in the Southern Workman
for October 1898, vol. XXVII, no. 10, pp. 209-210.
In place of the usual Motifs N571, "Devil (demon) as guardian of treasure," or N576,
"Ghosts prevent men from raising treasure,"
in this and the following experience Suggs believes that "magicking" and "vanquilling" —
magic and ventriloquism—kept him and his uncle from the treasure they sought. Motifs N563,
"Treasure seekers find hole from which treasure has recently been removed" (Baughman),
and D1314.2, "Magic wand locates hidden treasure," pertain to this and the succeeding narrative.

This was in Saxton, Missouri, in '27. There was a
fellow named Sanford, a colored fellow, had a dipneedle
for finding treasure, and Preacher Bill he goes over
there and borrows it. So we knew where there was supposed to be money at this house—a double log house
with a double fireplace in it, it used to be a still during
the [Civil] war, and they claim he had his money hidden
there, and he never did return. This house was just off
the road, had been there since 1862. They'd seen a turtle drawn on the sycamore tree, and thought that was a
mark so he'd remember the spot.

I and Preacher Bill set out on Thursday night (I remember because we had to return it for Saturday) about
ten or eleven. We put the whalebone on the needle before we got there, and he carries it under his jumper.
He was in the road about a hundred and fifty feet from
the tree, and the preacher holds it straight to the house,
and the needle commence to pull to the left, toward the
tree. Then it begin to spark. So we followed it toward
the tree. We heard this mumbling, like people was talking low, coming from the tree. So we jumped back,
waited fifteen or twenty minutes. We started right back
again with the dipneedle—she straightened right out
again like she did before, and the sparks come out fast.
And we seed a little blue light down on the ground right
by the tree. (The moon was shining.) Then come like
half of a brickbat to the left of my hand—I dodged to the
right. Then another come right by—whoom. Well I begin to get scared—hair raising on my head (you ever
been scared and had your hair rise?). So I told the
preacher, "Let's go, the mosquitoes is biting bad." [Ges-
ture of hitting shoulders]. I just wanted an excuse, I
didn't know he'd had that experience.

So in a low tone he says, "All right," and wraps the

needle up and sticks it under his arm, and we went on
back home.

Two days after I was helping plant in the pea field,
in July, for Mr. Grosenore. It was his land and his
house, an old slavery time house, and he was over looking at it. He was an old man, and went up to the house
to get in the shade, and come back and told us how it had
been all dug up, and to come see. The fireplace was all
dug up, about four feet, and a big iron pot was sitting
empty on the floor.

I figured somebody had vanquillered us, and caused
that sound to go past us.

36. Hidden Treasure and Hypnotism

   In this vivid description of a treasure hunt,
   Suggs shifts from the third person to the first,
   placing himself in the role of his uncle from
   whom he heard the adventure. As in the previous story, he explains the apparition of the
   treasure owner as magical conjuration rather
   than a simple ghost.

Now this is really true. He found out after that it
wasn't hants but magicking. That was in 1900, in Goodman, Mississippi.

My uncle Jack's wife was sick. One day two white
fellows came up to his house. Said, "Is your name Jack
Suggs? I've heard that you've been living in this country all your life."

He said, "Yes, why?"

"We've got a proposal whereby you can make money."

Said, "I guess you're talkin' to the wrong man,
'cause I don't do crooked work."

One speaking said, "Neither do I." Said, "If you will
work with us, we all will be in good shape with plenty of
money."

Said, "Let's hear your propose."

Said, "We've found hidden treasures, money's been
hidden in the Revolution and the Civil War. And if you
know within three miles of where it's located, we can
find it. And we'll split three ways equally. And found
out from two other people's in your community that you
know more than anyone else would about this."

"Well, if that's the way you'll go I'll work with you."

So we made a date for the next night. So we set out
to where I heard there was money buried. So as we got
near there, something crossed the road. One said,
"What is that?"

I said, "Wait. I'll see." So I ran up to her. It stopped and laid down. I whispered to them, "It's nothing but
a possum." So they goes to the spot, and the white fellow
(he wouldn't tell his name), he takes his intrument out
his pocket—dipneedle they calls it—and they puts it together. Puts a silver point to it—made like a ballpen
and pencil.

The dipneedle has two whalebone handles that you
hold. It costs about five hundred dollars or more. It's
made like a flashlight except for the end, where you put
in a point of the same thing you're looking for—gold,
silver, zinc, any mineral. There's a little wheel inside,
which th'ows sparks from the top when it hits the metal.
It pulls toward the mineral, and when you're right over
it the whalebone pulls down. Some work three miles,
others only ten to fifty feet. This worked for two miles
—they was big shots.

When they put the point in and caught hold the handle,
it went three feet before she started to sparkling. We
goes about seven feet—she dips straight down, and the

man that had it said, "Ain't we lucky! You like to put
your hand on it yourself." We didn't have no trouble—
not anyone passed. (It was about two at night.) We dug
about six feet deep, put a sounding rod down in the
ground then.

Said, "Hey. I've hit something."

"Well, let's dig faster—I want to see what it is."
We all begin to work fast. In a little while we pull up a
cookpot with a lead top—the old kind that used to swing
over the fire. The lead would solder down around the
edges, to keep the gold dry. There was a little brick
wall around and underneath the pot, to keep the rain
from coming in the sides. They taken the pot out and
opened it up. It contained six thousand in gold. That
was divided equally between the three.

The next haul they made next week—they didn't
make but one a week—they found nineteen thousand. He
didn't see these men at no time during the day—only
when they'd come once a week. So on the third haul, it
wasn't so far from his home, that was on his old Marster's place where he was born and raised.

Well, we began to dig. One man would stay watch
on top, other two would dig. But I remained in the hole
all the time to dig. When we dug about ten feet, something like a chain fell in the hole with a great clash. I
stopped and look around. "What's that?"

The fellow was in the hole was on top by this time,
say "You'd better get out, you'd better get out."

I say, "I don't see a thing down here. I don't see
nothin'." He came back in.

All of a sudden somepin floppin' like about six chickens with their heads off in the hole. Said, "Hold your
gun Jack, don't shoot, hold your gun."

"What I'm goin' to shoot at, don't see nothin'?"

The one on top says, "What's the matter you guys

there in the hole?" All at once we heard a horse troop
comin' closeter and closeter.

Said, "Stay where you're at Jack, we and Bud can
take care of everything here at top." I remains in the
hole.

When I did look up, there was a man on a horse,
dressed in uniform, looked like a colonel. His eyes was
like balls of fire. Smoke was comin' out his nostrils.
He was panting, and his sides was going in and out like
he'd been running fifty, sixty miles an hour. The man
says, "What you done digging here? There's seven or
eleven men out here laying to devour you as soon as you
get the money up. So that's why I ran to you like I did."
Then he was gone as quick as he appeared. Didn't see
him come, didn't see him go.

One of the men said [excitedly, rapidly] "Come on,
Jack, let's go, let's hurry up, let's go."

Out I came a little excited. Said, "Can't get it tonight. That's the Colonel that had the money buried,
who was killed in the Civil War. I haven't got the proper
things tonight to hold him back. We'll come the night after tomorrow night—I'll come to your house."

So I goes home. They leaves as usual. I waited two
nights. Nobody shows up. So the third day I decided I'd
go look at the place. There was a kettle on top the
ground—about a fifteen gallon kettle, had been taken out
the hole. I could see the prints of the collars on the
sides.

All the time this one on the top was a vanquiller—
he'd hyp'tized him.

In the old days everything passed down from Old
Marster to the son. When the war came they dig holes
way back in the woods to keep their money from the Yankees. One of the servants would dig the hole, then they'd

kill him so he wouldn't squeal, put him on top of the treasure.

Where you see the apple trees and fig trees with the pine trees around them you know that's where the old country houses were (except in the Mississippi delta). That's where you'd look with the dipneedle.

V

HOODOOS AND TWO-HEADS

37. Magikin from Bombay

The replacement of supernaturalism by oc-
cultism in Suggs's thinking can be understood
from the impression the following scene made
upon him.

That was in Lumford, Arkansas, in '20. A white
man, a magikin, Professor Hicks—I never will forget
his name—had studied eight .years in Bombay, India.
If you were born between June 29 and July 2 he would
shoot a block off his wife's head. This person would
put two fingers right back of his neck—he was hood-
winked, by the doctor of the town. And he would say,
"Watch the object," and all the time he's shaking his gun,
pulling it on up, and all of a sudden he'd go "Pow" and
knock the block plumb off her head, and there he'd shot
a hole in it. A solid block of wood about four by four,
and he shot a twenty-two caliber rifle.

He say him and his brother-in-law was the only two
people doing that kind of work. Just anything you want
to know he'd tell you. He was a vanquiller and a morti-
cian—he could cure by rubbing.

He told this poor white woman that her husband—
he deserted her, went to Durant, Oklahoma—would come
home soon and never leave her. Seven days later Frank
Taylor, Bob's uncle, went and got him and brought him
back, and two days later he died, he was just a no-good
sporting fellow.

38. My Uncle and the Two-Headed

> Chapter 7 in NFIM, "Hoodoos and Two-
> heads," gives texts and references to hoodoo
> practices. The present episode shows the two-
> head in the role of fortune-teller, as in Suggs's
> story of the celebrated "Aunt Carolyn Dye,"
> NFIM 117-118.

My Uncle Jack Suggs was cou'tin' a lady, Mary, in
Shaw, Mississippi. She got in a fight with another
woman he'd been seeing, Francis, who was in the family
way, and cut her across the stomach with a knife. So to
keep her from being arrested he took Francis and skip-
ped off to New Orleans with her, to see the two-headed.
She told him to stay there seven days, and after the
seven days he could go back. And the lady that got cut,
she [Mary] would come to his house and beg her
[Francis'] pardon-ness.
My uncle asked her, "What is your charges? "
She said, "Twenty-five bucks. But you don't have to
pay that now. Whensomever she come, as I've said, and
beg her pardness, you can send me the twenty-five dollars—which I know you will."
It happened just that way— Mary came and apolo-
gized to Francis.

39. My Uncle's Mojo

> Puckett, p. 19, conjectures "mojo" in the
> sense of charm or amulet to be African in ori-
> gin, and gives a photograph of an informant
> wearing a mojo, opp. p. 385. An informant in
> Drums and Shadows, p. 55, did a thriving busi-
> ness in "Mystic Mojo Love Sachet, " a

commercial product; and see the index under
"hand," an equivalent term.

Henry Bates he was the mojo man in Goodman, Mississippi. He told my uncle Chase he would give him a
hand, and he could go to the store and anything he axed
for, the merchant would let him have it. Cost him five
dollars. So he paid him, and old man Bates gives him
the hand, a little piece of red flannel sewed up in a bag.
And then he gave him some root to chew, told him to
spit it around the merchant. So he goes to the store,
puts a big chew of it in his mouth, and he spit right towards him, nearly on his foot. So he moved a little, and
Chase he spit over there again. He [the merchant] said,
"I been moving and moving and you just keep spitting on
me. You keep doing it I'll take one of my ax handles
and beat hell out of you."
    Didn't stay in town long, he was going back to get
his five dollars from that mojo man. He went right on
over to his house, called him out, said "Looka here old
Nigger, you're gonna pay me my five dollars. I'd like
to got the devil beat out of me with an axhandle." So he
gave the hand back and got his money.
    My cousin opened one and found in it some gravel
and cotton seeds and coal cinders beat up. The hoodoo
man told him he was hoodooed, but the doctor cured him
of rheumatism.

40. Chuck-a-luck Sanders

Chuck-a-luck was a game they played twenty-five,
thirty years ago. That's where this fellow got his name.
I knew him personally. He could escape from a jail,

throw his bones out of joint walking along. He went for
a hoodoo.

41. Two Hoodoos

      Motif D1719.1, "Contest in magic," applies
here.

    Two hoodoos was arguing about who had the most
power. One threw his coat down, and said "Catch a fire
and burn up." It catched fire and started burning.
    The second took his coat off and threw it over the
other'n, said "Rain down water and put it out." The rain
came down and put it out, and though there'd been a big
blaze it wasn't burned bigger than a dollar.
    (Like if you had a big fire and called to Cass and
the fire department came and put it out without anything
burning. There's something in the Bible like that too.
. . . [story of Elijah]).

VI

CURES AND SIGNS

42. The Thrash

The same treatment is reported in Vance
Randolph, The Ozarks, New York, 1931, pp. 95-
96, and Ozark Superstitions, New York, 1947,
p. 136. During the past year, 1955, a friend
of mine, Reda O'Brian, told me that her father,
Wick Howard, born in the Kentucky hills and
now living in Stockbridge, Michigan, had
gone out looking for a man who had never seen
his father or a woman who had married without changing her name, to blow in the mouth
of his grandchild afflicted with thrash.

Most doctors say the child doesn't have the thrash.
When they're three or four or five months they have it—
it's white bumps that breaks out in the mouth—they can't
even suck the breast or the bottle, they can't draw with
their tongue. My boy died of the pneumonia (at twenty-
two months) had the thrash, and my cousin, M. C. Clark
in Vandalia, cured him by blowing in his mouth. Any
child that has never seen its father can cure that way.
Clark's father died before he was born. He's only twenty-
six years old, he was in World War II. He came over to
my house; my daughter went over and asked him to blow
in the baby's mouth.

43. Curing Nettle Rash

A white fellow names Oscar, bridge foreman for Frisco Railroad, was at Jonesboro, Arkansas. My baby sister-in-law, about four years old, had the nettle rash bad. So my father-in-law was telling Mr. Oscar about it, at a funeral, and he said, "Why my wife can cure that." So Dr. Lonnie (Rogers, my father-in-law) comes and gets Josie, told us that Mr. Oscar's wife could cure her. So she carried her out there, she taken and goes off in the wood, just about twenty yards from the road. She didn't give her anything at all, but walked around the tree and brought her back to the church. So Josie have never had the nettle rash since. She's grown now and has five chilluns.

She's been taking doctor medicine, but it kept coming back. Mrs. Oscar just walked around the tree, and the girl followed her.

44. Grandmother Clara Suggs

The same cure for toothache, along with a number of others, is reported by Puckett, pp. 372-373.

For toothache grandmother would take a splinter made by lightning where it hit a tree, and have you pick your teeth with it till it bleeds, and then it would stop hurting you.

For warts she'd just look at them and say, " Who told you I could cure them?" and walk on off. In about a week they'd be gone—it would pass right off your mind, and when you noticed it was gone.

For headache she just put her hand on your head.

(She died at 117, in 1927, in Missouri.)

45. Bloodstopping

> There is an account of "Bloodstopping" in
> NFIM 153, from Will Todd, although the belief
> is far more prevalent in White tradition. See
> my Bloodstoppers and Bearwalkers, Cambridge,
> Mass., 1952, pp. 150-165.

There's a verse in Psalms, "When I was polluted in
blood, then you passed over me" — that was David talking about the Lord— you use that to stop the bleeding.
The one who says it touches the cut, on the nose or the
arm, and you repeat it. I saw a young boy do it at Poplar
Bluff, Missouri. He said he learned it from his dad—
said anybody could do it.

I got a brother, "Son" Suggs, can put his hand on
your pain, on the chest, or toothache, and it leave. He
did it on my wife. Say "You feel it?"

"A little bit."

"You feel it?"

"No."

Won't charge for it, says the Lord didn't give him
that power to charge for.

Everybody's got to have a gift.

46. Death Bells

> Three informants of Puckett, p. 462, con-
> cur with Suggs that "a bell apparently ringing
> in your ear points to death in the direction
> from which the sound comes."

I ain't scared of no dead people. I'd just as easy sleep in a cemetery. When something going to happen you see different forms of people or lights, that's a token. Wherever your people live, east of you, north of you, is the way they travel. After it happens you never see it no more. Some people call it death bells. You ever hear that ringing in your ears—like a rattlesnake? Nearly all colored peoples hear 'em, and some white people.

Every time you see this object, it's going in the direction your people live. You'll see it more than once.

47. Ghost Hole

An informant of Puckett, p. 139, said you can punch a small hole in your own ear to see ghosts.

If you're born with a ghost-hole, a little hole right on the tip of the burr (lobe), you can hear or see things, spirits, any kind of little old noise. My girl at home, Be-atrice—nine—she's that way. She used to see babies on the wall terrible—"Look at that little baby." Last year or two hasn't bothered her much. I quit seeing things myself after I got up round forty.

48. Bad Luck Signs

Exact parallels to these beliefs in Puckett are: rabbit crossing the path, 472-473; fog on mirror at death, 81; itching palms, 450; quivering eyes, 448; cutting nails on Sunday, 401-402; cutting babies' fingernails, 338. Suggs uses

the same word as Puckett's informants, "roguish," to describe what will happen to the
baby whose nails are cut. In "Negro Tales of
Mary Richardson," pp. 25-26, "Beliefs and
Sayings," the itching-palm and covered-mirror
beliefs are included.

If a rabbit cross your road, if you go to the right
you can perceed on for you'll have good luck. Well if
you go to the left, you have to walk backwards three
steps, then make X cross marks, and then turn to the
right and then you can go on the way you started, that
knock the bad luck offa it.

When somebody dies, a fog gets on the mirror.
Nearly everybody cover the mirror up.

Lay your hat on the bed, you have to turn the bottom
up to keep from having bad luck.

I know these signs, they work on me, I don't know
about another fellow. Now mine is hand eetching [itch-
ing]. If the palm of my right hand eetches I'm going to
get some money in less than twenty-four hours. Now if
your left hand eetches, a letter is coming. The last time
that happened was just before I got your letter. And my
eyes work on sinus too. My right eye quiver, I'm going
to rejoice about something. My left eye, I'm going to get
mad or it's going to rain. Now that's true for me. I got
that from my mother.

If I cut my nails (toes or fingers) on Sunday, I know
I'm going to be sick before Monday.

They tell me if you cut little babies' fingernails,
they'll be roguish. My wife won't cut them, she takes
and bites 'em off. She says, "I won't take no scissors
and cut them off, they'll be roguish."

You know there's thirteen signs to the zodiac. If you
castrate a hog when the sign is in their private, they'll
swell up and apt to bleed to death. If you castrate when

the sign's in the feet you won't have no trouble with them,
not a drop of blood.

Same with a woman. If the sign is in the private
(when she's holding her flower), then that's when she'll
have her period. It's in McDonald's almanac. All
woman come thirteen times — the flower's doubled up
extra one month. There's thirteen new moons in the
year.

49. Intercourse

> Puckett, pp. 267-268, talks about ways of
> keeping one's lover faithful. Drums and Sha-
> dows, p. 95, reports that women frequently use
> love powders "so dat dey kin rule duh men."

They say if a woman measures your peter with a
piece of string, and ties it round her leg, you can't get
no stake up at all, you can't get ready at all, with no
other woman but her.

A fellow told me, an older man from Baton Rouge,
Louisiana, that he would kill a forked snake and take out
its tongue, its forked tongue, and carry that with him all
the time in his pocket, wrapped up in a little piece of rag.
Then when he was with a woman, he'd pretend he was
looking for the place, and he'd rub it against her, and
then no other man could get her. He'd get ready, but as
soon as he'd try, he'd fade away, melt away.

Tell you why I believe that. Down in Shaw, Mississippi, before I was married, there was a young girl,
Duck, had a boy friend who cut logs, but she promised to
go with me. He was trying to get together, and couldn't
when I lived in town, but when I moved to the country as
a cook, I'd know when he was out of town, and would
drive in on a Sunday. We tried for half a day, but as soon

as I got on top it dropped right away. We stripped stark buck naked, but I never could do nothing. That's the only time I failed.

VII

TRUE WONDERS

50. Dead Man Stands Up

John, Julia and Tobe Courtney each told
me a comic cooling-board story where the
dead man frightened the attendants. See Pine
Bluff, ante, no. 43abc, pp.82-86, "On the Cooling
Board." Clear Rock tells how he ran from a
corpse on the cooling-board who asked for a
potato, in John Lomax, Adventures of a Bal-
lad Hunter, New York, 1947, pp. 182-184.

This is one that really happened, out to Shaw, Mississippi, on the Bogue, a little old creek there. A man had
died, and they had swouded him, and laid him on the cooling board. (Swouding—that's putting bandages under
your jaws, till you get stiff, so your mouth doesn't open,
and pin your arms across your breast—can't bend them
after they get stiff, you'd have to break them.)

Sambo wanted to have him some fun. All of them
went to sleep. So he taken the dead man, stand him up
in the corner. He tipped over to where one was sleeping,
and would shake him, wake him up and point to the corner where the dead man was standing. He run 'em all
away that way, then he put him back on the cooling board.

They couldn't say it was their imagination, all saw
the same thing.

51. Buried Twice

This story is the serious counterpart of
the preceding one. In the humorous version,
pranksters play a joke with the dead man; in
the present form a live man in a trance sits up
on the cooling board or in the coffin and terri-
fies the bystanders. See "Negro Tales of Mary
Richardson," no. 21, pp. 18-19, "Dead Man Sits
Up," and a modernized situation by Suggs,
"Live Man Embalmed," in NFIM 96. Joe
Woods told me the same episode as it occurred
in his native Galicia, Poland, where his aunt's
sister-in-law lived ten years after her prema-
ture burial. See my "Polish Tales from Joe
Woods," Western Folklore, VIII (April 1949),
p. 145, "Sleeping Death."

That was in 1906, in Indianola. Isaac Ward died the
first time then, and died again four years later. He had
been sick for eight or nine weeks. Well they washed,
swouded, and then went and bought his coffin for him and
laid him out. So when they put him in the coffin, they set
the lid on the side, so people could interview the body,
you know, come in and look at it. So about nine o'clock
that night the house was crowded, setting up the wake.
The beer crowd was there. They didn't have embalming
or death certificates in those days.

He heard a voice from the coffin, asking him to look
back. I and my Katie we's going through thataway. I
met some people running. I axed them, "What's the matter, what's the trouble?"

They said, "The dead man sat up in the coffin, asked
for a drink of water." So Mrs. May Walker, a two hundred pounder, she got up and gave them the water.

In 1910 he died of a heartache and they wouldn't bury
him for five days.

(They used to put a sauce of table salt on the breast
of the corpse to keep from purging so much.)

52. Buried Alive

> This is Type 990, "Seemingly Dead Re-
> vives," and Motif K426, "Apparently dead
> woman revives when thief tries to steal from
> her grave," which has become widely localized
> in the United States.

That was told me by my a'ntie. Woman was named
Helen Carter. She was a rich man's daughter in California, and they buried her with her jewelry on her. These
poor boys wanted her jewelry. So that night after breakfast they went and dug her up. As soon as they opened
the lid, and the air hit her, she came to and she knew
them, when they opened the box. So she's able to get out
of the coffin, but she couldn't go nowhere. So she told
her daddy who they were. So he made them rich for saving his daughter.

53. Sells Wife for Beef

> A circumstantial account of the same re-
> volting murder in given by Mary Richardson
> in NFIM 95-96, "The Man Who Sold his Wife
> for Beef." She says it happened in Clarksdale,
> Mississippi.

That was a true story, happened at Itta Bena, Mississippi, when I was a boy. I did know the fellow's name.
He got mad at his wife and grabbed up a hammer and
first thing he knew he killed her — that's the way he

testified in the court. She was a great big woman, about
two hundred and sixty, and he was a little man. So he
didn't know how to expose her; he cut off her head and
her feets like a hog and buried them, and the rest he
sawed up, sliced in steaks, and he was peddling them
around, selling it as beef. The people who bought it all
got sick.

"Come over here, my wife's sick, my child's sick,"
"Well, it's the same way all over."

So they got the doctor and he said it was human
meat, and they arrested him and hung him.

54. Snake and Baby

For other texts from Michigan Negroes
see NFIM 149-150, from Leozie Smith, and
"Negro Tales of Mary Richardson" no. 20, p.
18, both with the above title. This is Type 285,
"The Snake and the Child." See note 101, p.
224 in NFIM, which refers to a text in Randolph,
Who Blowed Up the Church House, pp. 87-89,
and an informative note by H. Halpert, 206-207.
Suggs's final comment is a characteristic semi-
rationalization to explain the affinity between
the snake and the child.

This was a bottle baby. They carried the baby to the
field with its bottle, in the crib under the shade tree.
When they came back, if the baby was woke, all the milk
would be gone, if it wasn't woke only half would be gone.
The field wasn't far from the house. When it got so it
could walk it would go out in the yard and carry its bottle
out there. When it came in the house the bottle would be
empty, wouldn't be a bit in it. Then from three years old
she quit the bottle but she would take milk in a cup and
would always go outdoors to eat, but nobody paid her no

attention. And when she got five years old she went outdoors, and her Dad seen this big snake. And she was
reaching out her hand for it. When he ran outdoors with
his gun the snake turned and went crawling off. He kills
the snake and three days after, the baby it died.

It was a white baby, in Shreveport, Louisiana, not
far from the Arkansas line. My a'ntie told my father
and them about it.

(Maybe like a lodestone draws from metal and flesh,
there was something between the snake and the baby.)

55. Bear and Baby

In the text from Leozie Smith with the
same title, NFIM 149-150, the bear abducts
the baby for but one night. Note 102, p. 224
gives three references, to two Negro variants
from Texas and one in White tradition from
Kentucky.

I heard that in the lower part of California they
missed the baby, didn't see no blood, thought maybe it
had wandered off. Three years after this a man hunting
came to a hollow cypress tree, and found the baby asleep
inside. And when he got it up it fought like a wildcat. It
was naked. And the bear got on his scent and follered
him plumb home, and they had to kill that bear. He'd
brought the baby up, nursed it, gave it raw meat to eat.
Yes, it was a colored baby.

56. Alligator and Naked Man

An alligator won't attack a naked man. If you're
swimming on the top he'll go to the bottom. He'll fight

you on the ground but not in the water. Ralph Roemind,
a white fellow, said he would go into the alligator's cave,
his bed, and run him out. He went to gigging him with a
gig, a spear, and the other fellows shot the alligator
with harpoons under the fore shoulder. But he pulled off
his clothes before he went in.

57. Alligator Taken for Devil

     The general Motif J1781, "Objects thought
to be the devil," applies here.

Alligators will travel from one lake to another once
a year in the spring by moonlight—don't know who
teaches them, nature I guess. One lake was on the north
side of the road, one on the south side. A fellow moved
from the hills, a colored fellow. He had never seen a
alligator. So revival was going on at the church, Mt.
Zion Church. So all of his peoples had gone to church,
he was about thirty minutes late behind them, it was 'bout
seven, eight o'clock. He heard a rail fence popping (they
didn't have wire fences then). He looked up, he seen
someone climbing up on the fence. And after a while it
made a big crash and he fell backwards. He made a second try, he went to climbing up on another panel. He fell
off again. He looked, the moon was shining bright like
day, and he could see. He said to hisself, "Surely that
must be the devil trying to get to the church." So he
broke by him, ran to the church to tell the people. He
run in excited looking, say "Say peoples, the Devil's up
the road there, trying to get across the fence to get to
the church." He said the reason he knowed it was the
Devil, every time he'd get upon the fence he'd break it.
"You don't believe it you come on and see."

The crowd followed him. The crowd heard the rails popping and they stopped. Two young ones said, "Let's go up there and see what it is." When they got close enough they could see the alligator trying to climb up again. One of them hollered to him, "Come on up here." Say "It ain't nothing but a big old alligator trying to cross, to get up to another lake, Benson's Lake." Said "We should have knowed what that was, because they crossed here all the time before that fence was built."
(That was at Fasonia, just north of Indianola.)

58. Jesse James's Tunnel

> The standard works on Jesse James by
> Robertus Love, Homer Croy and Carl W.
> Breihan contain no reference to this tradition.

About twenty miles from Cairo on the Missouri side of the river, about five miles south of Wyatt—the cotton belt railroad runs through there and then you leave it and go down the river—Jesse James had his home. It was across the Mississippi from Weakley, Kentucky. He'd rob the Illinois Central and row himself across the river to the willows, and he'd disappear. He had a tunnel there going underground to the well in his house. Or if they'd surround the house he'd go into the cistern, and swing off before he'd get to the water and crawl into the tunnel. Wasn't no levee on the Mississippi then.
    Reason I know is that in '47 I was at Wyatt cooking for Morowe Levee Company, and the house burned down. And when they 'xamined it they could see the tunnel in the cistern. You could still go about a hundred yards in it each way.

59. A Bear Hunter Who Lost His Nerve

> This account reads like one of Davy
> Crockett's bear hunts as told in his Autobiog-
> raphy. The phrases chanted by one of the
> hunters suggest a formulistic development of
> the narrative.

No matter how brave a man is, he'll lose his nerve
if you catch him wrong.

John Hugens was about six foot four inches, a light
brown skin, weighed about a hundred and ninety, a mixed
breed—Indian and white too. He lived out from Indianola,
and was known as a great hunter, and used to run a ball
team.

He had a lot of sharecroppers and farmers and day
laborers, had about two hundred acres from Billy
McCleod, and subrented. He had a gambling house in
Sunflower City, another in Indianola, and one on the river
where he was at—a big sport. Teddy Roosevelt used to
come down and go bear hunting with him. (He appointed
Wayne Cox's wife postmaster of Indianaola, a colored
woman, and got to know Hugens through him. Wayne Cox
owned three to four thousand acres of land, was a thirty-
second degree Mason. Had a bank of his own, was a mail
clerk on the Southern.)

One day they were hunting over on Quiver River, and
jumped a big bear. The men were all on stands, waiting
for the bear. John took his in the fork of a tree that had
fell down, so he'd have a place to sit. So the dogs was
running right to him, and he was looking for the bear.
Then he looked around, the bear had turned off to his left
and was coming right behind him. John said when he
looked over he was about fifteen feet from him, walking
on his hind legs over the bresh. John said if it wasn't
for the bresh the bear would have had him before he seen

him. And when he seen him his bristles was raised up
over his head (like a dog's only bigger), and his teeth
were shining. The bear come in a different direction,
that's what threw John off and excited him. Well he had
a trained dog Bulger, old Bulger, said when he heard
John's gun shoot he'd know it from any gun there was,
and he'd make for him. John shot at the bear sixteen
times.

So we was off, we heard the shots. Sam Johnson
(white fellow) said, "Listen to that old John." He knowed
that was his rifle popping over there. Said,

> "Fry some, stew some, brile some."
> [Hummed softly]

John was a crack shot, never knowed him to shoot
that many times. The bear weighed about five hundred,
and he was within two feet of the bear when he fired the
last shot, and then he missed him. So he grabbed the
barrel—he'd emptied the Winchester—and he was going
to hit him with it; he couldn't run because he was between
the fork. That time he seen old Bulger leap right on the
bear's back. So the bear was trying to reach behind and
get him. So John dropped his gun and pulled his dirk—
his Bowie knife, long hunting knife, a dirk they usually
call it—and stabbed the bear right in his heart.

(In switch cane that's the way they kill bear all the
time, when the bear gets hot and sits down and swipes
at the dogs. John sneaks up behind and stabs him. He'd
never use no steel arm either, would rather depend on
old Bulger.)

60. Moleskin the Brakeman

I knowed a brakeman didn't know A from B, but he would take the switch list (with the numbers of the cars on it) and go find his car even at night. He called an 0 a goose egg, 1 a cigar, he knowed 6, he called 9 a six bottom up, 4 was a cross-legged man, 5 was a fishhook. Two 0's he'd call two goose eggs. You work your own cars, and he never made a mistake. We called him Moleskin, he was just slick and black as a mole. That was in Memphis.

61. Tommie Suggs

This is no folktale. Suggs told me his son came out and lived near him in Calvin, but later moved away to Elkhart, Indiana. "I was no different to him than any other man, 'cause I didn't raise him," he explained.

When I was in the Army in 1917 I got a letter saying that I had a son, and had to support him. I was going to marry his mother when I got back, but she died, and her sister brought him up. I saw him when he was six months. I lost track of the whole thing. I used to cook for Mrs. Cook in Bono, Arkansas, and Albert, a colored boy, got acquainted with Tommie at Newport, Arkansas, after he came back from Alaska (early 1950). Albert told Tommie he knew a Suggs, and wrote to Mrs. Cook and got my address, in Vandalia, Michigan. Tommie was oil-milling. When Tommie got back to Seattle he heard from Albert and wrote me a letter.

"My name is Tommie Suggs. My mother was Ida Justice. They say my father was J. D. Suggs. If this letter mean anything to you you are my daddy."

So I wrote him and in three weeks he came, and he went to work with me for Fattore in South Bend. Then he sent back for his wife and boy.

VIII

PROTEST TALES

62. Guard on the County Farm

Chapter 6 in Pine Bluff, ante, describes
and presents protest tales. The first narrative in this group is an eye-witness account of
a Negro convict being whipped to death. Compare the descriptions by Mary Richardson in
NFIM 90, of "The Prison Farm," and of "Grandmother Whipped," no. 14, pp. 14-15, in "Negro
Tales of Mary Richardson." Brutal whippings
recalled by slaves are in Botkin, Burden,
"Praying to the Right Man," pp. 14-15, 163-170.

My first public working job was at Itta Bena, as a
guard at a county farm. I was twenty, and thought I was
doing something big to carry a gun. But I didn't like it
at all, standing out there in the cold while they were
working, and my heart wasn't in killing like I thought I
would be. But I had to stay six months on the contract.
They were chopping cotton, and shackled a fast man
with a slow man, a new man with an old hand. And
every once in a while the new hand would holler for
slack, because the other one would be pulling at the
shackle. Then they whipped the one who couldn't keep
up. It tickled lots of them to see their partners get
beat up. After they whipped Charlie with a leather strap
(about eight inches long and four inches wide, with a
wooden handle, to pitch it straight down while the guards

held him by the arms and legs off the ground; the straps
had holes to suck up the skin into blisters), he wouldn't
work any more, and told him they would just have to kill
him. The driver said, "Wheel him over." That gives
the left side to him. He hits him three licks over the
heart. He don't quiver or nothing, just quiver like when
you shoot a cow, and just lay like he was going to sleep
when they lay him down. He was dead.

63. German Atrocity

Atrocity stories belong to the folklore of
wars, and probably interest Negroes from the
resemblances to brutality stories in their own
tradition.

A French lady told me and Henry Allen that she'd
put up some German soldiers, a lieutenant and a cor-
poral. They told her to fix breakfast, called them down
to eat. So after they ate they told her to go upstairs,
she'd see how much they appreciate what she'd done for
them. And when she went up she said the baby was laying there with its stomach just ripped open with a bay-
onet.

64. Old Missy, the Mule and the Buggy

An exaggerative folktale has here grown
out of the realities of Southern mores. The
mule obviously represents the colored man, as
Suggs's parenthetical comment makes clear.
Compare Hyatt no. 10606, p. 637, "They say
down in Georgia if a black man sees a white
mule he must bow to it." Suggs's story "The
Fast Runner," in NFIM 181, in similar vein

develops a tall tale from the consequences re-
sulting when a colored man strikes a white
man.

Old Missy was going to town to carry some eggs.
So she was driving a mule to a buggy. The mule got
scared and runned away and throwed Old Missy out. It
didn't kill her, just bruised her up a little. So they got
the mule and buggy and drove it up to town, and had the
mule and buggy tried. They found the mule guilty for
running away with the buggy, and the buggy guilty for
running away and throwing Old Missy out. So the J. P.
he sentences the mule to be hung, and sent the buggy to
the penitentiary for life.

(Anything happened to Old Missy you going to suffer
for it, right or wrong. It's the middle class what had
to work you had to worry about— the big shots let you
do anything, the doctors, lawyers. They won't work.
Old Missy was working, she was going to town to carry
eggs. The middle class don't like the colored because
they won't get out of a job, and that makes them preju-
diced. If the colored got money they won't work for
nothing. There's fifty colored folks to one white in the
South. But the rich colored men can fry the poor ones
just like the whites do. Since the war things is better.
The white boys didn't like saying "Yes, sir" and "No,
sir" in the army.)

65. Will Kimbro Defends Himself

Here appears the realistic narrative of the
colored man fighting for his rights and triumph-
ing, a tradition going back to slavery times.
See Botkin, Burden, "The Slave's Chance," pp.
174-178.

Will Kimbro taught school from November till March—we only had four months. Then he would rent ground and raise cotton and corn. His mother-in-law was renting from a white man, too, and in the settling he beat her out of sixty dollars. She carried the bills over to her son-in-law and asked him to figure up the cotton. Then she goes back and asks for her money, and told them her son-in-law figured it out. One morning he woke up and found a note on the porch, telling him he had ten days to leave the country. He took the note to town and showed it to Mr. Will Brown, a hardware and grocery merchant he dealt with. Said "I hate to leave you all, but I haven't got anything to protect myself."

Walter Brown, the brother, said, "You furnish the grit and we'll furnish the guns and ammunition."

He agreed. They gave him two Winchesters and seven boxes of cartridges. His friend George Smart (colored) agreed to sit up with him and watch. Kimbro took his wife to his daddy's house and went back with Smart. They did this for four or five nights.

The sixth night Smart didn't show up. Will's father Ned said he'd go with him. The crowd has caught Smart eating supper, and sent him to the door to call Kimbro. He knew Kimbro wasn't in the house, but down in the new ground in front of the house, where he had been sitting up with him. Kimbro had left the light on, turned down low, to make them think he was in. It looked like about three hundred men in the mob—some was riding, some was walking. He saw one man walk up to the door and knock. He shot him—it was his buddy. The others were all crouched around in the thicket—they commenced shooting at him. His father shot two or three times and got nervous, and wanted to leave—he was an old man of seventy. Will said, "Ned, if you won't shoot, at least load my cartridges." He was lying behind a

stump. After a bit his father said he had to go. So Will
said, "If you have to go, leave your ammunition and your
gun." Last he saw of his father he was crawling off on
all fours. He disappeared for three days. Will kept
shooting until he heard no more shots. Then he walked
three miles to town—this was out in the country—and
called the sheriff from Silas. The sheriff came down
with his deputies, and they found or heard of sixteen
dead men, fifteen white and his buddy. They put him in
jail under protection, and at the trial he come clear.

That was in the spring. That winter he had his trial
at Circuit Court, and in November he was teaching us.
He was about thirty then. He was a brownskinned man,
about a hundred and seventy-five pounds, about five foot
nine. He didn't look hard at all. He ended up as a
United States detective.

66. How Jack Farmer Escaped the Law

An element of hoodooism here assists the
colored man in eluding his white pursuers.

Now this a true story. It happened in 1914, in Sunflower City, in Sunflower County. Jack Farmer was on
a farm, not far from Sunflower City, and this white fellow who owned it also stayed on the farm. Jack Farmer
had a daughter was married. So she got sick one Tues-
day morning. So her husband taken her in the buggy and
was carrying her to Sunflower to the doctor. Mr. Casey
met 'em—that's who they was working for—and he
taken a buggy whip out of the buggy, and whipped 'em
both, and told 'em to get back to the farm and go to
work. When they come back she was crying and her
daddy axed her what was the matter. She told him that

Mr. Casey whipped her. So he just picked up his shotgun and called Mr. Casey to the door and killed him.

Then they got three or four hundred men along with the law to try to catch him. They run him about six weeks in about a fifty mile square block, but they never could get close enough to lay their hands on him. They was trying to keep him from getting to his daddy, who was a hoodoo. They'd see him going into a thicket, in the day. They'd surround that thicket. 'Gainst they get it surrounded, they'd look off about a quarter of a mile, they'd see him just going off in another bunch of woods. So he had a brother lived at Shaw, named Henry Farmer. One night he made it there, to his house. He said, "Give me something to eat and I'll be on my way." He said, "Tell 'em I've been here, don't tell 'em no story, they's right behind me and they're coming here, but they can't catch me."

They came in as he went out the back door — he'd been gone about five or ten minutes before they got there. So they axed him had Jack Farmer been there. "Has your brother been here, Henry?" He told them "No." He didn't want to betray his brother.

They axed his wife Annie (I knew them better than I knew Jack, she was maid where I was cook, but she was older'n I was, she had a son old as I was). She told them "No." Then they slapped her and tried to make her own it. Then they taken him, Henry Farmer, and tied his feet and hands, and pulled him down the road with the car, trying to make him own it. So he wouldn't own it, and they turned him loose, they didn't kill him.

That day Jack Farmer made to the Bogue — that's a great big thick woods, an old creek there they called it the Bogue. So John Carroll was out there looking for him the next day. Jack was standing behind a tree and

he walked right up on Jack before he seen him. Said
"What you hunting, Mr. Carroll?"

    Carroll said, "I'se squirrel-hunting."

    Said "No you wasn't, Mr. Carroll, you was hunting
me." Said, "You got a wife and chilluns—the best thing
you can do is get out of these woods as quick as you can."
John Carroll got so excited he got to running and run into a vine and tripped over a log and broke his hip, and
he's crippled to this day, least he was last time I saw
him; I don't know if he's still alive. And that's the last
anyone saw of Jack Farmer. But his brothers knew
where he was. But they won't tell where he's at.

    He got to his father, who went for a two-headed guy.

    (Jack was around fifty, I was twenty something at
the time.)

67. The New Dance Step

    In Pine Bluff, ante, no. 61, pp.112-113, "Chas-
tising the Negro," E. M. Moore sets a similar
episode in Corning, Arkansas, but contrives a
ludicrous ending; the white man makes the Negro jump over the fence and pause suspended
in midair.

    Morehouse, Missouri, was a big sawmill town on
Little River. Every time a colored fellow come through
they made him dance and run—the young white fellows
did, eighteen to twenty-one. These two colored boys
come along, and they made them dance, and then chuck
rocks at 'em and run 'em out of town. One of the white
fellows, John, was in the bunch, told me they was the
best dancers he ever saw. They were gone about five
or six months. One day the same two boys come back
along there. John said to the gang, "Here come the

same two, let's make them dance again today." "Boys,
I want you to dance some for me today."

They says "Okay," just sets their suitcase down.
And the white fellows begin to pat for them (to make the
music). They done all kinds of dancing. After awhile
one of 'em stopped, said "Did you ever see that step,
Get Your Gun?"

He said, "No."

The colored boy said, "If we had our light shoes on
we'd show you something. That beats any step we know."

They said, "Well get your light shoes out; we sure
wants to see that."

They went to the suitcases, unlocked it, retched in
like they was going to get the shoes. Both of 'em come
up with a gun at the same time. Said, "Now let's see
you all dance." John said none of them couldn't dance
at all. He said they just made them jump up and down
for forty minutes till they couldn't get their feets hardly
off the ground. Said then they just picked up their suitcases, said "That's pretty good, boys," and walked off.

And they never did bother nobody after that. (My
cousin moved out in '27, and I went there in '25—this
was the year before. There was no coloreds there when
I went there. He come out there to see me, and went to
work for the same man I did.)

68. First Seeing a Train

        This and the following two tales deal with
the backcountry Negro who has never seen a
train. In "Negro Tales of Bolivar County, Mississippi," no. 18, p. 114, Rev. J. H. Lee tell's
of the "Obstinate Man" who refused to believe
a train could be built, could start, or could stop.

Old farmer was carrying his children to see the
train. They stayed about sixteen miles from town. So
he gone out to town, seen 'em laying the tiles and rails.
He wanted to know what was they doing that for. Said,
"Well we're going to make a railroad here, carry milk
and butter and p'duce to St. Louis, so you won't have to
drive your team a hundred and fifty miles." (It would
take them three or four weeks to carry it to market.)
He wanted to know how long would it be. They told him,
oh about a year and six months they would have it ready.

He made about two trips in that year and six months.
So he asked the depot agent what date would it start,
when were they going to put it on. Said "Oh, about the
fifteenth of August, when they would run the first train
over the road."

So he went back home and told his wife there was
going to be a train about the fifteenth and he was going
to carry them all out and let 'em see it. So he started
on the tenth, so he'd be sure be there on the fifteenth
to see the first run. So on the fifteenth he was there on
the side of the railroad good, be sure he'd see that train.
So he had his horse hitched to the wagon, just a one-
horse wagon, his nine kids piled in the back and the old
man and the lady sitting on the spring seat before.

Old man said, "Old lady, I'd better take this horse
loose, he's liable to run away, and hurt the kids and all
of us." So he taken his horse loose and hitched him
about twenty feet down the railroad. He looked up, he
seen a black smoke coming down the railroad. Looked
and he seen a big black something behind it, coming on
up towards him, making a lot of noise. He said "Old
lady, I'd better get out and pull this wagon off a little
piece from the railroad."

Here come the train with a lot of fuss.

"Chugachugachugachug—chug along, chug along."

So he get scared. All that fuss and that big black
thing and the smoke coming out of his head. So he lit
out to running. He got excited and forgot about holding
the shares (in the one-horse buggy the shares was strap-
ped to the horse so he could pull the wagon.) So he run
away, spilled out the kids and the old lady.

Last time I seen him he was yet going. I don't know
whether he come back and got 'em or not.

69. Po' Thing

Close variants with the same title are in
Pine Bluff, ante, no. 74, pp. 121-122, by John
Courtney, and "Negro Tales of Mary Richardson," no. 22, p. 19. This tale deserves a separate type number alongside Type 1315, "The
Steamship thought to be the Devil." In variants
told me by Walter Winfrey and Idell Moore a
handcart and a bull are mistaken for a train.
Joe D. Heardley told me of a family running in
fright from a streetcar, thinking it a train that
had jumped the track, and Clarence Grier gave
me one about the Irishman in Philadelphia who
thought a streetcar was Pat's house on wheels,
because it had the same number.

Aunt Dinah, she's about fifty years old. So she went
to town, her first time in fifty years. So she got there
about train time. It was a passenger train. She asked
what was that. The depot agent said, "Well, that's a
train." She had a load of fodder on her wagon, was carrying it to town to sell.

Said, "How fur did he come?" Said "Po' thing, I
know it's tired and hongry." So she begin to th'ow off
one bundle after another, until she had unloaded about a

hundred and fifty sacks. Said, "I know you're hongry and
tired. Po' little thing."

It was going "Bim, bim, bim," puffing you know.
She knowed that it was tired with the load it was pulling.

70. Jacob's Cut

Compare "Jessup's Cut" in J. Mason
Brewer, Humorous Folktales of the South Carolina Negro, Orangeburg, S. C., 1945, p. 51.

Old lady she was on the train. She left her husband
at home, was going to visit her daughter one hundred
miles from there. (Old folks didn't get to ride on the
train much then—that was her first trip—she was sixty-
nine.) Well after she got on the train the porter comes
through calling the station. He said, "Jacob's Cut."
[Loud, sharp]

Old sister jumped up, th'owed up her hands, said,
"Lord, who cut Jacob, for he don't bother nobody?"

Porter replied, "This is the station I'm calling."

She said, "Lord a-mercy, I thought you was talking
about my Jacob."

IX

SCRIPTURAL   TALES

71. Biblical Bits

Suggs, whose father was a preacher, and
who acted in Biblical plays in his youth, con-
tinually refers to Scripture for examples of
miracles and wonder, which he reinterprets in
the light of his own culture, emphasizing the
Negro personages in Biblical history. See his
reinterpretations in NFIM 156-158, "Mangeliz-
ing" and "How Hoodoo Lost His Hand." Roark
Bradford in Ol' Man Adam an' His Chillun,
New York, 1927, and Samuel G. Stoney and
Gertrude M. Shelby in Black Genesis, New
York, 1930, have portrayed Negro folk-chroni-
cles of the Bible in literary form.

In one place of the Bible it tells you God created
male and female and called them Adams. Then next
chapter it tells God created man out of the dust of the
earth, and called him Adam. So there must be more
than one Adam and Eve. Otherwise how could there be
so many different people?

After Cain killed Abel he ran away to the land of
Nod. He married his wife there. Now I never hear a
preacher preach on that text.

Nimrod was so black he was called the Choice of
Darkness. He was the descent of Ham. He became a
mighty hunter before the Lord, slaughtering the beasties.
People washed him up [worshipped] just like he was a

239

warlord. Like Hitler. He build the great city of Baby-
lon, of wickedness. Beasties people had never seen before he would bring in, slaughter them.

Jethro was a colored man. Moses married his
daughter. Jethro started all courts.

72. Aaron and the Rod

    Abundant references are given under Mo-
tif F971.1, "Dry rod blossoms."

They wanted to see who was going to be the choice
for the King of Israel after they was delivered from the
Pharoah. And they had all the smart people get walking canes — some was crooked, some straight, made out
of dry wood, hard as a bone — Charlie Chaplin used to
use one all the time. So they laid down their canes in
the ark of the covenant, this sanctuary of holiness, and
opened the ark in the morning, and Aaron's had budded
out. So they knowed he was their leader.

73. Elijah and the Ax

    See Motif F1047, "Anchor floats on water."

The childrens of Israel wanted him to prove that
there was a supreme being, God, who was capable of
doing anything. They had to have more proof then than
now. They had to have signs — we can read. Elijah took
his ax and th'ew it in the water, and it floated.

74. Christ and the Mule

See Motif A2561.1, "Why mule is sterile."

The mule can't breed you know and the old tale says
that Christ was riding on the mule to Jerusalem and the
mule got scared and th'owed him. Christ said, " Thou
shall be cursed, thou shall not bring forth any increase."
And that's the reason a mule won't breed colts.

(You can't cross a jenny and a stud horse, but you
can cross a jack and a jenny and make a mule. A jack
is a little short fellow but a mule is seventeen hands
high. A jack and jenny make another jack and jenny.
Did you ever see a ball game played on jennies? Funni-
est thing you ever saw. A man goes around in a tent
with the jennies, and you pay the quarter to get his
jenny.)

75. God Punishes the Dog

A variant from Tommy Carter is in NFIM
162, "God Names the Dog," Motifs A2234, "Animal characteristics: punishment for disobedience," and A2494.1.2, "Enmity between cat and
dog," apply here.

When the Lord made Adam, he put him in the Garden of Eden. And he made all beasties, and put every
kind of foul dirt in there. And Adam he named them.
So the Lord put him to sleep, made them all helpmeet.
Well Adam didn't have no helpmeet, so he put him to
sleep, and cut out of his ribs. Cat and dog was standing
around there growling. So he laid the rib down to close
up the room. Dog grabbed her rib and lit out with her.

So the Lord couldn't catch him, he cut the dog's tail off, and they been growling ever since.

(If there were only three women, two will talk about the other.)

76. The Beginning of Mhm

> Variant texts are in NFIM 162-163, "How
> the Devil Kept the Soul," from Mrs. John Grant;
> and Hurston, pp. 204-205, "How the Devil
> Coined a Word."

Well the Devil he's out getting up souls. So he caught a sackful of 'em, as many as he could put on his back in a sack. So he goes down the road a little piece and grabbed some more—his right hand full. So he goes on a little further and sees more, grabs them—his left hand. So he goes on a little further, he sees another handful. So he taken his right handful and he th'ew them in his mouth, and he grabbed the other handful he seen standing there. So he going on down the road further, he sees Christ.

Christ says, "Devil, do you want some more souls?"

He's afraid to open his mouth, for fear he'd lose them souls. So he nodded his head and kept his mouth shut, and said "Mhm."

(Now you'll have to figure out that part of it—I never did know anybody knew how to spell it.)

X

TALL TALES

77. The Big Watermelon

Five Southern Negro tales of enormous
vegetables are given by Arthur H. Fauset, "Negro Folk Tales from the South (Alabama, Mississippi, Louisiana)," JAF XL, 1927, pp. 260-
261, under "The Marvelous Potato." Herbert
Halpert has a case of "Fast-Growing Watermelons" in Western Folklore, "Tales Told by
Soldiers," IV, 1945, no. 18, p. 373, with full
references, and in his following text, no. 19,
pp. 373-374, "Great Pumpkin," animals eat
their way into and live inside the giant vege-
table. I have a similar text from Mrs. E. L.
Smith. Motif X1042.2, "The great melon," refers to Bolte and Polívka, II, 516. Baughman
classifies these motifs under X1402.1 (ca), "Lie:
the fast-growing vine," where he summa-
rizes the first half of Suggs's tale, and gives
one Negro and six white references; and X1401.1*
(b), "Animals eat into large vegetables, live
there for some time," for which he cites two
Negro and six White examples.

The preacher who told this said it happened down
in the Mississippi delta. He was born down there but
raised up here, in Niles—the Rev. Haynes. He told me
that last week right on the job (housing project at South
Bend, being built by Place and Company).
Fellow told him about the richest ground he ever

seed. He went out to plant a watermelon, and he went
back to get a stick to put in the ground with a paper on
it to show what kind of a watermelon it was — it was a
Tom Watson. Had his knife out to cut the stick and when
he looked around the vine had done caught up with him
and was wrapped around his feet. He fell down, he
couldn't get out of it, and before he could get up the
vines had done covered him up. He looked over on the
other side and a big watermelon had growed right up.
Whereas he already had his knife out to cut the stick, he
went to cutting a hole in the watermelon. That was in
June. So he ate and slept in that watermelon to about
the 28th of October (they have frost late down there) until it frosted, killed the vines (you know they wither and
fall down) before he could ever get out to go home.

78. The Big Punkin

A close variant is in E. C. Parsons, Folk-
Lore of the Sea Islands, South Carolina, no. 90,
p. 98, "The Giant Pumpkin," which encloses a
schoolhouse and a train in motion. In Hurston,
p. 135, a mule-team and wagon get lost inside
the pumpkin. Giant pumpkins frequently turn
up in tall tales, but with the motifs mentioned
in the preceding note; see e.g. my Jonathan
Draws the Long Bow, Cambridge, Mass., 1946,
pp. 129-132, "Big Connecticut Pumpkins."

They got to arguing about raising stuff. One of the
boys said, "My granddaddy is the best farmer around
here. He raised a watermelon— it weighed five hundred
pounds."
The second fellow said, "Shaw, that's nothing. Right
out of town right down there on the levee (that was in
New Orleans) my granddaddy raised a punkin was so big

they had forty men to pull the saw, they had a scaffold forty feet high, and the punkin was eight hundred rods long. And the saw was four hundred feet long. The saw cut it in half. Then they cut one of them halves into quarters. Then they prised it loose so they could get in to the seeds. And the seeds was so big they was making ships out'n them. And they used the other half for the roundhouse for the I. C. [Illinois Central] in New Orleans."

79. Big Cabbage

> The present text closely follows the variant summarized under Type 1920A, "Contest in Lying," and Motif X1024.1, "The great cabbage."

One fellow said, "You know, my grandfather was the best farmer in Florida. He raised a cabbage so large a regiment of soldiers could stand under one leaf."

Other fellow said, "Well my granddaddy made him a pot so large it takes a train running ninety miles an hour six weeks to go around it."

Other fellow says, "What do you want with a pot that big?"

"Well, to cook that lying cabbage your granddaddy raised."

80. The Big Dog

> Under Motif X1215.2, "Lie: large dog," Baughman gives seven examples, none Negro.

Fellow was talking about how big a dog he'd seen.
One fellow said, "Why the biggest dog I seen didn't
weigh over two hundred pounds."

Other fellow said, "Shaw, that wasn't no dog at all.
Dog over in New York bit a little boy and the police shot
him, and they had to telephone back to Chicago, told him
to tell the tail to lay down and die."

81. Far-Sighted Man

> In NFIM 182, Walter Winfrey tells this
> tale on "The Two Remarkable Irishmen," and
> see note 146, p. 229.

Two fellows was arguing about who could see the
further. One said, "I see a gnat over on that tree yonder about half a mile." [Gesture of sitting up, peering]

The next one peeped in the same direction and said,
"Yes, you sure did, 'cause I seen him wink his eye."

82. Turning the Buffalo Around

> This is Motif X911.1, "Man turns wolf in-
> side out," a popular American tall tale.

When I was in Wyoming in 1923 I heard an Indian
tell how he was running from a buffalo. (There used to
be lots of buffalo there.) It was seventy-five acres
across the plain to a big oak tree, and the bull was right
behind him as he was running around the tree. And he
run so fast he caught up with the bull, and run his hand
down his throat and caught him by the tail, and turned
him wrongside out, and the bull went running right back
the other way.

83. Clever Chinches

"Bob White in Chicago told me this," Suggs recalled. A well-told variant, "The Michigan Bedbug Story," localized in Kalamazoo, Michigan, was printed in the Wisconsin Superior Chronicle for Oct. 6, 1857, credited to the Grand River Eagle, and has received a modern reprinting in Michigan History, XXXIII, 1949, p. 255. After the hotel guest tarred the ceiling as well as the floor, the bedbugs built bridges of straw to cross the tar. This last touch is used in two variants in A. H. Fauset, Folklore from Nova Scotia, MAFLS XXIV, 1931, no. 89, pp. 73-74, "Bugs." In an Ozark text in Randolph, The Devil's Pretty Daughter, "The Drummer's Magic Circle," pp. 148-149, the hotel guest outwits the bedbugs with his circle of molasses, but as H. Halpert points out in his note, p. 222, the usual variants result in triumph for the bugs. Here again Suggs switches from third to first person.

Fellow went to the rooming house to stay all night. So they gave him a room right next to the kitchen. So he goes to bed, but the chinches begin to bite. So he felt like they were two or three hundred the way they were biting. "So I'll just get out of bed and take and make me a pallet on the floor." He knowed he'd get rid of 'em then. (They hatched in the wooden bed.) "Well here they come, a line of 'em." He say, "Well I know what I'll do. I'll just go there in the kitchen and get me some syrup, and pour them all around me. They sure will stick up when they crawl up in that."

So I lays down and goes to sleep with that ring of molasses around me. So I felt something hit me in the face and I woke up. "Tip tap, tip tap." Do you know what they had done? They had climbed up the wall, run

across the ceiling, so they got over me, then they was
dropping, like drops of rain, over in the ring where I
was lying. But there wasn't a single one that misjudged
his drop, and dropped in the syrup. So I didn't get to
sleep at all that night.

[Business of looking up at the ceiling, wiping face]

84. Chinch Bugs

> This unusual variant of the preceding form
> permits the harassed lodger to overcome the
> bedbugs. "There are two kinds of chinch bugs,
> one in the cornfield, the other in the bed,"
> Suggs added.

Fellow went to a rooming house. He got him a
room from the landlord, one dollar and fifty cents for
a night's lodging. So he goes to bed pretty early, he was
tired. So when he goes off to sleep the bedbugs begin to
bite. Felt like it was a hundred or more biting him. He
goes to the landlord's door and knocks on it. Say "Miss,
I can't sleep, these bedbugs just eating me up."

Say "All right, I'll fix that." She sprinkles a little
powder on the bed. He gets back in the bed.

No sooner he's in the bed and blew out the light, the
bedbugs started on him again. He gets up and goes to
the landlord's room again. Says "Say, these bugs eating
me up. I paid you a dollar and a half to sleep, not to
stay awake and kill bedbugs."

Landlord say, "Oh, I'll take care of them." So she
goes to the dresser, open the drawer, gets out a pair of
glasses. "Now lay still and put these on. You won't be
bothered with any more tonight. I forgot to tell you to
put 'em on."

So when he put 'em on he lay down, turn out the light.

One of the leading chinches, he went up and peeped in his face. Say, "He's not asleep." So they looking at the glass and thought his eyes was open. And so he got a good night's sleep.

XI

IRISHMEN

85. The Irishmen and the Frogs

The second part of this tale is Motif
J1851.1.1, "Numskull throws money to frogs
so that they can count it," which corresponds
to the first episode in Type 1642, "The Good
Bargain." Baughman gives two Negro references under Motif J1811.5* (c), "Frogs' cries
misunderstood." In Alcée Fortier, Louisiana
Folk-Tales, MAFLS II, 1895, "The Irishman
and the Frogs," no. 5, p. 21, the Irishman first
throws his jug to the frogs, then enters the water and drowns. I have other texts from Carrie
Williams and Andrew W. Smith.

Pat been to town to buy his tobacco and groceries
for the weekend. So he buys a caddy of tobacco (that's
about twelve pounds). It was a warm night in May, warm
and cloudy. (Frogs begin to holler in May when it gets
cloudy). Pat walked up on the bridge, the bullfrog commenced to holler, "Knee-deep, knee-deep." [Bass]
Pat was afraid of the bridge, and when they said
knee-deep he thought he'd wade. He kept getting deeper
till it was over his head, so he scrambled back and went
over the bridge, said "You don't know what you're talking about, it's head deep." He crosses the bridge then,
buys the tobacco.
When he's coming back and gets to the bridge the
little frogs holler, "Chew-tobacco, chew-tobacco, chew-

tobacco," and they keep a-hollering. So he th'owed the whole pack in there, a piece at a time, told them to take all the tobacco.

Then he thought about his money, said "Vell, I'll just count my money to see how much I have to buy me tobacco tomorrow." He counted, "One-two-three-four-five."

Old frog said, "Tenk, tenk, tenk, tenk." [Deep] He counts it the second time up to five. He thought the frog was saying, "It ain't."

So he th'owed it in there and said, "Vell, count it yourself." So the next day he had to go back to town and when he looks over there he seen the tobacco laying on the water—it done swelled up. Said, "They take the darndest big chews of tobacco in little fellows I ever seen."

(The water gets in the leaves and swells them.)

86. Irishman and Watch

> A similarly titled variant in NFIM 182-183 from Walter Winfrey contains a customary initial episode where the Irishmen discover a watch in the road and beat it to pieces, thinking it a serpent. This is Motif J1781.2, "Watch mistaken for the devil's eye." See note 148, p. 230 in NFIM.

Irishman was coming along and he heard tell of a watch. And it had a little short thing on it, and it was round. So Mike says, "Pat, what's this?" They seen a terrapin crawling on the road.

He says, "This is the watch they was talking about." So he picks him up, puts a string on the end of his tail for a watch chain. It was too big to put in his watch

pocket, so he let him down between his breeches. Terrapin began to scratch.

So he goes uptown and meets Mr. John (he knows
Pat and Mike). Mr. John sees the string fastened on
there, know Pat bought him a new watch. Says "Pat,
what time is it?"

Pat says, "Vell, eleven-thirty, and scratching like
hell for twelve."

87. Irishman and Punkin

> See the longer variant in NFIM 182 from
> Marvin Rice, where the pumpkin is sold as a
> mule's egg, and note 147, p. 229. This is Type
> 1319, Motif J1772.1, "Pumpkin sold as an
> Ass's Egg."

This I'shman he went to town and he seed a punkin.
He axed him what was it.

He said, "Well that's a mare's egg."

He axed him, Well what did he want for it. Told him
fifteen dollars. So he paid him the fifteen dollars, was
on his way home with the punkin. So he was on side of a
hill and he stumbled and fell. Punkin went rolling down
the hill. Up jumped a rabbit. I'shman said, "Cup caller,
cup caller, here's yo' mammy."

Thought it had hatched that quick, and rabbit just
setting down there.

88. Irish Bricklayer

> Halpert has a Pat and Mike form of this
> jest, in Folktales and Legends from the New
> Jersey Pines, no. 181, "Easy Work."

I'shman from Old Country, he came here from Iceland. He got a job as a hod carrier, carrying bricks and mud, on a two story building, had to go up a ladder. He wrote a letter back to his brother Mike saying, " Come at once, I've got a good easy job, a dollar and nine cents an hour carrying brick and mortar on the second floor. The other fellow does all the work, so come at once. Your brother Pat."

89. What Darkens the Hole?

Two variants I collected from E. M. Moore and Silas Altheimer are in Pine Bluff, ante, no. 46ab, pp. 87-88. This is Motif X911.3, "If the wolf's tail breaks." Halpert in Folktales and Legends from the New Jersey Pines, no. 187, gives a White text, and Negro references from six Southern states, besides White references from Canada and Scotland. Suggs has left out the punch ending here, "If the bear's tail breaks you'll find out what darkens the hole," and gives the form of Type 1900, "How the Man Came out of a Tree Stump."

Pat and Mike went out to catch 'em two cubs. They knew where a bear had some cubs in a hollow cyp'ess tree about twelve foot high. And the cubs they was in that holler down in the bottom of the ground. Pat and Mike knowed that was where the baby bears was.

Mike says, "Pat, I'll go down and get the baby bears, you watch for the mother." So Mike see the mother bear coming, he ran off. Mother bear she climbs up the snag. Then she begins to back down in the hole.

Pat say, "Mike, who darkens the hole?"

Mama bear backs on down (a bear can't go down frontwards). Pat out with his penknife—he didn't have

nothing in the hole but a penknife, he couldn't run. So he
begin to gig him with his penknife. So out he came, he
grab the bear by the tail. So he pulled him out. So the
bear went through the woods one way, Mike went the
other way, so Pat went the other way.

And it was raining, and I had on my paper suit, and
I made a short cut home as quick as I could.

XII

PREACHERS

90. What Did Paul Say?

> This is Type 1835A, Motif X435.1: "What
> says David?"—the boy, 'Pay your old debts.'"
> A variant I collected in Mound Bayou, "What
> Did John Say?" from Mrs. I. E. Edwards is
> in "Negro Tales from Bolivar County, Missis-
> sippi," no. 14, pp. 112-113. Baughman gives
> nine English and American references, of
> which only one is Negro. Suggs also told the
> closely related form of Type 1833, "The Boy
> Applies the Sermon"; see NFIM 170, "Abra-
> ham, What is Thou got in thy Bosom?" and
> note 128, p. 227. The present text is tran-
> scribed from a tape recording.

Well there was a preacher you know, way down
South—he was a preacher of the Hardshell Baptist
church. So his brother Deacon Jones, he's making
moonshine whiskey. Well he's always get it on credit.
So he gets up this Sunday morning, he's going have a big
day there. He wanted to preach a good sermon but he
had to get half drunk you know. And so he says, "Hey
son, go and tell Brother Paul to send me a pint of good
whiskey. I'm going preach some today." Say "Now listen, when you come in, get there 'fore I start." And
says, "Now I'll come out the back." Say "When you
come, I'll go out the back, you go back and you give it to
me."

So he says, "All right, Dad." So he goes out. So while he stayed so long, the preacher father kept waiting on him, waiting on him, he didn't come, so he had to open up the revival, his meeting.

He says, "Well now, Sisters and Brothers," say "what did Paul say?" Say "I seen Paul when he was coming down from Gotha." [Chanted]

Sister say, "Yes I did." [Chanted]

Here come his son walking in. He [the preacher] say, "What did Paul say?" [Loud]

Boy just kept walking up to him, shaking his head. He said, "What did Paul say?" [Chanted]

He said, "Now listen Dad, Paul say you pay him for that first quart of whiskey you had and he'll let you have another'n."

So, he hadn't paid for the first one. So the father got so mad, he just walked right out of the back of the poolpit [pulpit] hollering "What did Paul say?" Just went right out of the back of the door, hollering "What did Paul say?"

91. Preacher and the Mule

Walter Winfrey gave me a close variant in Inkster, Michigan. In a Texas form a deacon lays his hat on the side road while he cusses the oxen, saying "Lie here, Deacon" (A. W. Eddins, "Anecdotes from the Brazos Bottoms," Straight Texas, Publications of the Texas Folklore Society XIII, 1937, p. 96).

Preacher coming along going to church. Young man was on the side of the road plowing, he was just cussing his mule. Preacher got down off his mule, says, "Sonny, you shouldn't cuss that way." Says "Let me have that

plow, I'll show you I won't cuss." So boy give the
preacher the plow. Preacher say "Git up there, go on
now [loud], I'll break your neck directly." Say "Get up,
I'll cut your throat directly, better go on" [harsh]. He
used them words till he got back up to the other end,
where he started. He said, "See now sonny, I didn't
curse."

"Yes Reverend, but you told so many dark lies. You
said you was going to beat them to death, and you didn't
do that. You said you was going to cut his throat, and
you didn't do that."

'Bout that time they rung the bell for me to come
home to dinner—I was cutting sprouts near there—so I
don't know what the preacher said.

92. Mistakes Preacher for Stump

In Arthur H. Fauset, "Tales and Riddles
Collected in Philadelphia," JAF XLI, 1928,
a similar tale has old man Simpson mistaken
for a stump by two Indians: no. 42 p. 548,
"Live Tree Stump," told by a Negro from Virginia.

That was in Mississippi. They was having revival
at Bunker Hill First Baptist Church. So old man Steward,
Angus Steward, he was the old preacher, about eighty-
five years old, and he 'cided he'd pray before he got to
the church, he heared them singing in the church. So he
got on his knees praying.

There come another preacher named Willis Love.
He seen Brother Steward, he thought he was a stump.
Say, "I bet I been long here a thousand times and I ain't
seen that stump before." That's what he was saying to
hisself. So when he got even with him he aim to lay his

hand on the stump; old man Steward moved his head. Old man Love ran up to the church hollering, "Lord have mercy, help, Lord have mercy, help." [Very high]

My father was there. He was laughing when he come to the church that night.

93. The Preacher and the Jew

> A variant appears in Arthur H. Fauset, Folklore from Nova Scotia, MAFLS XXIV, 1931, no. 149, pp. 96-97, "Believe Anything for Rum." A colored deacon gets his friend to believe the Biblical wonders, even to Jonah swallowing the whale, for a drink of rum.

The preacher comes along and stops in at the Jew. He says "Good morning, Mr. Cohen, how's business?"

Says, "Vell, dull, business dull."

Preacher says, "Bloodsaw's business is good, down the block there." (He was another Jew.) Said "I'll tell you the reason Bloodsaw's business is so good. He believes that Jesus is the son of God."

Cohen said, "You say Bloodsaw's business is good?"

Preacher says, "Yes."

"Vell, I believe that, too."

"Another thing, Bloodsaw believe they put Daniel in the lions' den and they didn't bother him, didn't hurt him."

He says, "Vell, does Bloodsaw believe that?"

"Yes."

"Vell, I believe that too then."

Preacher say, "Another thing Bloodsaw believe, the whale swallowed Jonas and th'owed him up on land."

Mr. Cohen say, "Does Bloodsaw believe that?"

"Yes."

"Vell, then I believe that."

Last thing he believes is that they th'owed the three Hebrew children in the fiery furnace—Shadrach (Daniel), Meshach and Abednego. And it was so hot it killed the men that th'owed them in there. When the king looked in the fire he said, "Didn't you th'ow three men in there?"

And the guards said, "Yes, we th'owed three men in there."

And he said, "Behold I see four, and the fourth one look like the Son of God." Then he beckoned to Daniel, and they come out and there wasn't a hair scorched on their head, and none of their clothes was burnt."

Preacher said, "Do you believe that?"

Jew said, "No, and I didn't believe all those other damn lies."

(What made the Jew turn was that none of the old Jews believed in Christ.)

XIII

NOODLES

94. Discovering the Fool

See ante, Pine Bluff, no. 54, pp. 96-98, "The Fool Discovered," by Julia Courtney, and note.

There was a pretty big fellow, around twelve years old, or fifteen, and they was always telling him he was a fool—"You don't have sense to do nothing." So one day the father's going to town to carry a load of watermelon. So he carried Johnny along to sit on the wagon and watch them. He'd go and peddle some and come back. He says before he got to town, "Johnny, now don't you say a word to nobody no matter what they says to you, they'll find out you is a fool." So he got in town he had to go to Mr. Jones's store, left Johnny sitting on the wagon. Two men come along walking.

"Say sonny, whose watermelons? You want to sell 'em?" Johnny wouldn't say nothing. One of 'em says, "Come on," says "he's a fool."

Just about that time his daddy walked up. He says, "Oh daddy, oh daddy, they found out I was a fool and I didn't say a word."

95. The Biggest Fool

This text includes variations of Type 1210,

"The Cow is Taken to the Roof to the Graze"
and Type 1245, "Sunlight Carried in a Bag into the Windowless House." See ante, Pine
Bluff no. 56, pp. 102-104, "Three More Bigger
Fools," by Julia Courtney, and note.

Captain John told Bill to go out see how many fools
he could find. And if he found the biggest fool there was
in the neighborhood he'd give him a suit of clothes and a
quart of whiskey. So he goes down to the creek, he sees
a man trying to make a cow drink water by pushing her
head to the water.

He goes back up the streets further. He sees a man
with his cow and a rope on her, had a sack tied over her
mouth. Bill axed him, "What you going to do?"

"Oh I'm going to git on top so she can eat some hay."
Bill said, "Just untie her mouth, she'll eat."

Then he goes on up the streets. He saw another fellow with a wheelbarrow. He'd roll it into the shade and
he'd wheel it out. He axed him, said "What're you doing?"

Said "I'm trying to get some sunshine under this
shade tree."

So Bill tells Old Marster about all three of 'em, and
the one with the wheelbarrow is the one he won his suit
on.

96. Young Man in the Morning

This is Type 1479* and Motif X753, "A
youth promises to marry an old maid if she
will sit all night on the roof." Texts with the
same title are in NFIM 193, from Mary
Richardson, and see note 156, p. 231; and "Negro Tales from Bolivar County, Mississippi,"
no. 16, p. 113, from Archie Tyler.

There was an old lady she was wanting a young man.
Big frost at night, clear and cold, about twenty above.
The next man made the promise, if she could stay on the
house all night, she'd have a young son for a husband, if
she lay naked on the roof. They asked, "Grandmother,
ain't you cold?"

She'd say "Oooh, yes, but young man in the morning."
And she never did come down. She'd turn to one side,
and then to the other, "Ooooh," but she was just sticking
right with it.

97. Can't Call Them

> Archie Tyler told me this tale in Cleve-
> land, Mississippi. See "Negro Tales from
> Bolivar County, Mississippi," no. 13, p. 112,
> "The Two Deacons." A year later, at Chapel
> Hill, North Carolina, in August 1954, I re-
> corded a variant from playwright Paul Green.

This fellow named John he was down praying — that
was at Indianola, Mississippi. He said, "You know you
said, 'Go work in my vineyard.'" And he said, "Oooh,
oooh. Good as I know both those fellows I can't call
neither one of their names." [Chanted]

That was the Lord and the Devil. He was aiming to
say, "And what's right I'll pay you."

98. Oh Lord Oh Devil

A fellow was topping a tree (cut the top out so it will
spread and make shade — it's dangerous but there's big
money in it). Well he stepped on a rotten limb and it
broke. Here he come tumbling down. He hit on one limb,

that would break his fall. Say "Oh Lord, oh Devil."
About that time he'd fall offa that limb down on another.
He was falling awful slow. He was hollering all the time,
"Oh Lord, oh Devil, oh Lord, oh Devil." So he fell and
hit the ground and he didn't get much of a jar, the limbs
had broke his fall, and he didn't have to fall more'n five
feet to hit the ground.

People asked him, "Why were you calling on the
Lord first and then the Devil, what were you calling on
both of 'em for?"

He said, "Well, I hadn't been too good, and neither
too bad, so I didn't know which one of 'em's hands I was
going to fall into. So I called on both of 'em." So he'd
be right, didn't care what hand he fall into.

99. Funny Letter

This man ran away from home. Jake he had a wife
and one child, he got in some trouble. So he wrote her a
letter. He put the heading on it.

Cotton Plant, Arkansack.
September the toot, nineteen o toot and a toot.

Dear wife and one chilluns,
I now sotten down wroten to you. I am in the
Buffalo, New Yock. I'm doin' tolluble well some I
thank you. I would send you a cow and a calf but the
hole in the post office too small and I cannot get
them in the mail sack.
Your husband, Jake.

XIV

JOCULAR TALES

100. Wait Till Martin Comes

See ante, Pine Bluff no. 41, pp. 78-81, "Waiting for Martin," and headnote.

That was a hanted house, and this fellow was going to stay there. If he stayed the night they were going to give him the house, it was a fine house, couldn't nobody stay there. And so he build him a big hot fire. So he was setting up there by the fire warming. In walked a a big old rooster, he didn't have no feathers anywhere except on his tail, and a few round his head, and about five or six in each one of his wings; he was picked clean in all of his feathers except that.

So he looks around the house, says "Hm, there ain't nobody got here but me."

Just about that time in walked a little kitten, a sore-eyed kitten. He turned his back to the fire and warmed up. Then he looks up at the rooster. Says "Well is we going start now, or wait till Martin comes?"

And Jake says, "I'll be dogged if I'll be here when Martin comes."

So out the door he went.

(So he didn't get to win the house because he didn't stay all night to see what happened.)

101. Haunted Castle

This tale begins as the related type of the
preceding form that uses Motif H1411.1, "Fear
test: staying in haunted house where corpse
drops piecemeal down chimney." It then shifts
into a sober use of Motif E371.5, "Ghost of
woman returns to reveal hidden treasure," for
which Baughman cites one Negro reference.
See "The Spirit and the Treasure," from Katy
Pointer in NFIM 132-133, for a realistic use
of this theme with a male revenant.

There was a hanted castle [pronounced castul] —
nobody could not stay there. It was a fine place, well
furnished, everything comfortable, so that's why people
would want to stay there. A fellow would be coming
along, walking, asking for a place to stay — "You can
stay there, if you can stay there all night you can have
it." That's why so many people tried it, but none of
them stayed out the night.

The fellow goes in, everything's all fixed up, he sat
at a big table looking at a book — there was plenty of
books there — says, "I'll set up all night." A leg dropped
down on the table. Just looked over and another leg dropped down. He looked back and a right arm dropped down,
by the side of it. Then a left arm drops down. He looks
off and he looks back — a body dropped down. Well he
looks at his book, he looks back, a head drops down. So
there was a whole woman laying there on the table. Out
he goes. [Slap of the hands to indicate rapid flight]

Next week here come along another man hunting a
place to stay. Says "There's a castle over there, if you
can stay all night you can have it."

"Well I know I can stay." So he goes in, light the
lamp, set on that table, reach over and get him a book,

begin to read. It was kind of cold, in the fall of the year, he had a fire going.

In walked a big black cat. Say "Phew, it's cold to-night." He looked at him, went back to reading his book.

After awhile in walks a big old rooster, no feathers but on his neck and head. He says, "Boys, ain't got here yet?"

The cat says, "Naw."

After awhile he look up, in come a little bitty kitten with the mange and the sore eyes. He turned his back to the fire (just the way a cat does). He says in a low whiney voice, "You gonna start now or wait till Martin comes?"

Up jumped the man, say "I won't be here when Martin comes."

So he was gone. Next two or three nights here comes an old poor man, raggedy—he had a Bible under his arm. He axed him, "Is there anywhere I can stay to-night?"

Man says, "Yeah, see that house there, you can stay there all night."

"Okay, I thanks." So he goes and makes him a fire, open his sack, get him a cold lunch; a little piece a bread he got, and meat. So he goes over to the table with his Bible and begun to read. So down come a leg on the ta-ble. Well the man he looked up and he just move around a little further, went back to reading. Next time he looked up it was the right leg. Well he just moved around a little bit further, goes back to reading again. Next time he looked up it was the arm dropped down. He looks up, goes back to reading. Next time he looks up a body drops down. Bloh—it was kinda heavy. Next time he looked up a head dropped down and united to the body. He just looked around and went back to reading. Next

time he looked around there was a woman, she was
dressed up and standing on the floor.

Said "What in the name of the Lord do you wants
yere?" That's what he axed her.

So she pointed to the door, said "Follow me." They
went outdoors, and there was a big apple tree, and she
pointed straight down by it, said "Dig here." Said, "Go
to the house and get ye a spade—you'll find one in the
closet there. You go and get your spade and come back
and begin to dig." He digs about seven feet, and he hit
a pot. It was about a ten gallon pot. Under the cover it
was full of gold. The lady say, "That's why I been coming back. I wanted to give it to some poor person that
needed it. I was murdered for money but no one never
did find it."

(The others was wicked people, no doubt they was
gamblers and murderers—she kept coming back till
somebody axed her what she wanted. But he was a Christian, he had a Bible and said, "In the Name of the Lord.")

102. The Lady's Pet Bear

Usually this story is told as a hunting joke
of the live bear catch, where the frightened
hunter running from the bear explains to his
companions that he is bringing it back alive.
Baughman assigns this jest Motif X584.1*, and
gives two Negro and two White references, and
see Irvis, p. 174, where the wife shoots the
bear. Suggs has given the tale a novel context.

This lady had a pet bear. He wandered away from
home and got lost, and she offered a five hundred dollar
reward for him.

Rastus he's out in the woods hunting. So Rastus seen

the bear, and the bear seen Rastus. The bear hadn't
seen a human in six months and he was glad to see somebody. So he shook hisself and started towards Rastus.
Rastus shook hisself and started meeting him. The bear
was so glad he laid down and rolled over, he was so glad
at seeing some human. Rastus he laid down and rolled
over. Both gets up and goes to meeting each other again,
going towards each other. The bear gets close, he
reaches out to hug Rastus. So Rastus wheel and begin to
run. The bear was right after him. He come to old
Miss's house. Say "Ol' Miss, open the door, I got your
bear." So round the house he go and the bear right in behind him. He gets back and say, "Ol' Miss, if you don't
open the door this time I'm carrying him back to the
woods, where I got him." So the door wasn't open, down
into the woods he goes, him and the bear. And the bear
was right after him. Then he runs back to the house
again, and Ol' Miss happened to have the door open.
Rastus run in the house and the bear run in right behind
him.

Ol' Miss said, "Lord, here's my pet bear." And the
bear knew her, and they begin to hug each other.

Rastus say, "I told you I'd bring him in."

So she gave Rastus the five hundred bucks.

103. Imitating the Bear

Suggs here tells how he actually used a
folktale to distract a game warden. I heard
a French-Canadian dialect variant of this tale
from Burt Mayotte at Sault Ste. Marie; see
"The Bear on Sugar Island" in my article "Dialect Stories of the Upper Peninsula," JAF LXI,
1948, pp. 127-128. The hunting party Suggs
served practiced a custom of cutting off the

shirttail of every hunter who missed his deer,
a culture trait described by Fred Kniffen in
"The Deer-Hunting Complex in Louisiana,"
JAF LXII, 1949, pp. 187-188.

We was deerhunting, that was in the Ozark Moun-
tains. I was the cook. Well they bought my license, so
I could hunt in the evening while they were watching supper. So Hollis Craft he goes out and kills him a deer.
He came back, before he get to the camp he hollers out,
"J. D., go get your gun, and your coat."
   I grabbed my gun and coat and out the tent I goes.
Say "What you want?"
   He say, "I got a big buck killed up here. Get in the
truck, and we'll go on after it." I gets in the truck, we
goes on around the mountains. So we gets out and goes
down, he says, "Here's the deer right under the hill
here." I takes my hunting knife and cuts him in the
same gash where Hollis had cut him—I got to get blood
on my hands, no mark on my knife. We goes back to the
camp, takes that deer out the truck, hangs him up in the
tree. About that time I begin to take his intestines out,
up come two game wardens.
   Say "Who killed that buck?"
   I says, "I killed him."
   Says "Let's see your hunting license." I showed
him my hunting license. Says "Is that the first one you
ever killed?"
   I told him, No, that wasn't the first one I ever killed.
I said, "Listen, let me tell you a funny story." (I'm getting him off talking about the deer.)
   I said, "I went bear hunting. They told me all I had
to do was do what the bear do, and he wouldn't hurt me.
The bear shook his fist, I shook mine. The bear laid
down and rolled over. I laid down and rolled over. Then
he turned around and dug a hole. So I dug one. So he sat

down over his. I told him, I said, 'I beat you to that. I done it when I first seen you.'"

They forgot all about the deer. Then Hollis said, "Say J. D., let me borrow your gun, I'll see if I can get one."

"Okay, I'm through today, I got my limit."

104. Biggest Liar in the County

> This is a widely told hunting joke in American White tradition. For a Negro example see J. Mason Brewer, "John and the Constable," Mexican Border Ballads and Other Lore, pp. 102-104, in his article on "John Tales."

Fellow going hunting out of season. Just as he come up out of the woods into the main road he meets a man. The man says, "Well Sam, you have any luck today?"

Says "No sir, I hain't had no luck today but I had good luck yesterday." Said "Right out there I killed one big buck. I went out on the lake and I got twelve ducks out there. And out there on that hickory ridge where squirrels is cutting nuts, I got twelve squirrels."

Man says, "Gosh Sam, you sure had some luck." Says "Sam, do you know who I am?"

"No sir, I don't know who you is." Says "I'm the game warden."

Sam says, "Mr. Game Warden, do you know who I am? You can ask anybody round here about me and they'll tell you I'm the biggest liar in the county."

(So he didn't have no evidence against Sam so he let Sam go.)

105. Farmer and the Bull

The farmer wanted to borrow some money on his farm, so he went to the bank to try to get a mortgage. The banker let him have the money. And he was telling him about the fine stock and bull he had on his farm, how swift the bull was. And the farmer invited the banker to come out the next day and take dinner with him, to see the bull. So the farmer knew that he didn't have no such bull on his farm—he was just making it up, bragging and boasting his stuff, to get the money. So the farmer gets up early the next morning. He had a boy about ten or eleven years old, told him, say, "If the banker come out tomorrow tell him I'm gone, I won't be here today."

So about ten-thirty the banker come out to look over the farm, inspect the bull and see how swift he was — came out in the forenoon, before dinner. So the banker drove out in his car, honked his horn. The farmer's boy goes out to the car. Banker says, "Where is your dad?"

Boy says, "He's in Florida."
Said, "When did he go?"
"He left about nine o'clock."
"When will he be back?"
" Oh tomorrow about eight o'clock, I guess."
"Well, how did he go?"
Said "He rode that bull." (He knew he had to go by plane, but there wasn't any place for the plane to land.)

Boy knew his dad was shooting the bull all the time. Everybody in the country knew he was a bullshooter.

106. Gambler Fools the Judge

The law raided Jim's gambling house. So all of 'em

got away but Jim. They come in the front door, didn't
guard the back. So the law taken Jim up before the judge,
carried his craps before the jury. Judge says, "What
you got him booked with?"

Say "For gambling."

Says "Where's the rest of 'em, you only got one?"

Says "They all got away but this one."

Judge says, "You guilty or not guilty?"

Says "Something like this, Mr. Judge." Says "You
got ten dollars?"

Judge says, "Yes."

Says "Just lay it down here then, up here on this
desk, and I'll show you what I was doing when the law
came in. Is these the dice they said I had?" So he puts
down his ten dollars, says "Look Judge, it was something
like this. I shuck them in my hand, and I rolled 'em out."

The Judge said, "That's 'leven."

Says "Please your honor that's the way it was, Mr.
Judge." So Jim picked up the twenty dollars put it in his
pocket.

Judge said, "Case dismissed."

107. The Blank Dice

The law arrested two fellows for gambling. So the
law carried them up before the judge, say "I caught
these two men shooting dice, down there on the corner."

Judge axed the officer, "Where is the dice?"

Officer said, "Your honor, here they are, sir."

They passed the dice over to Jim there, said, "I'm
going to let you th'ow your own sentence, whatever you
th'ow that's the time you got to serve out." So Jim
th'owed two deuces, two one spots. Judge says, "Two
days."

"Well, Sam, it's your shot next." Sam was awful slicker you know. He done slipped a pair of blank dice didn't have nary spot while he was shooting. When Judge had th'owed him the straight dice he taken them and shaken them. When the Judge told him to shoot he shot the one didn't have no spots on it at all.

Judge told the jailer to lock him up and let him stay until some spots come on the dice.

By that time I had a paper suit and it was getting cold and I had to go back South where it was warm, and I couldn't stay to see how long he stayed in jail before the spots come.

[Shows by twisting his hand how the gambler held the dice]

108. Woman's Confession

> This belongs under Motif J1270, "Repartee concerning the parentage of children."
> Brewer has a tale in The Word on the Brazos where a dying woman similarly confesses her aberrations; her husband says, "Hit mought be Judgment Day tomorruh, but hit's gonna be hell heah tonight!" (p. 32).

Woman on her deathbed, she told her husband, "I want you to get all the children round my bed, for I know I'm going to die. I want to confess the truth." Say "Now I been saying that these here was all your chilluns." And she had about nine. Said "Well this un ain't none of yours (that was the oldest one), and this one ain't none of yours, and this one," until she got to the ninth one. He was a freckle-faced boy. And said, "And this one ain't none of yourn."

Then the freckle-faced boy looked 'em all over

good. He said, "Say why don't some of you bastards
say something."

(Many a man rocking one thought it was his'n and
it wasn't none of his.)

109. Hobo Slang

A timber cruiser in the Upper Peninsula,
Norm Thompson, told me an analogous jest in
lumberjack idiom describing an accident in
the lumberwoods. A similar specimen of oc-
cupational slang from the secondhand car
dealers of Livernois Street in Detroit, relating a shady deal put over on a customer, appeared in Life, XXXVI, March 22, 1954, p. 108.

A hobo was hiking up main stem. "I spied a guy
with his dukes on and his soup in his mitt and I was going to the finshop to flop. And he trotted me in the soup-
house because I did not have my dukes on."

The police carried him up the judge and that's what
he [the hobo] told the judge when he went up there. He
thought nobody there could interpretate, and so the judge
told the police get somebody what knew what he was talking about. Police had learnt slang, and so he begin to
testify what he was saying. Say "When this dusty knight
of the road was coming down the main street he saw a
policeman with his badge and uniform on, and his club
in his hand. He was going down to the electric light
plant to get his sleep. The policeman put him in jail because he didn't have clothes on, just rags."

Judge gave him twenty minutes to get out of town.
He told him he could keep fifteen of it, he only wanted
five to get out of town.

(Gang of sporting fellows would be standing around

talking about a fellow and he wouldn't even know we was
talking about him. Everybody in sporting class used to
talk that way. Fellow we called "Ouch," even when
death hit him, said, "In case I go to Croakerville, be
sure to close the slammer."

They'd say, "I was out on the last half of the gos-
pelitis, I was sticking with the weed. I seen a guy that
was sticking with salt, because I was out with the weed
at the crowded crib." It means that he was out taking
a girl out last Sunday night, the church house was
crowded, and this fellow seen me with his girl and was
mad at me.)

110. Quarrelsome Couple

> This is Type 1365, "The Obstinate Wife,"
> the C form, "The Wife Insults the Husband as
> Lousy-head," and Motif T255.3, "The obsti-
> nate wife: sign of the louse."

A man and his wife were fighting. She called him a
lousy rascal. He beat her so till she couldn't talk. He'd
knock her down and she'd get up and every time she'd
get up he'd knock her down again. She called him a
lousy rascal every time she'd get up till she couldn't
talk no more, then she went to mashing her fingers.
[Gesture of "popping" two thumb nails]

111. Minstrel Show

I worked with the Rabbit Foot Minister [sic] Show
in 1907 for about a year. It went to Alabama, Florida,
Texas, New Mexico, Wyoming, Utah, South and North
Dakota. I sang, danced, told jokes—danced stop time,

buck and wing, schottische, polka. About twenty-eight
in all, mens and womens together, all colored but the
boss.

They had a professor, like you, he comes on the
stage. Here comes Sambo, he walks on the stage, he
meets Doc. Says, "This big word glatitude, 'Fess,
what do it mean?"

He tell him the right way first, but Sambo couldn't
understand, he had to have a demonstrate.

So say, "Now Sambo, suppose there's a cow, and
her and a little calf was right on the bank of the water.
The calf falls in the water. I waded in up around my
waist, and got the calf, brought it out on the bank with
its mother. The cow walks up and licks me on the head.
She's so glad that I rescued the calf—now that's what
glatitude means."

He say, "No, no, 'Fess, you wrong."

"Well, what did it mean then by her licking me on
the head?"

"She thought she had twin calves."

112a. Minstrel Dialogue

"Say, 'Fess, you been to all the big cities in the
country, ain't you?"

"Yes, Jim, I been to every big city there is in the
United States."

"You ever been in jail, Profess?"

Say "Well no, I never been in no jail, do I look like
I ever been a criminal?"

"'Fess, if I call off these places can you answer all
the names where you been?"

"I been to lots of places myself."

"All right, Profess, now I'll call 'em off, and you
can't take it back if you say that's where you been."

"All right, that's a bet. I'll bet you twenty-five dollars, I know where I been."

"Okay, 'Fess, here I go. Been in New York?"

"Yes."

"Memphis?"

"Yes."

"Chicago?"

"Yes."

"Wales?"

"Yes."

"Jail?"

"Yes."

"Oh ho, doc, I thought you hadn't been in no jail."

112b. Minstrel Dialogue

"Doc, can you spell? Can you spell, Perfess?"

"Why sure, I been to one of the biggest colleges in
the United States, I made this Webster Spelling Book."

"Profess, I got one word I want you to spell. It's
a hard one too. I'll see whether you a professor or not,
can spell. Spell stovepipe."

Professor spells it. "S-t-o-v-e stove, p-i-p-e pipe."

Rastus goes to laughing at professor. "Ohoho."

Professor says, "What's funny?"

Say, "I know you couldn't spell stovepipe."

Say, "Well, let's hear you spell it."

Rastus say, "Okay here I go. S-t-o-v-e stove."
Then he goes to buck dancing—boompity boomp, boompity boomp, boomp. Then he say "P-i-p-e pipe."

"What all that bumping had to do to go with it?"

"Well, you see Profess, you never put the pipe together, I was putting it together."

"Well you win Rastus, I didn't put it together."

XV

RIDDLES

What's the biggest saw you ever saw in a saw or that anybody said that they saw in a saw?
>A bandsaw in Arkansas

An old man shuck it and shuck it and an old lady pulled up her dress and took it.
>An apple.

The old lady forgot it, the old man forgot it, the old man woke up in the middle of the night and stuck it in.
>Key in the door.

You ain't got it and you don't want it, but if you had it you wouldn't take the world for it.
>Bald head.

It go in hard and stiff and come out limber and greasy.
>A collud green.

I met a little boy and he was crying. I axed him why. He said his mother died six months before he was born.
>She dyed his clothes.

279

White run into white and run white out of white.
A white dog run into a cotton
patch and run out the cow.

What is all outdoors and you can't catch a spoonful?
The wind.

What have been here ever since the world is, and
never got five weeks old?
The moon. At the end of four
weeks it's gone.

113. A Riddle About God

I have seen something that God have never seen.
Oh that's not so. God have seen everything. He
made the world and everything that's in it. Now if you
call yourself smart, tell me something God has never
seen.
I have seen my equal, God have never seen his
equal.
(There never has been a man hasn't seen his equal.
The Devil tried to be equal with God. He was chorister,
leader of the angels in heaven, a pretty angel, and God
when he created man made him the Overlord. But
Luceefus tried to give the orders himself, and had them
eat the Tree of Knowledge. Then they was ashamed of
their nakedness and pinned fig leaves on themselves.
The Devil came in the form of a serpent and told her,
"No, you won't surely die. God knows that the day you
will eat of this you will know good from evil and be his
equal." So God gave her the curse that she should have
childbirth and the man be her boss. And Adam had to

eat by the sweat of his brow and till the earth until he return to the earth.)

114. Endings

   I had on a paper suit, so it looked like it was going
to rain, so I couldn't a stayed to see it end. (Wouldn't
a had nothing to wear home, you see.)
   Had on a pair of old shoes and no heels and I stepped on a slippery plank and got to sliding, and I couldn't
stop to see the end.

INDEX OF MOTIFS

References are keyed to Thompson's index, except those marked (*) which refer to Baughman's index. (See p. 289)

A. Mythological Motifs

A2234 "Animal characteristics: punishment for disobedience." P. 241

A2494.1.2 *Enmity between dog and cat." P. 241

A2494.4.4 *Enmity between dog and rabbit." P. 165

A2561.1 "Why mule is sterile." P. 241

D. Magic

D1314.2 *Magic wand locates hidden treasure." P. 199

D1719.1 "Contest in magic." P. 209

E. The Dead

E275 "Ghost haunts place of great accident or misfortune." P. 190

E320 *Dead relative's friendly return." P. 194

E371.5 *Ghost of woman returns to reveal hidden treasure." P. 265

E423.1.1 "Revenant as dog." P. 192

E423.3.6 "Revenant as hen." P. 192

E530 "Ghosts of objects." P. 187

F. Marvels

F402.1.1 Spirit leads person astray." P. 185

F971.1 *Dry rod blossoms." P. 240

F1047 "Anchor floats on water." P. 240

G. Ogres

G273.4 "Witch powerless to cross stream." P. 187

H. Tests

H1411.1 "Fear test: staying in haunted house where
        corpse drops piecemeal down the chimney." P. 26!

J. The Wise and the Foolish

J1270 "Repartee concerning the parentage of children." P. 27

J1772.1 "Pumpkin sold as an ass's egg." P. 252

J1781 "Objects thought to be the devil." P. 222

J1781.2 "Watch mistaken for devil's eye." P. 251

J1782.1 "Robber or dog in church thought to be a ghost." P. 1

J1811.5* (c) "Frog's cries misunderstood." (J1811.2
        in Thompson rev. ed.) P. 250

J1851.1.1 "Numskull throws money to frogs so that they
        can count it." P. 250

K. Deceptions

K237.1 "Heaven entered by a trick." P. 178

K426 "Apparently dead woman revives when thief tries
        to steal from her grave." P. 219

K651 "Wolf descends into well in one bucket and rescues
        fox in the other." P. 167

K1241 "Trickster rides dupe horseback." P. 161

K1956 "Sham wise man." P. 172

N. Chance and Fate

N563 "Treasure seekers find hole from which treasure
        has recently been removed." P. 199

N571 "Devil (demon) as guardian of treasure." P. 199

N576 "Ghosts prevent men from raising treasure." P. 199

N688 "What is in the dish: 'Poor Crab.'" P. 172

Q. Rewards and Punishments

Q223.6.2* "Person is punished for hunting on Sunday." (Not in Thompson rev. ed.) P. 194

T. Sex

T255.3 "The obstinate wife: sign of the louse." P. 275

X. Humor

X435.1 "What says David?— Boy, Pay your old debts." P. 255

X584.1* "Bear chases man back to camp: explains to fellow hunters that he is bringing it into camp to kill because he did not want to have to carry it." (Slightly reworded in Thompson rev. ed.) P. 267

X753 "Youth promises to marry old maid if she will sit all night on the roof." P. 261

X911.1 "Man turns wolf inside out." P. 246

X911.3 "If the wolf's tail breaks." P. 87

X1024.1 "The great cabbage." P. 245

X1042.2 "The great melon." P. 243

X1215.2. "Lie: large dog." P. 245

X1401.1* (b) "Animals eat into large vegetables, live there for some time." (Reworded in Thompson rev. ed.) P. 243

X1402.1 "Lie: fast growing vine." P. 243

INDEX OF TALE TYPES

According to Aarne-Thompson's index. (See p. 289)

I. Animal Tales

III. Jokes and Anecdotes

BIBLIOGRAPHY*

Indexes

Aarne, Antti, and Stith Thompson, The Types of the Folk-Tale. Helsinki, 1928.

Baughman, Ernest W., A Comparative Study of the Folk-tales of England and North America. 3 vols.: Indiana University doctoral dissertation, 1953.

Flowers, Helen L., A Classification of the Folktale of the West Indies by Types and Motifs. Indiana University doctoral dissertation, 1952.

Klipple, May A., African Folktales with Foreign Analogues. Indiana University doctoral dissertation, 1938, abstracted by Stith Thompson.

Thompson, Stith, Motif-Index of Folk Literature. 6 vols. Bloomington, Indiana, 1932-1936. Enlarged and revised, 1955-1958.

Collections

Bacon, A. M., and E. C. Parsons, "Folk-lore from Elizabeth City County, Virginia," JAF 35 (1922), 250-327.

Beckwith, Marth W., Jamaica Anansi Stories, MAFLS 17 (1924).

Botkin, B. A., ed. Lay my Burden Down, A Folk History of Slavery. Chicago, 1945.

Brewer, J. Mason, "John Tales," Mexican Border Ballads and Other Lore, ed. M. C. Boatright, PTFS 21 (1946), 81-104.

. . . .

*Abbreviations: JAF—Journal of American Folklore; MAFLS—Memoirs of the American Folklore Society; PTFS—Publications of the Texas Folklore Society.

Brewer, J. Mason, "Juneteenth," Tone the Bell Easy, ed.
    J. F. Dobie, PTFS 10 (1932), 9-54.

_____, The Word on the Brazos, Negro Preacher Tales
    from the Brazos Bottoms of Texas. Austin, Texas,
    1953.

Browne, Ray B., "Negro Folktales from Alabama,"
    Southern Folklore Quarterly, 18 (1954), 129-134.

Dorson, Richard M., "King Beast of the Forest Meets
    Man," Southern Folklore Quarterly, 17 (1954),
    118-128.

_____, Negro Folktales in Michigan. Cambridge, Mass.,
    1956.

_____, "A Negro Storytelling Session on Tape," Mid-
    west Folklore, 3 (1953), 201-212.

_____, "Negro Tales" [of John Blackamore], Western
    Folklore, 13 (1954), 77-97, 160-169, 256-259.

_____, "Negro Tales from Bolivar County, Mississippi,"
    Southern Folklore Quarterly, 19 (1955), 104-116.

_____, "Negro Tales of Mary Richardson," Midwest
    Folklore, 6 (1956), 1-26.

_____, "Negro Witch Stories on Tape," Midwest Folk-
    lore, 2 (1952), 229-241.

Drums and Shadows: Survival Studies among the Geor-
    gia Coastal Negroes. By the Savannah Unit of the
    Georgia Writers' Project of the Works Projects Ad-
    ministration. Athens, Ga., 1940.

Faulkner, W. J., "Dean Faulkner Folk Stories Series,"
    World of Fun Records S251, S252, S253, distributed
    by the Methodist Publishing House, Nashville, Tennes-
    see, with four-page leaflet, "Uncle Simon's Folk Tales."

Fauset, Arthur Huff, Folklore From Nova Scotia,
    MAFLS 24 (1931).

_____, "Negro Folk Tales from the South. (Alabama,
    Mississippi, Louisiana)," JAF 40 (1927), 213-303.

_____, "Tales and Riddles Collected in Philadelphia,"
JAF 41 (1928), 529-557.

Halpert, Herbert N., Folktales and Legends from the
New Jersey Pines: A Collection and a Study. 2
vols.: Indiana University doctoral dissertation,
1947.

Harris, Joel Chandler, Nights with Uncle Remus: Myths
and Legends of the Old Plantation. New York, 1883.

_____, Told by Uncle Remus: New Stories of the Old
Plantation. New York, 1905.

_____, Uncle Remus, His Songs and His Sayings: The
Folklore of the Old Plantation. New York, 1881.

Hurston, Zora Neale, Mules and Men. Philadelphia and
London, 1935.

Irvis, K. Leroy, "Negro Tales from Eastern New York,"
New York Folklore Quarterly, 2 (1955), 165-176.

Parsons, Elsie Clews, Folklore of the Antilles, French
and English, Part III, MAFLS 26 (1943).

_____, Folklore of the Sea Islands, South Carolina,
MAFLS 16 (1923).

Puckett, Newbell Niles, Folk Beliefs of the Southern Negro. Chapel Hill, N. C., 1926.

Randolph, Vance, The Devil's Pretty Daughter and other
Ozark Folk Tales. New York, 1955.

_____, Who Blowed Up the Church House? and other
Ozark Folk Tales. New York, 1952.

Smiley, Portia, "Folk-Lore from Virginia, South Carolina, Georgia, Alabama, and Florida," JAF 32
(1919), 357-383.

Smith, Richard, "Richard's Tales," Folk Travelers, Ballads, Tales, and Talk. ed. M. C. Boatright, W. M.
Hudson, A. Maxwell, PFTS 25 (1953), 220-253 (recorded by John L. Sinclair, transcribed by Stella A.
Sinclair).

South Carolina Folk Tales: Stories of Animals and Su-
    pernatural Beings. Compiled by Workers of the
    Writers' Program of the Works Projects Adminis-
    tration in the State of South Carolina. Columbia,
    S. C., 1941.

Stoddard, Albert H., Animal Tales Told in the Gullah
    Dialect. Library of Congress, Music Division Re-
    cording Laboratory, 1955. Long Playing Records
    L44, L45, L46. With booklet of text transcriptions.